STUDIES IN RUSSIA AND EAST EUROPE
formerly Studies in Russian and East European History

Chairman of the Editorial Board: M.A. Branch, Director, School of Slavonic and East European Studies.

This series includes books on general, political, historical, economic, social and cultural themes relating to Russia and East Europe written or edited by members of the School of Slavonic and East European Studies in the University of London, or by authors working in association with the School. Titles already published are listed below. Further titles are in preparation.

D. G. Kirby (*editor*)
FINLAND AND RUSSIA, 1808–1920: DOCUMENTS

Michael Kirkwood (*editor*)
LANGUAGE PLANNING IN THE SOVIET UNION

Martin McCauley (*editor*)
THE RUSSIAN REVOLUTION AND THE SOVIET STATE, 1917–1921:
  DOCUMENTS

KHRUSHCHEV AND THE DEVELOPMENT OF SOVIET AGRICULTURE

COMMUNIST POWER IN EUROPE: 1944–1949 (*editor*)

MARXISM-LENINISM IN THE GERMAN DEMOCRATIC REPUBLIC: THE
  SOCIALIST UNITY PARTY (SED)

THE GERMAN DEMOCRATIC REPUBLIC SINCE 1945

KHRUSHCHEV AND KHRUSHCHEVISM (*editor*)

THE SOVIET UNION UNDER GORBACHEV (*editor*)

Martin McCauley and Stephen Carter (*editors*)
LEADERSHIP AND SUCCESSION IN THE SOVIET UNION, EASTERN
  EUROPE AND CHINA

Martin McCauley and Peter Waldron
THE EMERGENCE OF THE MODERN RUSSIAN STATE, 1856–61

László Péter and Robert B. Pynsent (*editors*)
INTELLECTUALS AND THE FUTURE IN THE HABSBURG MONARCHY,
  1890–1914

Robert B. Pynsent (*editor*)
T. G. MASARYK (1850–1937) Volume 2: Thinker and Critic

MODERN SLOVAK PROSE: Fiction since 1954

Evan Mawdsley
THE RUSSIAN REVOLUTION AND THE BALTIC FLEET

J.J. Tomiak (*editor*)
WESTERN PERSPECTIVES ON SOVIET EDUCATION IN THE 1980s

Stephen White and Alex Pravda (*editors*)
IDEOLOGY AND SOVIET POLITICS

Stanley B. Winters (*editor*)
T. G. MASARYK (1850–1937) Volume 1: Thinker and Politician

Alan Wood and R. A. French (*editors*)
THE DEVELOPMENT OF SIBERIA: People and Resources

Modern Slovak Prose

Fiction since 1954

Edited by

Robert B. Pynsent

Reader in Czech and Slovak Literature
School of Slavonic and East European Studies
University of London

M
MACMILLAN

in association with
the School of Slavonic and East
European Studies, University of
London; and the Slovak World
Congress, Toronto

First published 1990

Published by
THE MACMILLAN PRESS LTD
Houndmills, Basingstoke, Hampshire RG21 2XS
and London
Companies and representatives
throughout the world

Typeset by Wessex Typesetters
(Division of The Eastern Press Ltd)
Frome, Somerset

Printed in Hong Kong

British Library Cataloguing in Publication Data
Pynsent, R. B. (Robert B.), *1943–*
Modern Slovak Prose: Fiction since 1954.
1. Fiction in Slovak – Critical studies
I. Title II. University of London. *School of Slavonic and East European Studies*
891.8'73
ISBN 0–333–51596–X

Series Standing Order

If you would like to receive future titles in this series as they are
published, you can make use of our standing order facility. To place a
standing order please contact your bookseller or, in case of difficulty,
write to us at the address below with your name and address and the
name of the series. Please state with which title you wish to begin your
standing order. (If you live outside the United Kingdom we may not
have the rights for your area, in which case we will forward your order
to the publisher concerned.)

Customer Services Department, Macmillan Distribution Ltd
Houndmills, Basingstoke, Hampshire, RG21 2XS, England.

Contents

Acknowledgements

I wish to thank the British Academy, the British Council and the Ford Foundation for their generous grants which made the original conference possible; and the Slovak World Congress for their help towards the production of this volume.

Robert B. Pynsent

Notes on the Contributors

Yuri Bogdanov is Professor in the Institute of Slavonic Studies at the Soviet Academy of Sciences in Moscow. He has published books and articles on Slovak and Czech literature.

Karel Brušák is Visiting Lecturer in Czech with Slovak at the University of Cambridge. He was educated at Prague and London. He has published numerous articles on drama and literature and he also initiated the serious study of Slovak literature in the United Kingdom.

Rudolf Chmel is Secretary of the Czechoslovak Writers' Association, research worker at the Slovak Academy of Sciences and editor-in-chief of *Slovenské pohľady*. He was educated at Bratislava University. He began his academic career as a specialist in Hungarian literature, but has published books also on Hungaro-Slovak literary contacts and on Slovak literature.

Manfred Jähnichen is Professor of Slavonic Studies at the Humboldt University in Berlin and has written on most Slavonic literatures, but has concentrated on Czech and Slovak. He is the author of the authorative account of Czech-German literary relations.

Sonia I. Kanikova, formerly Lecturer in Czech and Slovak Literature at the University of Sofia, until recently academic editor at Sofia University Press, was educated at Sofia. She has published articles mainly on Czech and Slovak literature. She has recently defected.

Jozef Kot is Deputy Minister in charge of Arts at the Slovak Ministry of Culture, and translator of Shakespeare and other English-language authors. He was educated at Bratislava University. He has edited literary monthlies and for a time was chief editor of the Bratislava publishing house, Tatran. Apart from literary criticism, Kot has published novels and short stories.

Marián Kováčik, former Lecturer in Solid-state Physics at Bratislava University, has been since 1976 editor-in-chief of the journal *Romboid*. He has published literary criticism and five books of verse.

Giuli Lezhava is a research worker in the Institute of Georgian Literature at the Soviet Academy of Sciences in Tbilisi. She has published articles on Czech, Georgian and Slovak literature.

Slavomír Magál is Reader in the History and Theory of Film at the Academy of Fine Arts in Bratislava, where he was educated. As well as translating from English and American literature, he has published books and articles on the cinema.

James D. Naughton is Fellow of St Edmund Hall, Oxford, and Lecturer in Czech and Slovak. He was educated at Cambridge. He has written articles on Czech and Slovak and is the author of a textbook of Czech for beginners.

Vladimír Petrík is Vice-Chairman for the Arts at the Slovak Academy of Sciences. He was educated at Bratislava University. Ever since he was an undergraduate he has been publishing articles and books on Slovak literature.

Peter Petro is Associate Professor at the department of Slavonic Studies at the University of British Columbia, Vancouver. He was educated at the Universities of Bratislava, British Columbia and Alberta. He has published a book and several articles on Czech, Russian, Slovak and comparative literature.

Robert B. Pynsent is Reader in Czech and Slovak literature at the University of London. He was educated at Cambridge. He has published books and articles, mainly on Czech and Slovak literature.

Donald Rayfield is Reader in Russian and Georgian at the University of London. He was educated at Cambridge, where he also read Czech with Slovak. He has published books and articles mainly on Georgian and Russian literature.

Ludwig Richter is Professor of Slavonic Studies at the Academy of Sciences of the GDR in Berlin, and he has published books and articles on various Slav literatures. His main speciality is Slovak literature.

Norma L. Rudinsky is Instructor of Writing at Oregon State University in Corvallis. She was educated at Stanford. She has published books and articles in literary history and criticism, and also translations of Slovak literature.

David Short is Lecturer in Czech and Slovak Language and Literature at the University of London. He was educated at Birmingham. He has published translations and articles, mainly on the Czech and Slovak languages.

Halina Sivachenko is head of the Czechoslovak section of the Soviet Academy of Sciences in Kiev, and has published books and articles on Czech, Russian, Slovak and Ukranian literature.

Dušan Slobodník is a research worker at the Slovak Academy of Sciences. He was educated at Bratislava University. He has worked in various archives and academic institutions, and has published numerous books and articles on Slovak and comparative literature.

Ján Števček is Professor of Slovak Literature and Head of the Department of Slovak Literature at Bratislava University where he was educated. He has also taught at the Universities of Budapest and Strasbourg. He has published a large number of articles and books, mainly on Slovak literature.

Břetislav Truhlář is a research worker at the Academy Institute of Literature in Bratislava. He was educated at Prague University. Previously he taught Slovak literature at Bratislava University, the Trnava Teachers' Training College and the Bratislava Academy of Arts. He has published numerous books and articles, chiefly on twentieth-century Slovak literature.

1 Introduction
Robert B. Pynsent

This volume is the product of a conference on Slovak fiction since 1954 held at the School of Slavonic and East European Studies in September 1987. 1954 was chosen because it saw the publication of Alfonz Bednár's *Sklený vrch*,* which marked the beginning of the Thaw in Slovak literature, the beginning of a reaction against oversimplified, schematic, tub-thumping depictions of Communists heroic in war and peace such as written by the recently deceased 'dissident', Dominik Tatarka. On the face of it *Sklený vrch* is a construction novel with a female first-person narrator, Ema. Bednár, however, far from idealises the building site in an underdeveloped part of Slovakia which he describes; the site is plagued by absenteeism, accidents, badly drawn-up plans and a lack of worker solidarity, and one of the main themes in the novel is a racket with cement and other building materials. Bednár comes out strongly against the post-war expulsion of Hungarians. The intellectual Ema suffers from the consequences of hereditary sin, for, though she showed bravery in the Resistance, her father had been a pro-Fascist informer and, almost as bad in those days, her mother had been a Communist. Ema's life is a tragedy: her background provides unrestrainable Fate; her tragic flaw is her belief in Communism and the working class. She has to die; she is electrocuted through the negligence of a labourer. She approaches the granite stature of a Social Realist 'positive hero' only when she stands before the site Party tribunal to defend herself against false accusations.

Certainly the novel contains topoi of the genre, like the evil emigré, but the weakness of the Communist villain, the ex-partisan Tretina, extends beyond that of a standard, bourgeois would-be believer whose villainy derives from those dreaded residual values that dogged the lives of so many contemporary literary figures. Ema and her husband are accused by him of being foul intellectuals; Bednár cannot, however, yet make Tretina a true villain, for he is still too

---

* Translations of titles mentioned in this Introduction are given in the References which begin on p. 37. Writers' dates of birth will be found in the Index.

much part of early 1950s enthusiasm (though one must be careful
not to identify Ema with Bednár).

To find Communist villainy one has to wait for the collection,
Hodiny a minúty (1956, four stories; with another two stories, one
published separately as *Cudzí*, 1960 – it was intended to appear as a
cycle of six in 1982, but of the 1956 stories, 'Rozostavaný dom', was
banned; so five appeared as *Novely*; first complete edition not until
new Thaw, 1964). This banned piece expresses disillusion with the
new socialist state, but also with the Uprising (the Slovak National
Uprising of 1944 was, actually, one of the largest mass Resistance
struggles of World War II). Against the background of hypocrisy and
corruption in Stalinist Slovakia the symbolic centrepiece is a cross on
a hillside; the Germans had tried to blow it up, but only now a senior
local Party official has succeeded in removing it. Stalinist society
appears almost more ruthless than German occupation because it
works by cold manipulation on top of cruelty and violence. The Party
official, Dugas, had been tortured by the Germans, but he had also
betrayed Slovaks and in the 1950s he is little more than a gangster.
In another story, 'Súsedia', the son of a traitor becomes the dangerous
careerist chairman of the local council and in the title story the
beautiful collaborator, Gáborová, becomes a secret policewoman in
the new régime. Such careers form a theme of Slovak literature since
Bednár. In the now emigré Mňačko's *Ako chutí moc* Miklík was in
the Hlinka Guard (the Slovak SA), edited a rabid anti-partisan paper,
but because he was not a Roman Catholic, he attained no high office
in the Slovak State; as a Lutheran, he became a Democratic Party
journalist after the war and then, after the 1948 Communist take-over,
he became a furious Stalinist. He employed the same inflammatory
gutterpress language and style for whomsoever he wrote. In Šikula's
Vilma the erstwhile Aryaniser and Fascist Kirinovič, having invented
a Resistance past, takes over a German's house after the war, and
has a major job in local government after the Communist take-over.
In the largely non-fiction studies of the USSR, *Generál s levom*,
Chňoupek had already stated that the brutality of Beria's boys was
as great as the Germans'. For example, he depicts Soviet soldiers
who had escaped from German camps and then joined partisans
being tortured by the NKVD into confessing they were German
agents. In *Slony v Mauthausene* Johanides portrays a wheeler-dealer
Hlinka Guard lieutenant who joins the Uprising, then from 1945–46
thrives as a cakeshop owner and then joins the Communist Party. In
Najsmutnejšia oravská balada the same author depicts the typical

Slovak lot in the figure of Jano Brechár; he was an Agrarian anti-Populist in the 1930s, was against the Hlinka Guard but had himself made black boots and pranced about in black breeches; he had joined the Uprising, been a Democrat after the War, but ends up a fairly senior regional functionary in the socialist state.

It is clear that Bednár was among the first, probably was the first, to try to approach political reality with some realism in 1950s Slovak literature. In her chapter Sivachenko claims that Bednár clearly supports socialism; that may be so, though it has nothing to do with his stature as a writer. In *Sklený vrch* and *Hodiny a minúty* he certainly appears to have been an optimist, but that optimism diminished as the 1970s progressed and in the sardonic pessimism of *Ad revidendum, Gemini* (1988) he returned to subjects treated in *Hodiny a minúty* and his ex-Fascist narrator gives little chance to any one-party state:

> Political parties are probably the worst thing in this world. One day they swooped down on me like a flock of evil birds, dangerous archaeopteryxes, to tear me apart, gobble me up, and they swamped me with balls and bosh or cobbler's cock, and I had to choose one party so I could be someone, so I could lend slightly legal form to my tendency to violence. [. . .] As an individual I couldn't manage great violence, only very small violence – and political parties were for making great, immense violence, enough to destroy all other parties, and not only that, but capable of extinguishing all life on Earth in the interest of the party's own prosperity. [. . .] Perhaps because of that it is good if there is a whole bunch of political parties [. . .], a whole tangle of worms which would then eat each other and not do as much harm to human beings as a single party, whether the German Nazi or the Slovak Hlinka Party (pp. 27–8).

Violence is central to Bednár's work. He abhors violence but is desperately resigned to the ubiquity of naturally violent human beings, and hence of gratuitous violence. He fears that such violence can all too easily be embodied in political ideologies. Perhaps more crassly in Johanides than in Bednár, that violence may belong to the essence of post-industrial society: for Johanides's Malay, department-store crèches and toy guillotines perform extreme violence on mankind; the Americanisation of the world is the brutalisation of the world and soon the Americans will learn from the Chinese how to suck the brain out of a live monkey (Johanides, 1985, pp. 114–5). In

Bednár one finds the expression of wariness of all political authority: 'Many a ruler has [. . .] imposed his notions of good on people, thus incited people to hatred and violence.' (Bednár, 1985, p. 89); violence is the grey theme of *Sklený vrch* and of *Hodiny a minúty*. The title story of Jaroš's *Krvaviny* constitutes a study of violence, mainly the violent dreams of a violent, dull conformist journalist who fears he will be inspired by his dreams to knife to death his wife and children or to rape all the neighbours. These dreams arise out of his modern living, modern neuroses and body-consciousness. In *Za hrsť drobných* Bednár relates the violence of Cintľa's being beaten up by lager-louts with little detail, and certainly no sadism or ghoulishness, and the resultant sense of horror is possibly greater than scenes of German violence in *Hodiny a minúty*. Cintľa, however, survives. The menacing violence of the louts as they lurk at the central family's gate drinking and urinating epitomises late twentieth-century urban delinquency. Further on in this trilogy, however, referring to one Slovak killing another in pre-war America, the canine narrator muses, 'that sort of thing happens among human beings. One kills another for no reason whatsoever. How many have died like that?!' (Bednár, 1974, p. 163). The main character of *Ako sme sušili bielizeň*, a painter, is blinded by bleach (the violence of the scene is as sudden as Cintľa's beating-up); then the drying-shed shared by the neighbours is burnt down and in the end the painter kills himself and his sweetheart. Particularly clearly here the social violence of marital infidelity and business trips accords with individual physical violence. In *Ad revidendum* the ex-Fascist Mišo Danihel, who is haunted by the scene of his shooting the baby of a woman who refused to tell him where the partisans were, goes off with his brother's wife, when the former is put in prison by a Stalinist class-avenger. Perhaps Slovak life had always been particularly violent. One thinks of the fundamental violence of village life in Jaroš's *Tisícročná včela* (for example, the two young men's mighty brawl over Martin's daughter, Kristína) or, indeed, in the interpolated tale of Johanides's *Súkromie*, where a village idiot is beaten to death for unintentionally contaminating water. Vilikovský, whose conception of violence is closest to Bednár's, ends his first collection of short stories with a distillation of modern violence. Two young thugs put on an act that a thin man in a bar is a homosexual and had tried to buy one of them for a vodka. He brushes them off, but they pursue him in the tram and when he suddenly jumps off, so do they; they follow him and give him a going over. Then one of these thugs visits a woman acquaintance, bullies her a little and then rapes her. When he returns out into the snow, he strides along whistling merrily. Vilikovský gives the story its emotional force by his matter-of-fact style. In his novel, *Prvá veta spánku*, he produces a similar scene when a frustrated police captain well-nigh sadistically trounces a youth who had falsely admitted to a murder. The reader does not expect that from this ironic, sentimental policeman.

Violence in modern Slovak fiction is frequently linked with animals; here it is perhaps clearer that depictions of violence represent the force applied by any authorities on their subjects. Kanikova is, no doubt, right about Dušek's conscious or subconscious Freudism and so we must be circumspect in interpreting the death of the phallic horse in *Kalendár*, and the violence with which the sweaty, spluttery, 40-year-old nudist Adam (*sic*) decapitates and drinks the blood of his beloved sparrows may not have a predominantly sexual meaning. The swallows slaughtered in Johanides's *Marek koniar* clearly bear power-politics connotations and, when the mental casuality of the war, Mandarín, crazily thumps blue birds in Ballek's *Južná pošta* his action emblemises the repugnant futility of learned violence. The young Bitman's killing of sparrows in Ferko's *Proso* represents the moral violence of his go-getting father's generation as well as the boy's own total insensitivity. Bednár's picture of the vivisection of dogs satirises political man's tendency to perverted messianism in making his victims suffer pain for the sake of (tomorrow's) progress: 'Injections, operations, transplants, vivisections and what have you, autotransplants, heterotransplants, homotransplants, calisections – all those are only brief, painful stretches of the glorious road to a wonderful, joyous, splendid goal' (Bednár, 1974, p. 21). All dogs, the narrator maintains, should rejoice at their laboratory experiences, for they represent a great leap forward on the path into the cosmos.

Human cruelty to animals constitutes ecological violence like the building of, say, dams. As early as *Sklený vrch* building is conceived of as aggression against Nature – here aggression is embodied particularly in machinery. Thirty years later in Beňo's cumbersome *Kým príde veľryba* the effects of a hydroelectric plant are cataclysmic; the water is a 'stampeding' whale. Building a factory is inimical to Nature, and the surveying of the site is undertaken by an ex-seminarian (Roman Catholicism suspended by the new religion of technology) in Feldeková's *Veverica* – where, incidentally, the steam threshing machine, which Hardy had used to represent grim progress in *Tess of the d'Urbervilles*, explodes. Factories, once there, produce little but foul air (Baláž, 1983; Bednár, 1974 and 1977) and, anyway, civilisation appears to consist in reducing greenness; in Bednár (1985) a garden is greatly diminished for the sake of building a useless drying-shed and at the end of that garden the rumble of a building site is as importunate as it had been in *Sklený vrch*. In Dušek (1982) an old tree is felled for the sake of a motorbike-shed and in the studiedly unpolitical Puškáš's *Záhrada* an elderly gardener does everything he can to prevent a school being built on a garden; when he had bought the land he had deceived the authorities by saying he wanted a building plot, whereas he had always wanted a garden. The countryside itself is being ruined by artificial fertilisers (Johanides, 1978 and 1988; Ferko, 1984) and weedkillers (Baláž, 1983); Ferko's ironic intellectual Jaro links pesticides with the welfare-state mentality: 'the postwar quasitoxoplasmatic pesticide generation has a certain innate laziness; there is too much affluence and so the first generation who has to pay heavily – I mean drastically – will put some order into the environment.' (Ferko, 1984, p. 49). The new class, the socialist *nouveaux riches*, form the largest element of social pollution. Yuppies threaten society more than lagerlouts; apparently circumstances are, then, contrary to those in the West. Yuppies may include waiters (cf. Andruška, 1977), Vlado's 'barman' type, his brother-inlaw with all mod-cons, in Hlatký's *História vecí*, the couple who build a second house before they organise a smooth divorce in Bednár (1986), and the smooth new-class academic, Karol, who is always ready to flash his administrative prowess in Ján Beňo (1977). Baláž (1983) overdoes the vulgarity of the working-class Iveta who sells herself into marriage with the rich wheeling-dealing engineer Rišo. The callous self-centredness of the family in Johanides (1979) is more convincing than Baláž's high-flying couple, and that derives to a degree from Johanides's skilful use of Bratislava slang. Hudec presents a new-class man dying of cancer in *Čierne diery* and he names him after himself; 'Ivan Hudec's' soul is so corrupt that not even love can redeem it; he is swindled by an acquisitive colleen.

Composers of *Trivialliteratur*, like Krno, and of worthy tract novels, like Mináč, had earlier attacked a class with similar habits in their depictions of the bourgeoisie and *jeunesse dorée* of the Slovak State. It has become a convention of Slovak literary history to speak of the Uprising Generation (those writing since the 1940s or 1950s who witnessed the Uprising), the '56 Generation (those who, in or shortly after 1956, contributed to the periodical *Mladá tvorba*) and to the Younger Generation (writers born in and since the 1940s who began publishing in the 1960s or later), and many of the contributors to this volume abide by this convention. When I now try briefly to point out (generational?) varieties of approach to the series of violent acts which gave birth to modern Slovakia (Uprising and German Occupation, Soviet liberation and Communist take-over; in some Slovak writers' view I should add collectivisation), you will note that chronological taxonomies are not entirely helpful. It is, for example, silly not to put Ladislav Beňo into the Uprising Generation, even if he did not publish his first novel until 1972; the style of that novel and the author's approach to its contents belong to the early 1950s. Chňoupek's most original work on the Uprising, *Lámanie pečatí*, half fiction and half reportage, belongs to the 1970s or 1980s for its content, but to the 1950s for its political stance and its attitude to individual psychology, though by birth the author belongs to the middle generation.

Tatarka constitutes another anomaly: he moved from stolid Uprising writing via Thaw-jumping to mild dissidence. Tatarka first made his name with his account of Anabella who becomes a muse or an obsession for a group of young artists, because of what they imagine about her rather than what she actually is, *Panna Zázračnica*, a novel which owes as much to the Czech Nezval as Feldeková's *Veverica* does. In *Navrávačky* Tatarka admits that he had never 'developed his talent' (1988, p. 90), but from *Panna Zázračnica* to the Socialist Realist account of the Slovak State and the persecution of Jews and Communists, *Farská republika*, one either sees development or the beginnings of what might be perceived as literary-political opportunism. In *Navrávačky* he compares his thundering hard-line *Prvý a druhý úder* with Bednár's Uprising works, which is very unfair to Bednár. In Tatarka's novel the hero, Reptiš, becomes a partisan, first in the Ukraine, then in Slovakia and afterwards he is a mighty builder of socialism; he is involved in bridge rather than dam building. The novel ends: 'On 12th August both bridge details sent a delegation to greet the conference of the Slovak Communist Party and as a present they brought with them the announcement that both bridges were completed' (Tartarka, 1950, p. 237). In his *Démon súhlasu* (periodical form 1965, book form 1963) he makes fun of Reptiš and his exploits, to a degree makes fun of himself as a man who had been possessed of the demon of conformity; by *Navrávacky* he is no longer able to laugh at himself. In *Démon súhlasu* he has still retained his fringe-culture notion that literature is a political weapon, not art: literature should defend the citizens against the abuse of power. In

Písačky he calls his autobiographical narrator Bartolomej Slzička, which may be self-ironical (*slza*=tear), but otherwise he takes himself all too seriously; this seriousness includes self-pity and self-congratulation about being a banned writer. *Navrávačky* still retains something of the old man's sensual self-indulgence of *Písačky* but it is primarily a folkloristic account of the author's childhood, youth and his experience as a writer in the 1940s and 1950s; it ends with a paean to various members of Charter 77. Often in *Písačky* Tatarka behaves like a village story-teller who has decided by mistake to be an intellectual, but at least he does admit (or, claim to admit) he is an uneducated man (1988, p. 111). When he writes of Werfel's *Barbara oder die Frömmigkeit* (Barbara or: Piety) that Werfel had written 'Piety was a Czech maid in the Werfel household' (1988, p. 104), it is at the very least misleading, and when he says Christians are people who stepped into the Jordan to be baptised by John (1988, p. 110), it is wrong – but one should not be surprised that such a gynophil should forget Salome. Tatarka died in the spring of 1989.

The so-called Uprising Generation perhaps wrote more about the Uprising than subsequent generations and they were also the writers who were most aware of the palpable similarities of all types of totalitarianism. Here one might except those writers who went into exile and who thus knew nothing of socialism first hand. I do not count Hronský, was was imprisoned by the partisans and then the Americans and fled to Argentina, or Urban, who was imprisoned by the Americans but then returned to Slovakia to write Socialist Realism; Hronský and Urban belonged to an earlier generation (if I keep to chronological categorising). Ján Okáľ, who went into exile in America, was in German detention during the Uprising, and in his literary memoirs he is almost scathing about the partisans. The Uprising, he says, 'collapsed as much because of internal divisions as of the German intervention' and 'only the leadership of the Uprising was revolutionary' (1986, pp. 38–9). He also suggests that the partisans treated those they captured well and then released them as a 'propaganda trick' (1986, p. 22). In contrast to writers like Okáľ and many younger writers of the 1960s onwards, Tatarka and, say, Jašík make the Slovak State a thoroughly repulsive institution. In Jašík's conception the State, the Hlinka Guard and the German occupiers embody institutionalised violence and thus an offence against the chief value of life, love. Jašík is as down-to-earth about Slovak collaborators with the Germans as Bednár. Mňačko's account of the Uprising and the partisan war in *Smrť sa volá Engelchen* was unusual because of the extent to which Mňačko psychologises, because it was an exciting story and because the most heroic Resistance worker was a Jewess – in order to get information for the partisans she acts as the German officers' whore. After the war she cannot live with her own heroism; so she kills herself. However ordinary most of the Slovaks in it are, this pro-Communist novel is far from mythoclastic. Indeed their very ordinariness supports Establishment partisan mythology. And they are awfully competent at blowing up bridges and trains and taking German officers prisoner. The Russian partisan group leader Voloďa is just as heroic and ideal as Tatarka's Žilko or Chňoupek's Veličko. In contrast, the Russian commander, Ivan, in *Ako chutí moc* is not simply a cruel plunderer of peasants; he is a brigand quite willing to shoot a Slovak as a spy if he takes a fancy to his boots. In this last novel Voloďa's place is taken by the Slovak Great Man whose vigorous life and moral corruption Mňačko traces. The Great Man had had a mistress during the partisan war; he had hid from the Gestapo and the Hlinka Guard in her house and then she had fought side by side with him. After the war, when he already has senior rank, he visits her in his chauffeur-driven car, gets very drunk, tries to rape her, is prevented and so has both her and her father put in prison. The partisan hero becomes Stalinist tyrant. In the crass satire, *Súdruh Münchhausen*, Mňačko stalely depicts the rise to power of a type who is the opposite (during and after the war) of the Great Man. Because of Mňačko's disgrace and defection Mináč's mythopoeic *Generácia* trilogy (1958, 1959, 1961) has achieved a place in Slovak literary history which it does not deserve for either artistic or political reasons. Perhaps it did serve to replace Bednár in the brief Re-Freeze which took place between about 1959 and 1963. The first part contains much overgeneralisation concerning people from different social and political backgrounds during the State; in this moralising novel the characters are not entirely black or white, though its schematicness might lead the reader to imagine they are. At the end most of the characters have rushed off to join the joyous Uprising – the kind of solution Šikula comments on sardonically in his 'Majstri' trilogy. In the second Mináč novel the Uprising shows what stuff country-born Slovaks are really made of; urban Slovaks turn out to be undependable or weak. Most of the third novel consists in straight propaganda writing to show how only the Communists could clear up post-war Slovakia, which was returning to Fascism with the help of the West. In the trilogy Mináč plays down the Soviet liberation; certainly we have Soviet and

Russian-trained partisans but the author's own patriotism keeps us
with the Uprising forces rather than the Red Army. His argument is
that the natural pure spirit of the Slovak country or country-town
dweller leads naturally to Communism; in his conception, then, there
is hardly a need for Soviets.

Not until the '56 Generation was the role of the French in the
Uprising dealt with. Though French participation was mentioned by,
say, Jaroš in *Krvaviny* or Šikula in *Vojak*, Chňoupek was the first to
treat the French seriously, in *Lámanie pečatí*. This generation
probably proffered as many nasty wartime Slovaks as the previous
generation. Now, however, one senses a growing urge, if not to
demythologise, at the least to re-assess the Uprising and the German
occupation. Thus Šikula writes in *Vlha*: 'You're often surprised at
all the places you find a Slovak! Honest Injun, sometimes even in
German uniform. Suddenly you realise one of your own is kicking
you, that Slovaks know how to knock out your teeth too, especially
if he's got a decent German boot on his foot. If he hasn't got a boot,
he'll beat you to death with a sandal or a carpet-slipper' (1978,
p. 260). Ordinary Slovaks are usually not in the slightest interested
in the war until the partisans or the Germans actually come knocking
at their doors. Jozef Horák showed that in the first proper Uprising
novel, *Hory mlčia* (1947), and that picture is reproduced in Papp's
Kára plná bolesti. The main character in Ťažký's *Aj v nebi je lúka*
becomes a Communist sympathiser between the wars, but shows no
political consciousness concerning the Slovak State; he might then
help in the Uprising and partisan war, but he more or less just gets
caught up in it like the peasants and artisans (with the exception of
the tinker Karčimarčik) in Šikula's *Majstri*. Mňačko and Chňoupek
seemed to be deliberately reacting to Jozef Horák, when they made
the hill-farmers the true heroes of the war, and in *S Rozarkou* Šikula
states explicitly through an old partisan that he wishes to change the
way people speak and write about the Uprising: 'so much has been
said about it that it's actually harmful; some people cannot talk about
great or beautiful things, can't look at them, like they can't look at a
pretty woman, for instance, without soiling her with their eyes. And
the Uprising was more than a pretty woman' (1966, pp. 50–1).
That also prepares us for the mythopoeia of the *Majstri* trilogy.
Nevertheless Šikula does not whitewash the Slovaks; nor does he
overblacken the Germans; he probably says so little about the Soviets
in the trilogy because of the reputation the liberator Malinovsky
gained when he had his headquarters in Modra, near where the

trilogy is set. Johanides shows the Slovaks' passive collaboration in the deportation of Jews in *Súkromie*, and in *Slony v Mauthausene* he depicts a religiose Slovak woman assuming the task of inspecting Jewesses' vaginas in case they should be hiding gold in them. There too a Jew is determined to die in his own garden before being deported to Germany and when the local synagogue is set on fire, former Jews' maids, including the wife of a Hlinka guardist, try to put it out. In *Najsmutnejšia oravská balada*, because of their respect for lawyers, Orava villagers will do nothing to the Jewish lawyer, but they make him watch them put his wife in a barrel into which they have knocked nails; as they set the barrel rolling down a hill the lawyer has a heart attack and dies.

The Younger Generation depict the Slovak State and events leading up to the socialist state more than the Uprising itself, for obvious reasons. The subject of Jewish persecution is also less frequently treated by younger writers than by those of the preceding two generations. The reasons for that are not so obvious. In fact, like Poland, Slovakia witnessed scenes of violent anti-semitism immediately after the War; Ballek points that out in *Pomocník* and in the following he ironises the blood libel as well as the old Party attacks on Zionism:

> A great many [of the Palánk Jews] have not survived the war and of those who have some are being baptised, Slovacising their names, scattering all over Czechoslovakia, or leaving for Palestine. They are complaining about the new postwar wave of hatred among some Goys who accuse the Jews of zealotry and other hypothetical blameworthy deeds like the crucifixion of Christ. They are particularly hurt by the absurd accusation that, through the ritual murder of Christian boys, they are collecting blood for the consecration of the new Temple in Jerusalem apparently dedicated to Jahweh because He had, after all, not permitted the extermination of His people. They are also hurt that some sinful person has now used axle-grease to daub swastikas on the walls of the synagogue (1977, pp. 264–5).

In his depiction of the periods up to, during and after the war in his *Kolonisti*, Habaj is as anti-semitic as he is anti-German. For the war and immediately post-war period Habaj speaks of the Roumanian participation in the liberation of Slovakia, as Ladislav Beňo had in *Nebezpečná zóna*. And as Beňo writes about the Ukrainian Fascist Banderites, so Habaj writes about the renegade Soviet Vlasov's army in Slovakia. Habaj also has a false hero such as we saw in Bednár or Šikula, except that Habaj's is a Hungarian, as one might expect from such a populist; a Hungarian Fascist thug becomes a Communist official (Habaj, 1986, p. 76). In the brief picture Ballek gives of the Uprising in *Lesné divadlo* he tries to be as truthful as he can; the insurgents listen only to the BBC and their own Banská Bystrica (not to Kiev, as many might well have done since the Uprising command was there); Ballek is usually a careful stylist, and so it is surprising here to find the anachronistic 'antifascist' and the jargon 'Anti-Hitler Coalition' (instead of 'Allies'). In *Pomocník* he tells us about the German leaflets calling on people to return down from their mountain hideouts, which is a topos of Uprising literature. Ballek's Riečan does, however, go down – he is immediately arrested, and for three days he is beaten with rubber tubing, until his father manages to exert his influence to obtain his release. No doubt equally realistic is the episode in *Agáty* when three drunken Uprising partisans kill a stray cat, then play football first with its whole body then with just its head. Then they eat their dinner and 'for a long time the astonishing relief and sense of victory, as if they had thrashed a troop of SS, did not fade from their cheeks' (1981, p. 90), but when they do sober up, they bury the cat. Ballek's Fate or God does not allow any of these three deheroised Slovaks to survive the war. Ballek is again unconventional when he points out the fate of Slovak soldiers immediately after the war. One is used to hearing of the soldiers who had joined the Uprising or who were in charge of the ackack around Bratislava or who were in the Fast Division in the Ukraine, but that is all. Ballek's brief description of detainees serves also as a picture of the variety of fates that could befall a Slovak family in the war: 'a military internment camp with a fairly large number of prisoners waiting for a court hearing. Some because they had decided to do a bunk at the wrong moment, some because they had not ended up on the winning side, some because they had been good racketeers, some because they had behaved improperly with civilian property and civilian women, and the next just because they had a simple outlook and after the first victories of the Reich has lost their belief in the need for a conscience' (1974, p. 96). Immediately post-war Slovakia in Karol Horák's *Cukor* is bleak indeed: families with members lost in the war, families with burnt-out houses, an outsider family of collaborators, families longing to thieve, and gendarmes of a lost morality: as a whole, human beings all hungry for something. The only glory of this Slovakia is the main character, Motylka's, private glory that she manages to exchange her tobacco for sugar for her pregnant daughter.

The main action of *Cukor* consists in memories, and memories and memoirs have as significant a place in modern Slovak literature as in any other. Okáľ's *Leto na Traune* consists of a stylised account of facts of the same, though less literary, sort as Chňoupek's *Lámanie pečatí*. Both works contain timid similes, occasional lapses into grandiloquence, some over-politicisation and lots of heroes. And both works are repetitive because they had been worked on over a number of years. Okáľ's work contains virtually no self-mythicisation, which cannot be said for Tatarka's *Písačky*, which is narcissistic. *Písačky* consists chiefly of repetitive, lush, sometimes mawkish, sometimes coarse and usually sensualist, descriptions of the *Ich*'s erotic play and copulation with a woman he calls many grand names like Lutécia, but mostly Čiča (Cuntlet). There is nothing audacious or shocking about Tatarka's memoir. It is simply tedious bad manners to go on about one's erotic experience for so long, and it is self-debasing in the sense that the narrator persists in invading the author's privacy. Some fiction works by other authors immediately occur to the student because they appear to contain a strong memoir element. Sloboda has his Socialist Realist account of a sojourn in the drying-out unit of a mental hospital, *Stratený raj*, but also his somewhat amorphous account of his days at Bratislava conservatory, *Hudba*, a novel to which Šikula's tale, *Liesky*, bears a striking, playful resemblance. The two authors were apparently fellow pupils. Neither Sloboda nor Šikula is nostalgic, but Tatarka is, in *Písačky* and *Navrávačky*, and in the latter he confesses that all his writing had consisted in recounting his memories of what had happened to and around him. One might argue that Ballek is also a sensualist and also nostalgic, but Ballek's nostalgia is not static nostalgia like Tatarka's or the Czech Karel Čapek's. Ballek's nostalgia, if his forms of creative memory can be labelled nostalgia at all, is dynamic; it creates a series of yardsticks against which one may gauge actions of today, just as today measures the first few post-war years when the action of most of his Palánk narratives take place. Even when he reaches the 1960s in *Lesné divadlo*, the 1940s remain the main creative impulse. Nostalgia certainly enters the title and the psychological action of Bednár's *Ako sme sušili bielizeň*: the old, clean ways of doing things, but nostalgia is also satirised, indeed parodied by the very blindness of the painter. The novel is too pessimistic to display self-indulgence of the kind nostalgia suggests.

Memory itself also makes for a theme. In *Južná pošta* Ballek declares memory part of a new beginning, a constituent naive optimism necessary to make something of the post-war world: 'I love the consciences of small children and the sound memories of adults. That is all that has survived this war' (1974, p. 71). The variety of points of view and the author or his narrators' moving backwards and forwards over the brief period covered by *Agáty* result in a true-to-life evocation of memory and varieties of memory. In Hlatký's view memory cannot, through piecing together impressions, recreate the relationship which had existed between the people who form part of an individual memory. 'Events, pictures and words are scattered', he claims, 'and feeling is brief and strong, and words and events live in feelings and impressions like lonely buoys on a wide, deep lake' (1988, p. 36). Puškáš's view of memory is less thoughtful, more banal, and suggests that lack of analysis which often marks his longer works. 'Time,' he says, 'sinks into the dense waters of memory like a papyrus scroll sinking into the dunes and patiently waits for a favourable wind to uncover it' (1984, p. 16). Chance or a favourable wind may, indeed, aid memory, but one may not say that is good or bad. Memory is in the broadest possible sense political. Narrowly, no authorities have any respect of individuals' memories, hence the bulldozing of the graveyard in Johanides's *Pochovávanie brata* and Hlatký's *História vecí*. In the second part of *Súpis dravcov* Horák considers the role of language in memory. In a factory language course the instructor jovially orders his pupils to forget their own language, that is to cast out all past experience (1979, p. 81). Politics enters here because the destruction of memory (to put it grandly, the destruction of history) constitutes the main philosophical concern of any society which claims it has evolved from logical laws of history and yet which denies or forgets or deliberately distorts its own past, particularly the past which can be remembered by the living. (In a society where historical re-interpretation is strictly limited by ideological dogma, literature tends to be given history's jobs, to demythologise and reconstruct.) Horák's first-person narrator, between the film and class dialogues, obediently tries to brainwash himself – which highlights the author's anti-historicism: 'The world is just arising, is constructing itself in my memory' (1979, p. 83). In *Cukor* Horák had looked at memory from another point of view; he had considered memory as a forger of this past. That capacity of memory is represented by a carefully tinted and prettied-up picture a photographer brings to the family he had snapped by mistake some years previously. That will remind any Slovak reader of the photograph revisions of the Stalinist period. Johanides's novel of initiation, *Najsmutnejšia oravská balada*, pays some attention to the impact of genetic or collective memory on the individual memory, and to the effect a person's death has on our recall of him. The memory may change the nature of its products without the interference of our will. The chief narrator in this novel, Poldo, realises that, when his father had been buried, his memories of him had become blurred; it was 'as if that funeral ceremony had intended to reveal that I had really had a father' (1988, p. 47). The second story of Balco's *Ležoviská* entirely concerns the unreliability of memory, the spatial and temporal games memory plays on us. Finally, Bednár's *Ad revidendum, Gemini* is for its action structure and psychology based on the paradoxical capacity of memory to charm and to menace simultaneously.

Memory is fast linked with a background element of literature that several contributors to this volume consider a theme of Slovak literature: home, *domov*, which is actually the same as *Heimat*, contains the same sentimentalising potential as *Heimat* and, indeed, the possibilities of conversion into *Blut und Boden*. Brušák points out the closeness of Habaj to the Czech Ruralist Prokůpek (in whose *Lost land* the central figure is also a colonist); other Ruralists like Knap (for his racism as well as his moralising) or Marcha (for his nostalgia and soil-love) also look forward to some modern Slovak writing. Apart from Habaj I think in particular of Ťažký. The concept *domov* constitutes the sentimentalisation of a notional home, place of belonging, and Slovak critics' (and writers'?) perception of it appears to have grown out of a combination of the feudal idea of belonging (*patria*) and the fashionable mid-twentieth-century invention of the 'identity crisis'. One is not concerned here with sentimental lauding of village as against city life, though there is still plenty of that in Slovak literature, say in Ján Beňo or, somewhat ironically, in Bednár's *Za hrsť drobných I*. Nor is one concerned with the creation of a fairy-tale small-town past, such as we see in Dušek's Piešťany in *Poloha pri srdci*, nor in the subrural quaintness of Sloboda's Devínska Nová Ves in *Hudba, Rozum* and *Uršuľa*. Though elements of both might come into our picture of what *domov* is. Dušek, Puškáš, Šikula and, in *Navrávačky*, even Tatarka, do tend towards *Heimatliteratur*. Johanides's conception of home is more or less the opposite of theirs. In *Najsmutnejšia oravská blada* home, the Orava region, is from a material point of view, a gene-bank and, from a spiritual point of view, a region whose sons and daughters are linked by a collective memory peculiar to themselves. In Johanides the background concept is 'tradition' rather than 'home', a basis rather than a pseudotheme imbued with nostalgia. The reader also notices that pain suffuses Orava as it does the Palánk of Ballek's *Južná pošta*. Johanides's Poldo has within him 'that pure, rough, vitreous bright air which besieged the spring-damp, barely twenty-year-old shingles on the wooden church's roof [. . .] and the wooden church steps which had been ground smooth by nearly two hundred years of coarse, heavy and also almost dainty soles, proud, dignified, deliberate steps, and he was able to recall the little clouds of breath on the icy air inside the log-built church' (1988, p. 17). Johanides's Orava is racially mixed – mainly Germans and Slovaks, Lutherans and Roman Catholics, but also Czechs. It is a region of incest. Pimps liked girls from Orava because they had learned such a lot from their fathers. Tatarka's Orava is a little more sentimental; he is proud of his sheepherding smallholder family and of a forebear who was executed for banditry, but his chief memories are of hawks (that is also influenced by the folk-tradition) and of sexual freedom. In Feldeková's neo-Surrealist deconstruction novel about growing up in Orava, *Veverica*, the sense of Polishness is strong through the presence of Jerzy and the sounds of the bells of Cracow which are heard on his Orava wedding day. The special feature of this Orava is provided by the herbalist or witch, with whom much of the novel is immediately or indirectly concerned – and so a fair portion of the story is magic. Perhaps, however, that is the magicality of remembering childhood. Certainly Feldeková's Orava lacks the depth of Tatarka's, let alone Johanides's. The witch constitutes a topos in depictions of the fairly recent past in the Slovak provinces. In Jašík's social novel concerning the growth of Communist political consciousness in a poverty-stricken Kysuce hamlet between the wars, *Na brehu priezračnej rieky*, the local witch Kvíčaľka has a fine sense of solidarity and down-to-earth Christian charity. In *Súpis dravcov* Horák parodies the literary witch in the figure of the fortune-telling Páleníčka who has thrombotic legs and so cannot move from her cottage. The village of Vyslanka or Vysranka, which is the object of such study in that tale, embodies a bizarre satire on the Slovak *domov* cult, on folksiness and on 'science'. Generally the village of memory is becoming a less and less pleasant place in Slovak literature. In *Tu musíš žiť* a village lad's mother comes to the city to inspect his bride; according to rural custom that inspection entails prodding and groping about all 'her female parts' (Baláž, 1983, p. 223). In Bednár's *Ad revidendum*,

Gemini Agáta displays herself to her brother-in-law so that he will not become a cow-shagger as others had before him. In *Ferko* the unnamed village where the old people's home is situated is a parody village lying on the river Tichá voda (Still Water, compare partisan scenes in Bednár's *Sklený vrch*) and between the two other settlements of Biely Majer (White Farm) and Lepšie Život (Better Life). Hudec sends up the *domov* myth in *Čierne diery* when his unpleasant narrator visits his native Nitra.

The memory of the village, town or area in which a writer grew up is generally stimulated by visual or olfactory sensation. In this volume Petrík speaks of that phenomenon in Ballek. Obviously enough, the acacias are the primary stimulus in *Agáty*: 'The acacias blossomed again in Palánk and new stories began' (1981, p. 557), and 'Acacias blossom and fade. And ever new stories of people come. What changes? Height, pressure, temperature, dew. Numerals change; the years of humanity slowly furl up' (1981, p. 291). The acacias represent, then, human continuum, and human sensuality, for the fragrance of the acacias is essential; thus the dotty Filadelfi would never dream of entering the acacia woods in May without a sweetheart. Dušek's Piešťany is also characterised by acacias (for example, 1983, p. 18), but also by gravel, pigeons and darkness, and in Habaj's *Kolonisti* one of the barbarous acts of the Hungarian occupiers is to hew down the Czechoslovak colonists' acacia woods. In *Poľné samoty* the acacias express continuity: 'The old Monarchy dissolved; a new state arose. And she took up into herself this meadow, this farmstead and the acacia wood' (Habaj, 1979, p. 5). Lilacs come second to acacias in Ballek, not because they are fewer in number, but because they do not so much characterise the surroundings of Palánk and Palánk's leisure as the streets, houses, workaday Palánk. Both lilacs and acacias are strewn about *Južná pošta* and in *Agáty* 'The town and the Stages of the Cross are one immense lilac bush, blue as the mantle of the Blessed Virgin' (1981, p. 162). In *Poľné samoty* a street has a lilac hedge, but the blossoms lack the emblematic value they have in Ballek: 'when the lilac fades, other flowers blossom. It is always full of fragrance here.' (Habaj, 1979, p. 231). In Hlatký the lilac also forms part of a general olfactory sensation – one which here casts a gently ironic light on a memory: 'When behind the thick walls of the National Health institution the lilacs blossomed and sated the air with intoxicating perfume, grandmother died and for Vlado heavy perfume became toxic stench' (1988, p. 11). Memory, past, history are evoked and transmitted sensually, for Slovak writers (often only first generation in the capital) are linked sensually rather than intellectually to their backgrounds (*patriae*?). Thus one of Ballek's narrators describes the confusion of memory as 'long journeys on foot, departures, returns, my near ones, acacia woods and their perfume, fairytales, stories and, ever more frequently, this my southern town which is my childhood brimmed with scents, colours and heathen joys.' (1981, p. 511). The dominant colour of *Pomocník* is lush green, the green of new beginnings after the war; in *Agáty* it is the yellow of mature middle-class society, the yellow of summer, heat and mindless, joyous buzzing; in *Lesné divadlo* it is brown and autumn pastels, the decay of socialism, the futile settling of old scores, the dangerous lure of the West. The main character in Puškáš's *Štvrtý rozmer* tends to have 'olfactory memories' so that 'ordinary potatoes sometimes gave birth to a picture of china-white shoots in a musty cellar with long lace-curtains of cobwebs hanging from its walls' (1980, p. 49). Poldo's memory of his father's funeral in Johanides's last novel is primarily linked with the smells issuing from spice-tins when his father had used to cook (1988, p. 56). In Dušek an ordinary olfactory memory may develop into an emotional generalisation, which, in the following case, encloses a paradox – indeed, the author suggests, perhaps unintentionally, that 'a good man' is an oxymoron: 'The snow spreads a silent, inconspicuous scent, a misty scent, something like ice. Good men have the same smell' (1982, p. 78). As the inhabitants walk down the street which opens *Náprstok* the smells of their occupations fuse with those of a soda-water and paper-flower factory. There is something of an olfactory fairytale in that. In visual memory Dušek has a predilection for autumn and its colours, where Balco, who shares some memory imagery with Dušek, likes summer. Balco's memory also has a genetic dimension, for in the present Dr Semely's heart 'his grandfather is scything down the meadow on a beautiful day in a distant June in the slow, lazy sun of the Monarchy' (1986, p. 17). *Heimat* or *domov* or the memory thereof is as intimately linked with female armpit and pubic hair in Balco (1986, p. 11) as it is in Dušek. In Dušek armpit hair is likened to nests (1982, p. 73) or little bushes where one can hide (1985, p. 74–5) and in the cycle *Kalendár* the reader cannot be sure whether the armpit described, or the linked excretions, belong to the girl Lenka or the countryside, Mother Nature (both grammatical feminines in Slovak): 'Everything was trembling in the hot body of the countryside. The smell of sweat was in her armpits. The smell of water in her mouth. And of spittle' (1983, p. 92).

Notions of *domov* may often be linked with national self-conception. As one might expect in a numerically small nation on the very fringes of Western culture, national self-conception not only includes a great deal of national or nation-building mythology, but also sometimes approaches outright nationalism. The novel mentioned more frequently than any other in this volume, Jaroš's *Tisícročná včela* exhibits the same sort of nationalism as Okál', nationalism such as Mináč satirised in the 1950s. Okál' writes with a false tradition which had been gradually built up during the nineteenth century and came to a ludicrous head in the 1930s. Okál' speaks, for example, of 'the thousand-year-old tradition of Svatopluk's warriors' (1986, p. 123). Mináč satirises such invented tradition in the words of the architect Ferkodič: 'we Slovaks have waited a thousand years to fulfil our historic task, to turn the idea of Slovak statehood into fact. A thousand years! How full of suffering was the road from Svatopluk and Pribina to Tiso [. . .]!' (1958, p. 47). When one returns to Jaroš, one wonders whether the national and political elements in the historical novel were not intended as a joke, but then all the critics have misunderstood the novel for a decade. Certainly the sexual topography of the novel would also have artistic value, if one interpreted it as satire. The novel's title is either based on or alludes satirically to two national myths which are widespread among writers, not only among the uneducated public. The first word refers to the historically entirely unsound notion that the Slovaks had suffered for a thousand years under the Magyars. The main stimulus to this myth was given by the Millenium Exhibition of the 1890s when the Hungarians commemorated the arrival of the first Magyars on Hungarian territory. The second word in Jaroš's title refers to the notion that the Slovaks were a hardworking nation of artisans or builders. The family at the centre of the novel is called Pichanda (stinger, but possible erotic meaning, too), and Martin Pichanda is a bricklayer; his eldest son, Samo, is first a bricklayer, then a miller (in Slovakia, with the butcher, top of the artisan scale), and Valent betrays his class a trifle by becoming a lawyer and marrying into the local rich petty nobility (though, naturally, he prefers a peasant girl, who symbolically dies bearing his child). Samo keeps bees (retains sound Slovakhood) and his apiary functions as a refuge from his immediate surroundings. Their buzzing sends him to sleep and so the bees create dreams for him. In one of them the queen bee speaks to him so that the reader understands her function as the lasting spirit of the Slovaks. 'I am,' she says, 'the thousand-year-old mother bee.

Only I never die; I remain living in the hive, for I am eternal. I know everything about your ancestors [. . .] and shall know everything about your children, grandchildren, great grandchildren . . . ' (1979, p. 15). Samo's copulation with his future wife keeps to the rhythm of the bees' humming. The other bee-loving character in the novel is the National Awakener, Orfanides; thus the bees are linked with the 1950s notion of the naturalness of Communism for the Slovaks. The ludicrousness of this manifests itself in the tipsy Orfanides's behaviour: 'he shouted loudly into the hive "Workers of the world unite!"' (1979, p. 52). Later on, Orfanides actually explains the novel's title: 'We have held out a thousand years only because we know how to work. Ten of us die, but twelve of us are born. Just like bees, just like bees . . . !' (1979, p. 135). Then, after that, Samo explains that the Slovaks may well resemble bees, but they do not have stings. That may be understood as referring to the unrevolutionariness of 1890s Slovaks or to the natural sweetness of the Slovak character. When Samo withdraws from politics his attitude to his bees changes; he loses his respect for the queen bee and becomes a defeatist, who expects the bee-like Slovaks to be annihilated one day, if not by a tsar or king, then by a notary or priest. Jaroš drives his banal political point home at the end of the novel: 'Neither priests nor schoolmasters nor Slovak capital nor the World War solved for us what we have to solve for ourselves. Honey is carried into the hive by bees . . . We are those bees!' (1979, p. 442). With his dying, poor, hard-working Slovak Ťažký echoes Jaroš: 'Chrobáčik's last smile, last sensation of life was when he declared himself a bee.' (1986, p. 23) I am not suggesting that Jaroš invented the Slovak-as-bee banality. In *Poľné samoty* the Hungarians burn down a Slovak's beehives at the end of October, 1938: 'The dear little bees are burnt to cinders. How could anyone do that? They set fire to the bees, God's workers . . .' (Habaj, 1979, p. 37) Hlatký appears to make bitter fun of the idea in *História vecí*, though it may be sheer coincidence that Hlatký links his theme word *med* (honey) not with good Slovak work, but with alienation or humiliation. The gingerbread-maker (*medovnikár*) is a pharisee whose daughter Vlado's father had first wished to marry, but the *medovnikár* defected when faced with the Communist take-over, and, anyway, he had been forced to make love to her in barns for she would have been ashamed to be seen in public with a poor boy. On the Christmas Eve Vlado spends with his simpering uncle he is told there is no Father Christmas and receives no presents; his grandmother, however, makes a cross of honey on everyone's forehead; then gingerbread is eaten at her funeral wake. At the wake the narrator points out his use of honey as a narrative principle, as the element which sticks together all events concerning various members of his family and the priest. Later honey becomes a disguise which had been adopted by bureaucrats to hoodwink the masses, to create a belief in social messianism: 'I suspect that villains like him [the uncle] smeared a honey rope beneath our noses to lead us by, so that we would not see what their hands were up to' (1988, p. 84). The third element is the circus bear (*medved*), which appears first as a simile for the clumsiness of Vlado's hard-working father in front of the flash new-classness of his son-in-law. Then it appears with the name Arthur (chivalry and spirituality), clearly close to death or in extreme distress; its paws bandaged, a circus artiste beats it up, so that the young children in the audience feel that this smart, white-shirted artiste is beating up a teddy-bear. Still, when the bear can endure it no longer and runs off, all the audience applaud the bully. All physical or spiritual simplicity is driven out by the sophisticated bullying of modern society.

The notion that the Slovak had always been bullied and despised by the Magyar is also part of national mythology. Even Ballek totes the legend that all Hungarians had said '*Tót nem ember*' ('Slovaks are not human'; 1977, p. 186), and Ťažký, more realistically, has Magyars call his wretched hero *butatót* ('Slovak simpleton'; 1986, p. 61). But this man reproaches Transylvanian Hungarians for knowing no Slovak, which is silly, and is not surprised that he can get by with Slovak in Pest. According to the legend transmitted by Ťažký the Avars had called the Slovaks *tót*s and the Magyars had taken the word over only as a term of abuse (1986, p. 114). (Actually *tót* is the same word as *deutsch* or *Dutch*.) In *Poľné samoty* Habaj has Hungarians hate Czechs, but despise Slovaks, and in *Kolonisti* Hungarians are willing to learn Czech, but not Slovak (there is historical truth to that). The Slovak grandfather of the main character in Mitana's *Koniec hry* had been murdered by Magyar nationalists. The anti-Slovak Liptay in *Agáty* has Grünwald's *A Felvidék* as his bible, and here Ballek has unthinkingly accepted Slovak nationalist propaganda, for Grünwald was a liberal who (in another work) advocated the Magyarisation of the Slovak intelligentsia for fairness' sake, to give them equal chances with the Magyars. Grammar schools should be sausage machines: one stuffs Slovaks into them and out pop nicely moulded Magyars. Grünwald rejected the teaching of Hungarian in Slovak primary schools. In the same novel Ballek repeats an element in the Slovak tradition which apparently has some truth to it. The assassination in Sarajevo had evoked 'greater sadness than elsewhere' (1981, p. 285), since Franz Ferdinand had conceived of an autonomous Slovakia and Transylvania. Another part of national mythology is more or less authentically related in Šikula's *Vojak* where Bartók appears as a collector of Slovak folk songs. Šikula makes his hero one of Bartók's informants. Hykisch is positively mythopoeic in his representation of Pressburg as a great centre of Enlightenment intellectual activity in his dryasdust didactic chronical *Milujte kráľovnú!*, where he also puts forward a non-nationalist version of history, where Magyars and Slovaks built Hungary together. In the same work, however, he propounds biological patriotism: 'Matej Bel switched into the Central Slovak dialect. Adam Kollár quivered. He had heard the voice of home. As if his father had spoken – ah, that gentle dignity' (1984, p. 116). The Slovaks' role as Slavs appears to be ever increasing, and Cyril and Methodius are gradually becoming Slovak saints. Slavness may express itself as linguistic sentimentalising as it does in Hykisch's chronicle when the rough soldier from Upper Hungary suddenly finds he understands the citizens of Prague: 'How wonderful it is to be a Slav and understand the people of this city' (1984, p. 239). Tatarka, having described the custom of going *na vohľady*, when village girls waited in their rooms or in the hay for the boys to come to sleep with them, indulges in Slav mythopoeia: '*Vohľady*: it is an ancient Old Slavonic institution that young men and women can freely make love before they get married' (1988, pp. 37–8). Bednár satirises much Slav consciousness in *Ad revidendum*: 'balls and bosh or cobbler's cock – beautiful, delicate expressions, much more beautiful and delicate than logorrhoea or verbal diarrhoea. Balls and bosh and cobbler's cock are expressions of an almost dove-like nature; one can see in them Slav dove-like nobility' (1988, p. 142). Still, the notion of Slovaks as artisans (together with reminiscences of glorious Slovak bandit heroes like Jánošík) probably forms the most important part of national mythology today. It is embodied in the master carpenters of Šikula's trilogy. Ballek's Riečan (*Pomocník* and *Agáty*) is a butcher who, however, does not find peace with himself until he becomes a worker in the 1950s. His assistant Lančarič is a more typical example of a Slovak artisan within Ballek's conception of Slovakhood, which is a comingling of races, Slovaks, Hungarians, Germans, Croats, Bulgarians, Armenians; there is even one Arab in Palánk. Lančarič combines South Slavdom with Magyardom and Slovakdom.

In modern literature there is a greater need to express Czechoslovakdom than Slovakdom. The Slovak State was vociferously anti-Czech and so, first, that atmosphere had to be righted. After the federalisation of Czechoslovakia on 1 January 1969, anti-Slovak feelings began to grow in the Bohemian Lands and so, secondly, Slovaks needed to demonstrate they were above such things. It is common for an educated Slovak to speak good Czech, but it is rare for an educated Czech to speak good Slovak. Among other things, that might suggest that Slovaks have a greater sense of Czech-Slovak unity than the Czechs. In *Leto na Traune* Okáľ cites Jozef Tiso's last speech before he was taken back to Slovakia for trial – and where Tatarka was chosen as the Establishment journalist to interview him in prison. In this last speech Tiso spoke of 'the fiction of Czechoslovak national unity' (Okáľ, 1986, p. 83) and Okáľ himself is clearly no great friend of that unity. In the pre-war republic the Slovaks justifiably felt themselves to be underdogs. Masaryk himself and many literary critics opposed Slovak linguistic 'separatism' and not always the best Czechs were sent to teach in Slovak educational institutions. The rancour felt by Slovaks in the First Republic is rarely mentioned in literature since the 1950s. One of the strongest expressions of it, however, comes from the lips of the eponymous hero of Šikula's *Vojak*. He claims that all the small factories there had once been in Slovakia suddenly disappeared because of Czech cartels. The result was that Slovakia was poorer than it had been as a part of Hungary, 'and so the liquidation goes on; that's democracy; let's swallow up everything; in Slovakia there are suddenly only shepherds and sheep, tinkers and tinkers' apprentices, rafters; you can die or go hungry!' (1981, p. 115). Hykisch sees the roots of Czechoslovak unity as lying in the Enlightenment, which is true insofar as the Czech Revival and Slovak Awakening grew out of the eighteenth century, and his *Milujte kráľovnú!* may be interpreted as a collage novel advocating, not so much 'Czechoslovakism', as the then fashionable notion of *Mitteleuropa*. Tatarka's Czechoslovakness shows itself in *Písačky*, but is positively strident in *Navrávačky*; just before its oneiric ending he declares, 'This nation, Czech and Slovaks [. . .] I am a citizen of this republic, even if they try to deny that fact . . .' (1988, p. 111). The declaration of the Uprising, while a quintessentially Slovak matter, was also a Czechoslovak matter; it is a topos of Uprising literature to show Czechoslovak flags being unfurled in August 1944 (cf. Chňoupek). The episode of the partisan friendship of the Slovak Jano with the Czech Janoušek in Šikula's

Vlha evidently expresses Czechoslovakism; the novel also contains a song on the unity of Czechs and Slovaks (1978, p. 266). Czechoslovakism is also expressed in the story 'Sandrik anticorro', where a Czech adopts Slovakia as his home and then joins in the partisan war (Šikula, 1987). Predictably enough, Habaj links the Czechoslovak idea with the 'first worker president', Gottwald, and the joining of Czechs and Slovaks to colonise southern Slovakia might itself express some unity – though Czechs are clearly not as reliable chaps as Slovaks in *Kolonisti*. What differences there may have been between Czechs and Slovaks during the First Republic and the War are, however, shown to disappear in the natural non-nationalist solidarity of socialist Czechoslovakia (Habaj, 1986). The very name of the 'colony' Lipová Osada (linden settlement) expresses Czechoslovakism, and it is notable that the Hungarians cut down the linden trees there. In Balco's *Ležoviská* Hungarian gendarmes hang a gipsy on a linden tree and their commanding officer then has the temerity to participate in the new Czechoslovakia; the grandson of the hanged gipsy has to kill him. In Šikula's *Vojak* the Germans hang the Slovak Great War veteran on a linden tree. Finally, national service may be used to emphasise Czech and Slovak unity. Roman in Baláž's *Tu musíš žiť* serves as a border guard in the Bohemian Forest as does young Jurkovič in Ballek's *Lesné divadlo* (see Chmel's chapter).

For Tatarka the unity of the Czechs and Slovaks in Charter 77 becomes part of a replacement religion; he writes of the 'dissidents' as a 'holy community' (1988, p. 105). Tatarka, however, rarely showed a spiritual side in his writing. For most modern Slovak writers religion or the failure of religion or the need for a faith is an aspect of reality they cannot leave unregarded. Rarely we find stock (more or less vulgar) Marxist statements like Jašík's 'Štefan knows that poverty breeds delusions and churches' (1956, p. 21). So too Puškáš's Rotarides dismisses 'non-materialistic religiomystic' thinking (1980, p. 11); the same author writes similar words twice in his later *Záhrada*: 'In Nature there is not one rosary bead's worth of teleology – and that is horrid, cruel and unjust of her' (1984, p. 185 and p. 212). For all his apparent sarcasm about religion and the spiritual, particularly in this novel, Puškáš does believe there is some universal moral imperative (1984, p. 213). In 'Rozostavaný dom' Bednár observes that the new socialist régime may build factories and houses, but that it demolishes souls. Thus the bourgeoise Soňa, who prostitues her body for her parents' and her own future, becomes a 'beautiful, enticing body without a soul, a naked, dulled serving animal' (1956,

p. 276). Sardonically he has one of his narrators in *Ad revidendum* refer to Stalinist terminology: 'Once I even heard about engineers of the human soul' (1988, p. 100). The first wife of one of Hudec's depressive first-person narrators, I.H. (one presumes again, 'Ivan Hudec'), dies of cancer of the soul. The sarcastic picture of this disease contains satire on woman as well as on the vacuous age which produces such cancers: 'A lotus grew out of her vagina – a real fairytale lotus! Hordes came to wonder at this strange cancer. Photographs of her lotus lap adorned the pages of every decent magazine for bored travellers' (1987, p. 125). Sick souls are faithless souls, and we remember Alica in Johanides's *Súkromie* who is so afraid of faithlessness. Most (all?) of today's Slovak writers had parents or grandparents who were believers and largely for that reason the believers we see in literature are elderly. True believers are also usually admirable. In Ballek's Palánk works old Jurkovič is the believer. He is also a repository of legend and folkloristic exegesis: the story of Jesus Christ is the story of a man who grows up. Thirty-three is the age of maturity, the age we all leave our mothers and go to reign at our fathers' right hands and run our own worlds. The Crucifixion emblemises the pain we experience when we leave our mothers for our fathers (1981, p. 315). Old Jurkovič fears that state-controlled atheism will produce the same dessication of the soul that Bednár fears. 'He who takes God down from Heaven', Jurkovič maintains, 'is destroying age-old man, his civilisation and culture and his nature as it has been hitherto; he who takes the Virgin Mary down, is taking the age-old mother down from the male Heaven. Who knows what will happen?' (1987, p. 102). Hlatký's grandmother represents a similar spiritual condition, though Jurkovič's faith is wise where the grandmother's is naive. Still Christianity is for her a source of strength and goodness. She never complained about shortages or hunger and through her thrift she had managed to feed her own children and her neighbours'. She did not know envy; 'she would not allow that people were different from the way she wanted to see them and saw them. She thought that everyone lived like her and that if they did not, if from time to time they drank too much, swore, lied, it was always just a little weakness' (1988, p. 15). She is more or less a perfect Christian, but she is believable, however idyllic she might sound. That has to do with her character, as far as the author is concerned, for another Christian woman in the work, Sutner's devout Roman Catholic mother, drives her son away from conventional religion by her priggishness. In Ferko's *Proso*, too, we witness the social failure of Christianity; a woman brings her children up as good Christians and they turn out to be selfish hypocrites. When she jokingly suggests she is old enough to go into a home, they jump at the idea. Ferko also laughs at bigotry; when the old people see a television film about Russia before the Revolution, a woman proclaims that it was all those Orthodox priests' fault that things had been so bad; what they had needed was a few decent Roman Catholic priests. That incorporates satire on Communist satire on the Church. When a character is shown who tries to combine loyalty to the Church with loyalty to the Party the writer describes a cowardly opportunist. Ballek has the weak, nosy postmaster Havrila who tries to be a good Party man while remaining a regular churchgoer (in villages away from Palánk). He had betrayed God by serving the local Stalinist leader, Mlynárik, and betrayed Mlynárik by composing anonymous letters condemning him for misuse of his power. If he had ever had any morality, now he had lost it: 'I wandered between sin and repentance; I flew between heaven and hell, guilt and absolution, the new régime and my old faith, my wife and mistresses, morality and depravity' (1981, p. 517). The cunning Šuhajda in *Lesné divadlo* describes growing up in Czechoslovakia in the 1950s for those who had practising Roman Catholic parents. Atheism in the morning, Cathechism in the afternoon, being simultaneously a Young Pioneer and a server at Mass, political posters and pictures of saints. Ballek makes a point that follows the tradition of nineteenth-century non-socialist Czech and Slovak intellectuals; Communism and strict Roman Catholicism are both messianic, although the Catholics tended to put Heaven before God's Kingdom on Earth, the Second Coming: 'The vicar taught us to cross ourselves in secret and the schoolmaster to listen, but think what we liked. From one: paradise on Earth, from the other: paradise and salvation in Heaven. The master mockingly told us that there is no air up there, that it's terribly cold up there, that even an aeroplane couldn't get there, and the vicar said that if the Almighty did not wish it, it would not rain on collectivised land' (1987, p. 77). Bohdan in Hlatký's *História vecí* resembles Ballek's Havrila. He is a Party man, a trusted personnel officer in a large factory and, when his believer mother dies, and he marries his sneak daughter to an unprepossessing Party apparatchik, he begins a career in the local state or Party bureaucracy. Previously he had devoutly prayed with his mother, pretended to be a good Christian, though afterwards he says he had done so only because she had needed it; in fact he had simply been fawning to her. He is a pharisee, a liar, disloyal and selfish. The priest in Hlatký, however, represents the failure of institutional religion. At least in the eyes of Bohdan's nephew, Vlado, he behaves automatically, with ritual solicitude. It seems an unthinking cliché to have him obese, and to have him appear to Vlado as some great black bird, and he has an unattractive personality, though he despises Bohdan: 'You rely on the confidentiality of the confessional. In this state no one demands of us that the people should believe us. But they do believe. Even those who do not believe in the Creation. [. . .] You must thank God you do not have to confess. It is people like you who need confession; everyone would gain from it' (1988, pp. 42–3). For Vlado (the same generation as the author) priests belonged to a different world, to history; they were little more than 'literary figures from the last century' (1988, p. 40) and when his grandmother was teaching him his prayers, his mind considered the omnipotence of fairytale royalty rather than that of God (1988, p. 29). Religion pertained to grand-mother's world. In *Za hrsť drobných I* the grandmother's religion is slightly comic. She does a great deal of praying when her eldest granddaughter has run away from home; she sometimes prays with the canine narrator, Flip, and at one point she terrorises the household into family prayers in the middle of the night. Bednár respects her Christianity and her praying, but her formalised religion is no weapon against the ills of modern society. In the dog's-eye view of a church in *Za hrsť drobných II*, Bednár, while indicating the popularity of a church in the countryside, satirises secular institutions' pursuit of deification; religion may have failed, but its political version is ridiculous:

A church is a big building with a tower pointing into the cosmos; it is always full of people, resounds with the hymn, 'Lord, when we bend before thy throne . . .' and the people who can't get into it stand outside – loads and loads of people. They sing, pray . . . It will be glorious when we're sent as gods to the developing planets! They'll sing to us like that there, or even more beautifully; they'll build churches to us, temples and who knows what else; they'll hang pictures to our honour, there'll be statues of us carved in wood, hewn in stone, cast in bronze . . . Oh, the glory of it! (1974, p. 61).

Other representations of the failure of religion hark back to the nineteenth century. When the spiritual begins to disappear from life,

man starts being god unto man: 'there always were many people who
wanted to be gods. And some really like to believe they are gods.
But then they do not want to have partners among the other gods.
Suddenly there are no gods. But there are no people either,
(Johanides, 1966, p. 78). In Johanides this leads to a variety of
Franco-German Existentialism that was particularly clear in *Podstata
kameňolomu* and *Nie*, but is still evident in *Marek koniar* and
Najsmutnejšia oravská balada; in these two works, however, the
influence of western (including Semitic) esoteric beliefs are beginning
to vie with Existentialism. In *Panna Zázračnica* Tatarka makes trendy
references to the *kundalini* of Indian mysticism; Dušek makes fun of
that notion in *Náprstok* (which witnesses that he expects his readers
to see the joke – and there is a veritable cult of Indian mystical
thinking in Czechoslovakia), and combines this fun with gratuitous
vulgarity: 'They nicknamed him Sekunda [second], but the lout Alino
changed this name too: he swallowed the first two letters' (1985, p. 30;
kunda=cunt; the two boys' names then join to make *kundalin(i))*.
Johanides sees the Renaissance as the beginning of the failure of
religion, the beginning of modern vulgarity: 'The Renaissance was
the first age to invite the lowest joke into the best society, for the
secret Renaissance recognised the immense power of vulgarity, if it
is given direction and made decorative; the Renaissance was the first
age to articulate the general desire of the majority for chewing-gum
and fairgrounds' (1988, p. 141). There Johanides is ironising the
whole industrial world, socialist as well as capitalist systems; both
are equally godless. Elsewhere he ironises his own Existentialism:
'We despised our weaknesses. We considered our egoism to be that
fateful aloneness that is talked about so much nowadays' (1965,
p. 40). The conclusion of Jaroš's *Krvaviny* works as both a parody
of Existentialism and an Existential statement, for this conclusion
begins, 'Everything robs me of my freedom, shouted M. Gorazd',
and ends, with a manifestation of a fine sense of the macabre and in
the spirit of late Surrealist banalisation: 'with firm step and head high
he reached the kitchen where he picked up a knife with his right
hand and with a single powerful movement he drove it into his heart.
He fell onto his back without uttering a sound and even many hours
later his face expressed that same surprise as it did when he last got
up from his armchair' (1970, p. 141). Sloboda's *Uršuľa* indulges
either in sentimentalised Existentialism or in that Islamic fatalism
which says one's fate is written on one's brow whatever one does.
Within herself she hears a voice telling her that, since you have

been born, 'you are to suffer' (1987, p. 71). Just as the roots of Existentialism lie in the nineteenth century so do those of love as a religion (if we discount Joachim of Fiore and so forth). For Jašík in *Námestie svätej Alžbety* love is a force rather than a religion, or a distilled version of Pauline charity, and bourgeois society consists of two battling forces, love and money. That makes for caricature, for example, in the figure of the rich *bourgeoise* Erna who longs for true love, but does not want to lose her money. Nazism is, in Jašík's conception, a creed of hate. Tatarka's mysticisation of copulation reminds one strongly of French love sects in the nineteenth century, though his is as banal as a faded Flower Person: 'My individual primal experience is that something sacred exists between a man and a woman. That is the place where the sacred fire burns from which the human being originates and comes into the world' (1988, p. 30). Johanides's depiction of love in *Súkromie* is of humble Christian love, *caritas*, which embodies a loathing of hatred. The head-waiter cannot understand Doval's love: 'I like Marta as I like all other people. [. . .] I had the intense feeling that he was trying to teach me hatred or at least to awaken my interest in hating' (1963, p. 56). So too, for Johanides's Marek hatred is the greatest deformity of the human psyche: 'Yes. He felt anger. He was capable of feeling anger. But he had not known hatred. When he found out what hatred was, he was sick for several months' (1983, p. 65). The author's later character, Poldo, a Protestant Orava German at least by adoption, reacts more robustly to the hatred he does not know: 'Poldo and Betka [his wife] did not even begin to understand what physiological hatred was until they were sworn at as Jews in the restaurant in Karlova Ves. They looked at each other and began guffawing with Lutheran loudness' (1988, p. 12).

Slovak writers, like writers in other socialist countries, having seen the results of the failure of religion, and having been more or less brought up to believe that religion was an historical event or an opiate for the lower classes in capitalist societies, and having witnessed the failure of the surrogate religion incorporated in the practice of Leninist-Stalinist ideology, express the need for the spiritual more strongly than their Western counterparts. Indeed the need for the spiritual may often seem offensive to their philosophy of materialism. Spiritual longing was once conceived of ideologically as alienation and modern man is often in fact so alienated, so divorced by tangible reality from true reality that he has lost any sense of the spiritual. A diseased narrator of Hudec's expresses that: 'They run away from the least expensive vehicle in the world, the simple beauty of their own aloneness' (1987, p. 63) Bednár's blind painter, Marci, himself constitutes an emblem of artistic alienation. In him the author both writes about that alienation and satirises the self-aggrandisement of artists. The unspirituality of his surroundings may lead him to suicide, but he claims to be seeking the spiritual: 'I am not concerned with the drying of washing; I do not paint washing, but the Breath of God. [. . .] If you like, I paint the breath of the cosmos, the universe. And wind belongs among the components of the cosmos. [. . .] Apart from that I paint all possible seasons, all times of day, day of work and day of rest; if you like, I paint contrast: filthy surroundings – clean washing; I paint its fragrance; I paint movement; I fill the vacuum with the Breath of God.' And he goes on to express the way Positivism and the materialist worldviews it had bred had denuded life: 'Science does all sorts of things, but beyond all those all sorts of things it has opened the terrible maw of the vacuum before us and over us and around us; the more science there is, the more terrible, and indeed, larger is that maw [. . .] The more science, the less security –' (1985, p. 189). And even before he is blind Marci paraphrases Revelation 6:12: 'Has the sun disappeared somewhere for ever? Has it become black? And has the moon really become as blood?' (1985, p. 34). That is, incidentally, echoed when he has just been blinded: 'the sun has become black for me as the prickly sackcloth of hair of a penitent's habit' (1985, p. 138). The danger of any hunger for the spiritual or metaphysical in a fundamentally (ex-) Christian culture is that it will lead to a cult of suffering. As by now you would expect, Tatarka luxuriates in that cult and the Czech 'dissidents' of the 1980s are the glorious sufferers: 'This is the question of Catholic mysticism: the Roman Catholic Church needs to be persecuted. Everyone becomes aware only through persecution' (1988, p. 109) Hudec disposes of the cult simply, though he omits to state that suffering is still evil: '*Suffering is not a category reserved for just a group of unfortunates! Suffering is part of life, of everyone's life!*' (1987, p. 29).

Another danger in an arid, materialist world is the pseudomystic, the spiritual conman. Unless one believes that only action open to someone in the Eastern Bloc who believes in the non-material is to defect, Ballek's Šuhajda is just such a pseudomystic. He exploits two types of mental mythology, metaphysics and psychology, to deceive his friendly captors into believing that he had not been trying to escape to the West. Indeed, he prostitutes the spiritual by employing it as an unfair ruse. He claims he has deserted his barracks in Prague and come to the Bohemian Forest in search of quiet. What he says about the soul, about its existence, however unfashionable it might be, and what he says about God as the little thread binding everything in Nature, is all aboveboard. So too is what he says about paradise: 'The vision of paradise [. . .] has already ruined [. . .] many, many people' (1987, p. 75). It is however, not all right for him to attempt to persuade his captors by his apparent Christian meekness that his fear of boredom is what had driven him to try to escape. He also makes that fear metaphysical. Because the border guards regard him as a harmless eccentric, they do not pay much attention when they are escorting him back, and so he tries to get over the border again. And fails again. In the second story of *Sny, deti, milenky* Puškáš pokes fun at such contricksters when he satirises fornicators' ability to create metaphysical excuses for sexual misdemeanours. Pseudo-mysticism, including its pseudoscience, the once fashionable teaching of such as von Däniken or Velikovsky, is satirised by Bednár in the undergraduate Cintľa (*Za hrsť drobných I*), and the popularity of horoscopes even among intelligent Slovaks is reflected in stories by Dušek and Hudec.

Awareness of the lack of the spiritual does not necessarily imply the desire for a religion, even if it implies a rejection of historical materialism. Vilikovský lampoons official anti-Christianity: 'Look, someone has thrown the moon into the water. A yob. A godless oaf. An atheist' (1965, p. 24). And in his first novel he suggests that modern man has lost a profounder understanding of God; there are times 'when God is only a metaphor . . . and between you and me, a metaphor thought up by a second-rate artist . . .' (1983, p. 53). In his satire on spies, secret police, Slovaks, Roumanians (especially chambermaids), Leninism, Nazism, Balkan homosexuality and police informers among university teachers, *Večne je zelený*, the narrator asks, 'Do you believe in God? Religion is the opium of mankind. Opium is the religion of mankind. Thus speaks the iron rule of dialectics' (1989, p. 27). Šikula has little to say about religion and the spiritual because his art lies in the earthy, but he does acknowledge the abilities of the spiritual man, for example, the organist Vincenc: 'He was religious and he respected everyone and other people's piety and that respect was at least as great as any seeker can have' (1987, p. 28). The irony there is sympathetic, but in Bednár one frequently does not know where the irony begins or ends. In *Ad revidendum* Mišo Danihel is a pantheist and that rural faith is contrasted with a vision of a second coming of Christianity, to punish Christendom. One of his narrators, the well-balanced Classicist Zátroch, certainly believes that some religion must come to purge the 1980s world: 'it is pretty certain that Christianity will come (I don't know in what form), and it will bare its teeth at us, growl, bite, and the more of it we hide, the sharper and longer its teeth will be. And if it doesn't come, that enchantress Islam will, with even longer and sharper teeth' (1988, p. 22). It might have distressed the persecution-élitist Tatarka, that the main narrator, Protáz, writes of the state of Christianity in 1980s Slovakia: 'few people have their children baptised nowadays, and when they do, they do it secretly, especially when some not entirely negligible person is involved. It's like the very beginning of the Church when the Christians gathered [. . .] only in the catacombs' (1988, p. 75).

Bednár rejects messianism, Hitlerite and Stalinist, in *Hodiny a minúty*, and he rejects the messianism implicit in the notion of progress in the vivisection scenes of *Za hrsť drobných*. Feldeková likewise satirises Stalinist messianism, for example: 'Although I had not yet learned to read and write, the word "happiness" was an exception. I knew how to read and write that word. After all, it was written on every street-corner' (1985, p. 58). Such rejection is, however, essentially negative. In Slovak literature there seems to be only one positive answer to the spiritual plight, and that is a proud, but humble, seeking for knowledge. In the 1980s the figure of the knower has arisen in two writers. The knower is essentially an isolated human being because he (not she) knows (is presented as knowing) things normal human beings do not, perhaps cannot, know. They represent the power of knowledge and are harmless, but are often or usually seen by those in power to be hostile or frightening. Johanides's knowers are described as such by hints rather than analysis. Djelefi probably is not a knower; as a young man he had been an epicurean, and, as the author puts it, later pain had not turned him into the fox that praises its own pain. Nevertheless he has some qualities of the 'mystic': 'He was able to go off into his prayers as if into a room, and to lock himself in them' (1983, p. 198). The real knower here is the eponymous hero, Marek de Molnay. The power he exerts over the two hostile factions in sixteenth-century Hungary depends on not only his skill in assessing the conformation and suitability of horses, but also on some hidden power. He is the mole (in a pre-spy-novel sense) who burrows through true knowledge and can appear anywhere, as if out of thin air. Marek is also intensely sensible of the genetic memory within him; this memory knows much more than he knows and yet supplies the reactions and impulses which make him a knower. He also has within him the calm which characterises a knower. Poldo Brechár in *Najsmutnejšia oravská balada* is a more complex version of the knower. Certainly in his childhood his mother called him a mole, but Marek had been an attractive, charming, if aloof, man, and Poldo weighs 130 kg, is 170 cm tall and has a migraine every month. He is as aware of the genetic memory within him as Marek. He is not actually a Brechár either, since his father was sterile and his ex-prostitute mother had conceived him with someone else (1988, pp. 19, 90); so his account of the Brechárs' coming to Orava is barely linked with his status as a knower. Poldo reads the German Cabalist, Johannes Reuchlin and the *Dunkelmannbriefe*, which allows him to make a formal link with a knower of nearly 500 years earlier who had been murdered and then buried with his horse and all his belongings on what was later Nedvedák-Brechár land. Poldo imagines this man had been a poet and physician who knew that there was 'on the background of this darkening world [. . .] a secret clock, in accordance with which nations grow or fade' and understood 'the laws governing the world's mechanism' (1988, p. 134). Johanides persuades his reader that the fat minor literary bureaucrat, Poldo, has within him this knower, the poet physician who tried to heal souls and bodies. A more rationally developed knower is the subject of the second part of Hlatký's *História vecí*, Sutner. Initially he reminds us of Ballek's Šuhajda. When Sutner is caught trying to get over into the West, however, he simply admits it, does not make excuses like Šuhajda. Sutner has some basic Christian attributes: 'Who should I hide from? No one can hide. People are distinguishable by whether or not they know that they cannot hide anywhere', and: 'he who listens to his inner voice is free' (1988, p. 114). But he is not just a Christian; nor is he, however, an occultist as was fashionable in the American and socialist-bloc 1980s. The knower Sutner's faith is a spiritual presence; pure feeling has allowed him to discover his spiritual essence. He stands against the moral relativism that has been created by codifications of law. The ever-increasing number of laws in the world reflects the changing forms of evil, 'the movement of evil from simple violence to complex, differentiated violence' (1988, p. 118). Sutner's faith takes in nihilism (Vlado actually labels him a nihilist) and Existentialism; it essentially outwits materialism. In this faith 'no one is threatened with punishment after death and no one will be rewarded.

[. . .] There is no guilt, where all are guilty' (1988, p. 119). Man's conscience will release him or her from moral relativism, but he or she will still come to realise that everything in the world is as it should be. Man has used his freedom to multiply evil and there is no point in trying to change that. In summary Sutner tells Vlado, 'All people who have a perceptive conscience are believers [. . .] A perceptive conscience is a gift which renders action impossible' (1988, p. 165). Sutner's somewhat Oriental passivity and his knowing calm drive Vlado to question his own Communist optimism – and the author is also questioning that: 'I am not a Communist because of, but in spite of, human nature; I have faith in society's capacity to purify itself; I believe that this century will destroy social conflict's power over individual human fates . . . I believe in the transitoriness of the catalepsy of the spirit; I believe in imagination, an imagination which will fill the emptiness' (1988, p. 133).

In a world where guilt has become unfashionable and where there is no firm religious basis to morality, the individual tends to devolve his or her responsibility on a mood, a psychological or physical state, as if he or she could deny that any of those states comprised him or her. This is an ever more common type of moral sophistry, more common than the habit of blaming things on an institution or another person. Jarunková treats that side of the matter in *Pomstiteľ* and, in *Rozum*, Sloboda considers the comfort of deciding one has no talents so that one does not feel honour bound to humanity, Bednár and Hlatký have the strongest and clearest comments on this moral alibism, which may well be wider spread in socialist countries than in the West because the welfare-state mentality had until recently been more widespread there than in most Western countries. One may certainly link it with the fatalism expressed by Ballek's Šuhajda, which one could conceive of as a bastardisation of notions of (historical) determinism: 'I'm only a little bird in a cage which I shan't fly out of, since I was born in a cage because that was what was allotted me' (1987, p. 75). Bednár's ex-Fascist Danihel expresses the modern moral sophistry three times: 'one is not responsible for many things; circumstances are responsible for many'; 'What was done to me and what I did. [. . .] Circumstances did those things to me,' and 'the human being is only a product of circumstances' (1988, pp. 34, 39, 255). Hlatký's version in *História vecí* is even more telling; the disgraceful words are Vlado's: 'Helplessness relieves me of responsibility' (1988, p. 85).

As the nineteenth century witnessed the apparent failure of religion, so it witnessed an increasing belief in the failure of language. Modern Slovak fiction is of itself linguistically highly self-conscious, but it is also self-conscious about language as an institution. That might result from a growth in national (linguistic) self-confidence, but it appears also to result from a sense of the failure of the public word. New ideological systems or even fashions within these systems bring with them new vocabulary and new meanings for old words. This state will be all the more strongly felt by writers in a language which was codified for ideological reasons. Bednár's Danihel describes something of the linguistic violence perpetrated by propaganda or police informers in the 1950s: 'soon some new, unexpected meaning will be stuffed into everyone of our words, like a worm in an apple – the worms of new meanings will eat away our language, and all that will be left will be balls and tosh and cobbler's cock' (1988, p. 72). One might indeed speak of *Ad revidendum* as a work on language almost to the degree that one can of Horák's *Súpis dravcov* (see Short's chapter). The public word is otherwise the public speech and Ballek's Filadelfi, not long after the end of the war, has the obvious to say about that: 'In my lifetime almost everything that rang from the lips of people in public was untruthful. All armed conflicts took place for the sake of peace and the brightest words always range out for some dark religion' (1981, p. 330). Kot's Moriak links political and linguistic corruption: 'I am myself guilty, for there is no more terrible guilt than to yield in silence when one sees evil, not to resist when big words are misused for opportunist reasons' (1983, p. 92). All Bednár's writing about metaphors in *Ad revidendum* actually concerns the political misuse of language, for example: 'There are nothing but metaphors everywhere. Verse has somehow ceased to depend on metaphor [. . .], but prose, particularly newspaper prose, journalese, even the sports page, is nothing but metaphors. [. . .] Slovak masters and mistresses [. . .] must envy us the way we easily and unreservedly believe everything these metaphors use to trammel up our brains' (1988, pp. 12–13). Loose language is capable, Bednár's Protáz suggests, 'of destroying not only an individual, but whole nations and empires, perhaps the whole of humanity' (1988, p. 198). Bednár's approach to language here, but essentially from *Za hrsť drobných* onwards (See the ghastly, meaning-free popsongs Cintľa and his friends compose), is that its corruption constitutes one of various kinds of pollution that afflict late twentieth-century man. For Bednár the Slovak overuse of hypocoristics is part of that pollution. Names are in the broadest sense political, since in the Judaeo-

Christian tradition to name is to possess. Tatarka calls the woman in *Písačky* Lutécia or Natália, Letícia or Ruska, Parízia or Čiča, Naj- or Naj-Naj. The soldier of Šikula's *Vojak* is actually Ďuris, but when he is labouring in Vienna he is nicknamed Martinengo after a Pressburg fire-chief and, then, as a soldier he is called Koko. Names here, then, connote positions in society. When the man is a war invalid and, thus, an outsider, the names lose their social function: 'when I felt lonely Ďuris was always walking along beside me and Koko was right beside him, but beside Koko or Ďuris was always Martinengo, too . . .' (1981, p. 81). Changes in place names in Slovakia have since World War I (they wanted to call Pressburg Wilsonovo before they settled on Bratislava), and particularly after the World War II (when, for example, most Saints and Crosses disappeared), been a touchy political business. Horák plays with the question. Šikula bases a long game with words on the fact that the 'cross' name of Svätý Kríž nad Hronom was changed after the last war (1979, p. 208). In *Ako chutí zakázané ovocie* Hudec levels a sarcastic gibe at such name-changes: 'Why is it Čalovo and not Veľký Meder? What did Štúr do in Štúrovo, in other words in Parkaň? Are we fighting against religion by striking out the Turčiansky Svätý on the notices saying you are entering Martin?' (1981, p. 30).

Linguistic self-confidence or just sheer joy in language manifests itself in punning and a great deal of other wordplay not only in Horák, but also in Bednár (particularly *Výpoveď* and *Ad revidendum*), Vilikuvský's *Večne je zelený* . . ., Ferko's *Proso* or Hlatký's *História vecí*, and Šikula even indulges in Hungarian wordplay in *Majstri* and in the first story of *Heroické etudy*. The pedantic or fanatical use of Slovak (or proper Slovak) is laughed at by Horák, but also, say, by Karvaš, who describes a public lecturer thus: 'When he pronounced "Hornopôtočskovcom" his small lips formed the end of a rifle-barrel aimed at the conscience of the forgetful, ungrateful nation' (1968, p. 127). In *Záhadný úsmev* Hudec has a story which initially concerns the [u] sound in ô; the scholar so concerned with ô has a fellow in the schoolmaster Hron in Puškáš's *Záhrada*, who has a passion for the Slovak ä. In *Heroické etudy* Šikula has a funny and clever story about Slovak diphthongs, which contains much vocalic punning and satire on school texts.

No doubt the roots of today's Slovak language consciousness do lie in the linguistic chaos of Slovakia after World War I and then again after World War II. In recent literature that is, naturally enough, described in most detail by Habaj. In Bednár's *Ad reviden-*

dum language–consciousness is seen to derive from isolation, for the two main narrators, Danihel and Protáz are the chief expounders of language consciousness. In Hlatký, on the other hand, the failure of personal language, the lack of correspondence of word and concept in the case of the word for 'reason' (*ratio*), itself creates isolation (1988, p. 78).

It is the Slovak language that has hitherto kept most scholars and readers in the West ignorant of Slovak literature. Slovak writers are translated into other socialist-bloc languages, but even that does not mean that they are widely read. Slovak literature has not grown up in isolation, however. Up to the end of the 1960s Czech literature dominated in Czechoslovakia, and Slovaks were great readers of Czech literature. Slovaks are also great translators and, because of their history, many Slovak readers over 40 read in Hungarian as well, as in German. Slovak literature has not grown in isolation but a certain isolation has been imposed on Slovak literature.

REFERENCES

Edition used is the first unless otherwise stated.

Peter Andruška, 1977, *Horúce letá*. Hot summers.
Anton Baláž, 1983, *Tu musíš žiť* (2nd ed, 1987). You have to live here.
Július Balco, 1986, *Ležoviská*. Places for lying.
Ladislav Ballek, 1974, *Južná pošta* (2nd edn, 1979). Southern mail.
    1977, *Pomocník (Kniha o Palánku)*. The assistant. A book about Palánk.
    1981, *Agáty (Druhá kniha o Palánku)*. Acacias. Second book about Palánk.
    1987, *Lesné divadlo*. Theatre in the woods.
Alfonz Bednár, 1954, *Sklený vrch*. The glass mountain.
    1956, 1964, *Hodiny a minúty*. The hours and the minutes.
    1960, *Cudzí*. Strangers.
    1970, *Za hrsť drobných (v kazete z Péšávaru)*. A handful of coppers (in the casket from Peshawar).
    1974, *Za hrsť drobných (o umelom Cézarovi)*. A handful of coppers (about plastic Caesar).
    1977, *Blok 4/B*. Block 4B.
    1985, *Ako sme sušili bielizeň*. How we used to dry the washing.
    1986, *Výpoveď*. The affidavit.
    1988, *Ad revidendum, Gemini*.
Ján Beňo, 1977, *Druhý semester*. The second semester.
    1986, *Kým príde veľryba*. Until the whale comes.
Ladislav Beňo, 1972, *Nebezpečná zóna*. Danger zone.
Bohuš Chňoupek, 1974, *Generál s levom*. General with lion.
    1984, *Lámanie pečatí*. A breaking of seals.

Dušan Dušek, 1982, *Poloha pri srdci*. A place on the heart.
1983, *Kalendár*. Diary.
1985, *Náprstok. Zopár idylických fotografií* . . . Thimble. A few idyllic photographs . . .
Oľga Feldeková, 1985, *Veverica*. The red squirrel.
Andrej Ferko, 1984, *Proso (Rezká humoreska)* Millet. A nippy humoresque.
Ivan Habaj, 1979, *Poľné samoty*. Isolated farmsteads.
1980, *Kolonisti I*. The colonists, I.
1981, *Kolonisti II*.
1986, *Kolonisti III*.
Edmund Hlatký, 1988, *História vecí*. The history of things.
Jozef Horák, 1947, *Hory mlčia*. The mountain forests are silent.
Karol Horák, 1977, *Cukor*. The sugar.
1979, *Súpis dravcov*. List of predators.
Ivan Hudec, 1981, *Ako chutí zakázané ovocie*. The taste of forbidden fruit.
1985, *Čierne diery*. Black holes.
1987, *Záhadný úsmev štrbavého anjela*. The enigmatic smile of the gap-toothed angel.
Anton Hykisch, 1984, *Milujte kráľovnú!* Love the queen.
Peter Jaroš, 1970, *Krvaviny*. Bloody tales.
1979, *Tisícročná včela*. The thousand-year-old bee.
Klára Jarunková, 1968, *Pomstiteľ*. The avenger.
Rudolf Jašík, 1956, *Na brehu priezračnej rieky*. On the bank of the translucent river.
1958, *Námestie svätej Alžbety* (2nd enlarged edn, 1960). St Elizabeth Square.
Ján Johanides, 1963, *Súkromie*. Privacy.
1965, *Podstata kameňolomu*. The essence of the quarry.
1966, *Nie*. No.
1978, *Nepriznané vrany*. Unacknowledged crows.
1979, *Balada o vkladnej knižke*. Ballad of a savings book.
1983, *Marek koniar a uhorský pápež*. Marek, master of horse and the Hungarian pope.
1985, *Slony v Mauthausene*. Elephants in Mauthausen.
1987, *Pochovávanie brata*. Burying my brother.
1988, *Najsmutnejšia oravská balada*. The saddest Orava ballad.
Peter Karvaš, 1968, *Nedokončená pre detský hlas*. Unfinished piece for child's voice.
Jozef Kot, 1983, *Kolkáreň*. The skittle alley.
Vladimír Mináč 1958, *Dlhý čas čakania*. The long time of waiting.
1959, *Živí a mŕtvi*. The living and the dead.
1961, *Zvony zvonia na deň*. The bells ring out for day.
Edition used, all three bound as *Generácia* (A generation), 1979.
Dušan Mitana, 1984, *Koniec hry*. The end of a game.
Ladislav Mňačko, 1959, *Smrť sa volá Engelchen* (6th edn, 1964). Death is called Engelchen.
1967, *Ako chutí moc*. The taste of power.
1972, *Súdruh Münchhausen* (published in Cologne). Comrade Münchhausen.

Ján Okáľ, 1986, *Leto na Traune* (published in Cambridge, Ontario). Summer on the Traun.

Ján Papp, 1969, *Kára plná bolesti* (2nd edn, 1976). A cart full of pain.

Jozef Puškáš, 1980, *Štvrtý rozmer*. The fourth dimension.

1984, *Záhrada* (*v piatom období roka*). The garden (in the fifth season).

1985, *Sny, deti, milenky*. Dreams, children, mistresses.

Vincent Šikula, 1966, *S Rozarkou* (*S Rozarkou. Liesky. Vlha*, 1984) Life with Rozarka.

1976, *Majstri*. The master capenters.

1977, *Muškát*. The geranium.

1978, *Vlha* (edn as 1966). The golden oriole.

1979, *Vilma*. Vilma.

1980, *Liesky* (edn as 1966). The hazels.

1981, *Vojak*. The soldier.

1987, *Heroiké etudy pre kone*. Etudes héroiques for a horse.

Rudolf Sloboda, 1977, *Hudba*. Music.

1982, *Rozum*. Reason.

1983, *Stratený raj*. Lost paradise.

1987, *Uršuľa*. Uršuľa.

Dominik Tatarka, 1944, *Panna Zázračnica*. The Miraculous Maiden.

1948, *Farská republika*. The parish republic.

1950, *Prvý a druhý úder*. The first and second blow.

1963, *Démon súhlasu*. The demon of conformity.

1984, *Písačky* (published in Cologne). Jottings.

1988, *Navrávačky* (published in Cologne). Tapings.

Ladsilav Ťažký, 1986, *Aj v nebi je lúka*. There is a meadow in Heaven, too.

Pavel Vilikovský 1965 *Citová výchova v marci*. A sentimental education in March.

1983, *Prvá veta spánku*. The first sentence of sleep.

1989, *Večne je zelený* . . . . Ever Green is the . . .

2 Narration and Analysis in Contemporary Slovak Fiction
Jozef Kot

Two hundred years ago, in 1787, Anton Bernolák, philologist of the Slovak Enlightenment, published his *Dissertatio Philologico-Critica*, a constitutent part of which was the codification of the first literary norm of the Slovak language. But three years earlier than this, the first Slovak novel, *René mládenca príhody a skúsenosti* (The adventures and experiences of young René), whose author was the Enlightenment priest Jozef Ignác Bajza, had been published. The fact that in his conception of the literary language Bajza was in controversy with his fellow Roman Catholic cleric Bernolák is not important, nor is it important that the dream of a literary language for the Slovaks was not fulfilled until the middle of the next century; that 1840s language was codified on the basis of a different dialect from that chosen by Bernolák. One cannot, however, ignore the fact that at the time when the Slovak men of the Enlightenment were endeavouring to establish the basic tool of literary production, a literary language, Fielding, Richardson and Smollett – to mention only the British Isles – were writing their best novels. In the beginnings of modern Slovak fiction, that is in Bajza's picaresque novel, we find a constant tension between the narrator's conviviality as a writer of traveller's tales and a philosophical, reflective approach which reveals the sensibility and morals of the times. This foreshadows an inner tension which has not disappeared from Slovak fiction even two hundred years later: narration and analysis meet as two inseparable sisters, but also as angry brothers.

One may ask why they should be angry and why it should always be like a see-saw, where the rise of one side automatically means the fall of the other. Angry, mainly because the traditions of nineteenth-century fiction impressed on Slovak criticism perhaps more than on the authors themselves the idea of fiction being first of all narration, the reproduction of experience. It could even be said that the aesthetic ideal of the fiction of 'critical realism' is, as some have suggested, more or less founded on the tendency to be anecdotal. Instead of the conscious arrangement of the prose text, preference is given to recording, to a sequence of epic microstructures. The prose writer threads his mimesis onto a string like beads; he evokes the impression of the authenticity of his world: sometimes he succeeds, especially if he is capable of historical and social thinking. It should be noted that the majority of Slovak writers took the place of historians, and it is to their credit that they always stood on the side of those who redressed social injustices, who had a programme for a more just world. They drew on popular, 'plebeian' traditions; they knew neither castles nor salons. They may have looked admiringly sometimes at Turgenev, sometimes at Ramuz and Giono, then at Sholokhov and Babayevsky, at Hemingway and Camus, but primarily they profited from the principles of the Slovak folk and fairy tale. With the criteria of comparative studies in mind, we might suggest that it may have been the Slovak folk and fairy tale which in earlier periods most often crossed the boundaries of Slovakdom and found its place in the European context. If we look closer, it is precisely the popular tale which provides a classical example of narration, not for an attractive, dramatic story, but for an effective metaphor leading to a moral. The triads of identical epic structures (parallels) typical of the folktale indicate that the unknown narrator is arranging his material, charging it with aesthetic function and thus subjecting his world to philosophical analysis.

Art, since it reflects the world, cannot but be primarily the materialisation of philosophical conceptions. From this point of view the Aristotelian definition that art is thinking in images has not lost anything of its validity: the history of art reaffirms that in every epoch it treats, and that goes particularly for the history of literature, where the concept and the word become almost identical categories. Let us take for example the Shakespearean world which, for all its universality, nevertheless retains its direct connection with neo-Platonism. Every comparison certainly has some little flaw. Shakespeare's greatness is measured by his immersion in existential human values, by the profundity of his archetypes of individual and social behaviour, and not by the fact that in his dramas he provides instructive stories about time being out of joint and about the violation of the heliocentric cosmic order.

In its most important achievements the Slovak fiction of the last three decades by no means abandons the analysis of the values of the world: its starting point is, therefore, philosophical, but also

42   *Narration and Analysis in Contemporary Slovak Fiction*

generalising in its intentions. It has very quickly overcome the infant diseases of a preconceived, over-simplified understanding of the world, as well as the popular tendency to see things in black and white terms. The process of emancipation of Slovak fiction (and for a long time verse had been considered the dominant genre, the genre which was somehow predestined to express the nature of the Slovak people) was implemented primarily by the departure from traditional prose structures and by the internalisation of the point of view, but above all, by a more decisive involvement of the author's intellect. In certain moments the boundaries between genres seem to have disappeared; prose seems to have more and more often taken over the creative methods of verse and in plot construction, the creative principles of music are also employed. A similar process has more or less intensely affected most European literature. But while in historically more developed literatures this usually took place only as a privilege of a narrow élite and formed an élitist segment of literature, in Slovak literature it represents a sudden geological fault, a break, a qualitative leap, which is marked primarily by the fact that literature manifests no split between élite and popular; thus modern Slovak prose can count on a wide, multifarious readership.

This volume concentrates on Slovak prose since 1954 because Pynsent considers Alfonz Bednár's *Sklený vrch* the turning point in post-war Slovak prose. 1954 was also the year in which attempts at creating an improved image of the contemporary world without its actual problems led almost to a caricature of literary representation. To be more specific: it is the time of publication, for example, of the novels *Družné letá* (Friendly years) and *Radostník* (The wedding cake) by Tatarka, which constitute the quintessence of over-simplification and schematisation of literary intentions. It is not until 1956 that a new movement in Slovak fiction occurs, when the much discussed *novelle, Hodiny a minúty* by Bednár, were published, and when gradually Mináč's project to represent the experience of a generation materialised – in the trilogy *Dlhý čas čakania, Živí a mŕtvi* and *Zvony zvonia na deň* – and when we witness the coming of a new literary generation forming round the literary monthly *Mladá tvorba*. At first this generation made itself heard more through criticism of the preceding period and the formulation of new programmes than through any tangible literary achievement.

Even before 1956, however, Slovak fiction did not lack important projects: it aspired to deal with the new social situation and primarily to contribute actively to the revolutionary metamorphosis of an economically backward and culturally impoverished Slovakia into a modern, economically, socially and culturally developed part of the Czechoslovak state equal to the larger part constituted by the Bohemian Lands. This effort, which continued the spirit of the social, cultural and political programme of the 'progressive' DAV group which was active in the period between the two world wars, rested primarily on the shoulders of those writers who had actively participated in the anti-Fascist struggle which culminated in the Slovak National Uprising (1944). But this generation of *Gründer* remained productive after 1956, when it assumed the task of performing a new qualitative step forward in Slovak fiction (for example, not only Vladimír Mináč and Alfonz Bednár, but also say, Rudolf Jašík with his belated *début*). The new literary generation grouped round *Mladá tvorba*, which started coming out in 1956, seemed (from the viewpoint of those times) to contrast sharply with their predecessors. Now, over 30 years later, it is, however, evident that they were bound up with the most important representatives of the Uprising Generation by their ideological as well as their artistic programmes. The '56 Generation, like their predecessors, also laid stress on an integral and veracious depiction of social movements; they also emphasised total social involvement. If there was anything questionable, it was at most the degree of transparency of this intention.

As far as this chapter is concerned, it was this generation in which the tension between the two basic approaches was manifested most palpably, namely: whether just to set down a record of the surrounding world or whether to subject it to analysis and, thus, to interpret it, but also transform it. Part of the generation arising in the mid-1950s instigated a cultivation of direct, immediate experience: the depiction of the writer's own childhood, the evoking of his or her own memory, not to illumine his or her relationship to the world, but to fascinate by the power of the story and of the experience, becomes a frequent theme of fiction. In polemics at the time I called this coming of the young generation a 'coming without weaponry' – by 'weaponry' I understood then (and still understand now) primarily the presence of an author's philosophy, his or her conception of the world and active approach to its transformation (cf. *Mladá tvorba*, 1958, no. 5).

Two decades later, when in the 1970s a new blossoming of Slovak fiction began, we met a similar phenomenon, although it was on a qualitatively higher level. The form of Slovak fiction had in the meantime matured. New, talented authors had appeared. Their thematic space had also expanded: their interest shifted from the micro-experience of an individual to the macro-experience of the people or at least of a regional community. It is no longer a matter of the evocation of an individual author's memory, but of the memory of the people, the search for the meaning of the progress of history. Some of the authors content themselves with the role of chroniclers, but the most important 1970s and 1980s novelists endeavour to raise historical experience to the status of a metaphor. Beyond presenting the history of the people, they attempt to characterise the people, but they also attempt to make certain generalisations about human behaviour in particular historical conditions. In this aspect, the most ambitious may have been Peter Jaroš's *Tisícročná včela*, which constituted an attempt at writing an apotheosis of the industriousness of the common people: it was a celebration of those who had overcome even the darkest periods of suppressed national life, of other nationalities' economic, cultural and linguistic expansionism in the territory of what is today Slovakia. If the symbol of the indestructible, eternal bee has an Ahasuerian quality, at the same time the author does not make a secret of his historicising concern and he intersperses the fabric of his novel with fictionalised factuality. This trend is even more palpable in the sequel to Jaroš's family saga, *Nemé ucho, hluché oko* (A dumb ear and a deaf eye, 1984), where the historicising principle dominates and what we see is, in fact, the recounting of stories illustrating the history of the Slovaks at the beginning of the new Czechoslovakia. Narration, which in the case of the first novel had led to the analysis of the character of the people, has returned to the description of history: the main character does not move history; he is just a tool in the author's hands which supports the author's intentions as an historian.

Such oscillations between points of view can be seen even better in fiction that delineates the history of southern Slovakia. The interest of prose-writers in southern Slovakia is, to considerable extent, influenced by the fact that the interests of two neighbouring peoples, the Slovaks and the Hungarians, meet in this relatively small area. While the cycle *Kolonisti* by Ivan Habaj constitutes an account of the dramatic social and national destinies of this part of Slovakia, the novel *Pomocník* by Ladislav Ballek has higher ambitions: it attempts to present an analysis of man's relationship to property, to ascertain the origins of the existence of the immediately post-war *nouveaux riches*. Moreover, in a graphic and authentic manner, it opens up the theme of Mephistophelean temptation in Slovak fiction. However, the study of prototypes of human behaviour in an extreme situation, when two social systems exchange the baton, does not seem to offer full satisfaction to the author as an epic writer, and so in the final chapter, an epilogue of a sort, he returns to the Dickensian narrative techniques: in a hasty, condensed manner further destinies of the heroes are recounted – and these might have provided material for equally stimulating analytical studies. Ballek's next novel, *Agáty*, draws in the reader by the story itself; an evocation of childhood memories somewhat in the style of Thomas Wolfe, but at the same time a theatrically arranged lyrical backdrop painted with ironic flashbacks, it is, in fact, an entirely inorganic jointing of independent *novelle* and short stories, connected only by the unities of place and historical time. The author seems to be fascinated by geographical space: parallels with Faulkner's Southern world come to mind immediately. Here we also have a limited territory with the same main characters of genealogical sequences of main characters. But while Faulkner raises his interest in the American South to metaphorical symbols and arranges his material as a poet, as a modern creator of myths, Ballek in his *Agáty* remains only a lyricising narrator. Whether this is a viable development will be confirmed by the author's further work, in which he will inevitably bring his main characters closer to the present.

Certainly, Slovak literature aims to reveal the special features of other regions, particularly western Slovakia and its villages. Vincent Šikula is the most consistent in his dedication to this area; in his short stories and *novelle* he comprehends the depiction of villagers more as a lyric than as an epic writer. On the surface we have a spontaneous, inorganic amassing of stories and reminiscences, but even a superficial reading may lead us to assume that Šikula's fiction is prototypical of the supremacy of narration. The fabric of Šikula's stories consists of numerous layers; the overlapping of these layers is intentional, since the author employs an associative method: not the association of words, but the association of larger epic wholes. Originally a musician, Šikula uses recurring *motifs* to create polyphonic stories. In his trilogy, *Majstri*, *Muškát* and *Vilma*, Šikula achieves an unusual depiction of one of the most important chapters of modern Czechoslovak history – the Slovak National Uprising. The picture of war in the preceding generation's fiction drew on authentic experience, and Šikula also tries to evoke authentic experience. It is the experience of not yet mature, but so much the more sensitive observer; moreover, the events take place in western Slovakia, where the Uprising barely penetrated. And so the war experience is refracted through the cognitive prism of the uncomprehending and inexperienced narrator. While Mináč's trilogy attempts an all-embracing historical and social view, Šikula renders cognition more subjective and relative; that seemingly creates the impression of fragmentariness and historical incompleteness: nevertheless, it may well be that in no other Slovak prose work has more truth been written about heroism, about the great self-sacrifice of a small people, about the absurd cruelty of the war. Although the method he has applied in short stories and *novelle* has not changed, the author has attained in his novels greater discipline in the direction of a sensitive diagnosis of the period.

Contemporary Slovak fiction also treats current events and movements – mainly in a smaller epic space. The programme of authors thus orientated is based on deep probes into the conscience of their contemporaries, on the realisation of the necessity of taking active stances at times of great or small decisions. Moral questions thrown up by an epoch of dynamic social change are in the forefront; we witness a persistent struggle for the ecology of human relations and only after that, say, for the natural environment. In this regard contemporary Slovak fiction differs a little from certain trends in contemporary Czech or Soviet fiction. It is not the problem that is in the foreground, but the attitude to the problem, how it impinges on the deeds of the individual. That is why prose dealing with contemporary themes tends to be introvert: it rejects wide epic screens; it does not try to depict the world in all its complexity. Rather, it abides by the rule according to which a drop of water should constitute the depiction of the whole ocean. This method has its merits and demerits. It influences the very choice of genre: short stories, *novelle* and short novels prevail. The writer answers urgent questions not with the insistence of a reporter, but with the topicality of a lyric poet. The traditionally orientated reader, however, expects a story, and sometimes even a critic impatiently raises his index finger and reproaches this type of fiction for its partiality.

Since I have been concentrating on the tension between the narrative and analytical approaches, it will be clear that this trend in fiction applies the analysis of the world as the decisive, sometimes even the only, principle of construction in a prose text. Ján Johanides consistently keeps to this principle; in his first works in the 1960s he was inspired primarily by French Existentialist literature and, later, also by Butor's vision of the *nouveau roman*; he then matures into a reflective prose writer. In the limited space of his *novelle* or novels he subjects the monstrosity of bourgeois morals to microscopic analysis, for example in *Balada o vkladnej knižke*, but also the brutal nature of Nazism which is still alive, in *Slony v Mauthausene*, or even the historical novel *Marek koniar a uhorský pápež*. Johanides's fiction tends towards sparkling style: the language is exact, gnomic, stripped of redundant connotations and descriptiveness. The problem of this type of prose consists mainly in its compositional principle: relegating the plot to the very edge of the writer's interest obscures the narration, sometimes it makes the text unclear, enciphered, and manifoldly decipherable.

The novels of Rudolf Slobada constitute a similar case. The compositional principle is saved here by the fact that it is for the most part of a first-person narrative; often it is a stylised autobiographical narrative. Sloboda, especially in his first novels, seems to project the Joycean world of *A Portrait of the Artist as a Young Man*. Sloboda's hero also constantly redefines his relationship with the world, with others; he asks basic philosophical questions; he indulges in unrelenting dissection, an almost masochistic dissection of his deeds and attitudes, in order to achieve catharsis. The prose works of Rudolf Sloboda, at first sight sad, even tragic, are, however, brightened by the author's faith in fundamental human values. Therefore the bizarre world of a drying-out clinic in the novel *Stratený raj* is simultaneously a parable concerning the potentials for man's self-amelioration. Sloboda uses sarcasm, irony and satire; we need think only of his veracious divagation on the mechanisms of film-making in the novel, *Rozum*. Johanides may be inconsistent in his composition, but Sloboda also tends to sacrifice the story to meditation and digression, although his material, precisely because of the simplicity, even bluntness, of language is clearer and therefore more readable. Sloboda as philosopher rejects closed schemes of thinking; he begins with the dialect and dynamism of knowledge; those lead him to a special form of social involvement.

The younger Dušan Mitana treats problems akin to those treated within Sloboda's conception of the world; in his novel *Koniec hry* he presents a stylistically, but also compositionally precise variant of the age-old investigation of crime and punishment. His hero is a murderer, who with the deductive ability of a chess grandmaster opens a game to conceal his absurd deed.

The novels and *novelle* of Jozef Puškáš also represent attempts at an analysis of contemporary thinking, but they sometimes surprise us with the lack of verisimilitude in the main characters' behaviour or with the vagueness or nugatoriness of the points at issue (the search for a flat in *Stvrtý rozmer*, and the saving of a strip of land in *Záhrada* (*v piatom období roka*) because of the extreme situations in which he places his characters.

Analytical fiction is today most successfully practised by Ján Lenčo, a prose writer who began with short parables and moralities, then acquired a liking for history, mainly classical Greek and Roman; but he profited most from his personal experience as a secondary-school teacher and a cinema manager. His novel *Rozpamätávanie* (Reminiscences, 1978) is something like a teachers' decameron: in a panoptically crowded common-room we follow the life stories of individual representatives of the teaching profession. Each narrative, is however, set at a different angle; indeed, each represents a different literary genre: nothing is repeated; the work almost surprises the reader with its consummate capacity to variegate. The author-narrator could content himself with a reproduction of droll stories; the author-analyst tries to turn each story into a metaphor or symbol. Thus *Rozpamätávanie* becomes perhaps the most complex picture of Slovak life at the end of the 1970s. Ján Lenčo exhibits this method also in his lengthy novel *Roky v kine Úsmev* (Years in a cinema called Smile). It is again a zoological study, this time of the cinema staff, of pursuers of occupations ranging from those of charwoman and boilerman to those of representatives of local 'cultural' authorities. The novel depicts a sense of honest human work, reveals the perversion of pretentiousness and careerism, mocks trivial human weaknesses that for the most part grow into a monstrous, devastating grudge against everything that is superior to the dull average of everyday banality. It displays a procession of modest heroes, some-times fanatics of their work or their hobbies but also chronic complainers, gossips and slanderers. Here again Lenčo allows his reader to gain an overview of both firmly-based and opportunistic attitudes; his decameron is, however closer to Fellini than to Boccac-cio; his background is naturally enough, not the Ancient world, but a Slovak county town in the 1980s.

At the beginning of my chapter I pinpointed narration and analysis as two antipodal forces. The experience of Slovak fiction indicates that, at present, the principle of analysis is more productive than any other principle. It is absolutely clear that this cannot be analysis which fully substitutes narration, analysis which surrenders the epic nature of fiction. It may result from the merit and good fortune of the works I have chosen to mention (which can in no case be considered a comprehensive picture of contemporary Slovak fiction) that, depending on the individual writer's talent and concentration on his or her intention, a worthwhile synthesis of these two approaches has been achieved. All this is because Slovak prose writers are forced not to ignore the readers; they cannot and do not want to resort to artificial narrative schemes, but even less to artiness. The favourable cultural and political conditions of the 1970s and 1980s have increased the authors' receptiveness, but also their responsibility for the logos they pronounce. Writing becomes literature the moment it is directed towards the universal knowledge of the laws of the world and man.

3 The Audacity of Tatarka
Peter Petro

Many of today's Slovak writers have managed to liberate themselves from the temptation of worldliness, of being trendy at all costs, and even from the totalitarian imperative which might handicap the writer as much as the imperative of nationalism which ruled Slovak literature in the first half of the twentieth century with a few, significant, exceptions: the imperative which commended Slovaks to catch up with the rest of Europe.

At the beginning of the post-Stalinist process of literary development there looms the figure of Dominik Tatarka who had written semi-Surrealist, then pre-Stalinist Socialist Realist, then Stalinist works, but still as an audacious writer whose temperament forced him to launch into the smallness, anxiousness and parochiality of Slovak literature and Slovak literature's inferiority complex, as he found it at the beginning of his literary career, in the 1940s. The Socialist Realist novels he published at the end of the 1940s and in the 1950s represent a conscious retreat, a suppression of his natural inclinations, and perhaps even a sincere attempt to come to terms with this, the only officially sanctioned, manner of writing. They represented a painful failure which could be explained only by the all-pervasive character of the totalitarian temptation that east central European intellectuals could hardly afford to ignore in the early 1950s. In 1956, after the Soviet XXth Party Congress, there arose the opportunity to begin writing free of strictures, free of administrative pressure.

Dominik Tatarka's *Démon súhlasu*[1] is the confessional declaration of a disenchanted intellectual's fight with the totalitarian temptation, with which he had essentially begun struggling by 1954.[2] Ten years later, commenting on *Démon súhlasu* Milan Šútovec wrote: 'And so it happened that the "timely word" pronounced by Dominik Tatarka with his *Démon súhlasu* has still remained in a certain sense until now, despite manifold changes, the only morally and artistically fully qualified event of Slovak literature.'[3] Today Tatarka's 'Fantasy Tract from the End of an Epoch', over 30 years after the end of the epoch that the subtitle to the *Démon* evokes, we are, perhaps, even less likely to find in Slovak literature anything more morally and artistically qualified regarding that period from any Slovak writer or critic. Even though the subtitle proved to be somewhat optimistic, a caesura in national literary consciousness did occur, despite the resumption of a restrictive cultural policy. The critic, Stanislav Šmatlák, pointed out the topical as well as the more profound and permanent features of this work when he wrote:

> Tatarka's *Démon súhlasu* is certainly a work characterised by a sharp reaction to the turn-about in Czechoslovakia social life which we associate with the XXth Congress. But its essential feature is not the readiness of the reaction, but its depth, the intellectual and aesthetic horizons it opened. That demonstrates that this work could not have been born in a day, but that the author had had to reflect upon it, to involve himself emotionally in it, even to agonise over it, if you like, long before he could publish it.[4]

Another element necessary for publishing or attempting to publish a work of this kind, which Šmatlák does not mention, is courage. Courage, audacity, would seem to be an adequate epithet to lend to Tatarka's work as a whole.

His inquisitive, caustic, reflective, almost naivist, manner apparently confused many of his critics whose stock responses pigeonholed Tatarka as an author influenced by Surrealism, Slovak Lyrical Prose, even Existentialism. Tatarka himself resisted identification with such labels: 'In my books, it seems to me, no Surrealism, nor Existentialism is echoed [. . .]. I was aiming elsewhere, at the source of my creation.'[5] The last statement comes from the mid-1960s, the time of the rediscovery of the importance of Slovak Surrealism[6] and it is characteristic of Tatarka that he declined to jump on this bandwagon. However, it is certain that in wartime Slovakia Surrealism was the movement that captured the imagination and loyalty of some of the best Slovak poets, painters and even critics. Today it appears that the Surrealist movement is almost equal in literary importance to the nineteenth-century Slovak Romantic movement. The appearance of Tatarka's *Panna Zázačnica* derived as much from Tatarka's originality and audacity, as from the receptive literary milieu, a milieu well prepared by the Surrealist movement.

Though *Panna Zázračnica* clearly signified a challenge to the Establishment, the novel won a prize and was published by the publishing house representing Slovak nationalism, Matica Slovenská. Tatarka boldly created a female character who was free and unrestrained and who lived among an equally unrestrained cast of characters the like of whom would reappear only much later, in the

1960s. It was not until the 1960s that Slovak literature tried to catch up with post-war European literary developments.[7] Tatarka returned to *Panna Zázračnica* in the mid-1960s when he wrote the screenplay for a film made by Stefan Uher.[8]

Tatarka's enthusiastic support of the changes brought about by the Communist take-over in 1948 included qualified support for Socialist Realism, which he saw as a vehicle for free experimentation, as he declared in his 'Manifesto of socialist humanism.'[9] That demonstrates that, when he came to write his *Démon súhlasu*, Tatarka objected most of all to the dehumanising elements of totalitarianism, elements like enforced unanimity:

> How is it, why is it that everyone, to a man, never agreed with everyone else so unanimously until now, even in decisive moments when our nation was in mortal danger? [. . .] Universal agreement is, in the human species, a heretofore non-existent phenomenon. Pause to consider, artists and thinkers, how this phenomenon of unanimous agreement could have arisen. How did it originate, who is responsible for it? Not I, but the people say that this is an unnatural, malignant phenomenon, more malignant than the cult which we uncovered (The Demon of Conformism', p. 293).

Since restrictions were to be ignored even in wartime, how could he abide by them in peace and in an avowedly humanitarian society? This is, however, a satire written by an insider, and there are definite limits to how far Tatarka was prepared to go, however courageous he might have been. He did not aim his sarcasm at the justifiable target of Stalinism, which is now euphemistically called the 'personality cult', of which he would say, in the 1960s: 'What we see today as strange and even mysterious, what we call today the period of the personality cult we'll see a few years later completely differently – or at least we suppose we will. We shall call it, and quite calmly, the period of the centralisation of the nations. The liberated nations will be called the centralised nations.'[10]

There is a sound sense in the idea that in *Démon súhlasu* Tatarka has exchanged his Roman Catholic education and his western European cultural orientation for a culture which did not quite fulfil his expectations and which, moreover, led to an Orwellian split personality. He does not yet say openly, but obliquely suggests, that the very desire for change, the desire to be progressive at any price, might be erroneous: 'Dissatisfaction with one's brain is, after all, a progressive emotion; many of my contemporaries actually burn with passionate desire to shape and mingle their brains with borrowed brains. And as a result of this commendable intention, they produce only pap.'[11]

It would not be altogether fanciful to say that in the background of the wholesale criticism of reality as he saw it in *Démon súhlasu* lies not only Tatarka's return to his early spiritual formation, his Roman Catholic education, which was not only formal (he attended classes in a seminary), but, above all, a return to the religious instruction he had received from his mother whom he clearly and unashamedly adores.[12] Such a reading of *Démon súhlasu* was not yet possible in 1956, though as early as in 1950 he had written in a short story, 'Apoštol rannej myšlienky' (The Apostle of a morning thought),[13] about a character who advises a Communist to start the day with a morning prayer, albeit a secular prayer.

Having rebelled against the faith of his mother, he now rebels against his new faith. To do that publicly demands courage and it would be hard to deny that Tatarka's satire was a great act of rebellion in the form of a manifesto. The title itself suggests exorcism of the demon (devils) of conformism. Those who fall victim to this demon are clearly possessed. They must be made to see the truth. Thus, Tatarka addresses his fellows as their comrade, a participant victim of demonic possession, one who is no longer possessed because he had 'died'. He has now come back to life to proclaim the truth:

the truth about Slovak society cannot be what kills, what angers and frustrates us, what forces us into isolation and madhouses, no matter what those standard government-issue brains say to us. The truth can only be what nurtures our human nature, nurtures that from which races grow and develop, small races, even the smallest of nations.

For me this is truth of our times. I have longed for it all my life. Because of it and on its behalf I have asked to speak, even if after death, when it will be too late for me.[14]

This audacious ending to his manifesto-like satire is credible and emotive because it is based on a grotesque, almost Surrealist, story. An appeal to rationality gains impact when made against the background of feverish, nightmarish irrationality.

In contrast, Tatarka has works where he is courageous by default where the great issues – political, philosophical and spiritual – are submerged, as happens in his *Prútené kreslá* (Wickerwork chairs, 1963).[15] There he returns to his youth and the time just following the

Munich Agreement, when he spent a year at the Sorbonne, pursuing a young French student intent on playing cat and mouse with him. The reader trained to expect a vigorous defence of democracy or a diatribe against Fascism is disappointed when he encounters a lyrical evocation of the last season before the whole world went mad; one might aver that this parallels Pasternak's *Last Summer*.

Prútené kreslá appeared at the time when Lyrical Prose had just been given official approval. Tatarka's great step forward consisted in acknowledging that not every poem has to propagandise. Tatarka succeeded in adumbrating grave issues, but not seriously dealing with them: in reversing the optics, as it were, and making clear that the personal world takes precedence over the social. As he later said: 'One has to struggle for freedom – even in the novel, and for the novel'.[16]

He insisted on the autonomy, the originality, and the uniqueness of artistic expression and, therefore, he never took kindly to literary historical explanations, which always treated Slovak literature as labouring under the overwhelming weight of foreign influence, and so Slovak literature consisted only of second or third-rate echoes of the great things happening beyond the world of the doomed Slovak writers. Tatarka could not accept that because he had seen the world. Though he was impressed by it, he, in his own way, managed to make some impression on it, and so was not overwhelmed. When listening to a learned account of foreign influences on the Slovak Avant-Garde, he remarked: 'With all respect, go to hell with such an account of the history of this sparsely populated Undertatrania! You don't realise how laughable it is'.[17]

This is the kind of courage that comes naturally to a man who was meant to die by machine-gun fire, after he had been captured by the Germans in the partisan war. In a painful and moving autobiographical story Tatarka recounts what he thought during those last moments before the execution from which he was saved by a desperate escape that few survived: 'Now what? You caught me, you put me in front of the machine guns. Now you have roasted me, you must eat me as well. But, even so, I won't stop thinking what I want. Yes, you can go to hell'.[18]

Having survived the Germans and Stalinism, Tatarka could not pretend that nothing had happened in 1968. Consequently even his former friends could not pretend that nothing had happened when he refused to 'normalise' himself, to accept the later, corrected official version of the military intervention of Warsaw Pact forces led by the

USSR in Czechoslovakia. Tatarka has no quarrel with the authentic version of the government which called a spade a spade.

Tatarka's hitherto most audacious work *Písačky* appeared only after his dismissal of the Establishment. It is divided into three volumes, *Písačky*, *Sám proti noci* (Alone against the night) and *Listy do večnosti* (Letters to eternity), which have been published in the West.[19] *Písačky* is an unprecedented event in Slovak literature. If it is true that every writer tries to reach a certain limit, that he charts out a certain course and then tries his best to follow that course, then one has to say that Tatarka in his *Písačky* attempts literature *without* limits.[20] Parallels are to be found in French writers: Léon Bloy, Céline; in Czech literature Jakub Deml also comes to mind. The contemporary Russian writers Yuz Aleshkovsky, Venedikt Erofeev and Viktor Nekrasov – if taken as a group – would give one an idea of the utterly unrestrained quality of Tatarka's prose in his *Písačky*. Such names suggest qualities like playful inventiveness, a monological, often downright diarist, approach, and a disdain for properties of any kind.

Perhaps the most shocking element, seen against the background of the history of Slovak literature, is Tatarka's eroticism. This is not eroticism of the commerical variety, designed to produce arousal. It is eroticism as an escape of a different kind. It is an escape to woman as the closest personification of Nature available to an urban man, perhaps even escape to 'das ewig Weibliche'. Tatarka's woman as a mistress is a last recourse after everything has failed. His fantastic trysts, however detailed and anatomical they may be, differ from morbid pornography because of Tatarka's linguistic inventiveness, unexpected lyricality and, finally, the all-pervasive sense of transcendence which accompanies the autobiographical character, Bartolomej Slzička's, peripeteia. Perhaps the passing mention of the *Kundalini* of Indian mystical thinking in *Panna Zázračnica* provides a clue to the more elaborate use of eroticism for the purpose of transcendence in *Písačky*.

If one accepts that Tatarka dispenses with traditional limits in his *Písačky*, it is only fair to state that these limits include the limit of good taste, or the limit which prohibits the disclosure of information embarrassing to one's friends and acquaintances. On the other hand, to stay bound by such limits would mean, paradoxocally, that a writer of Tatarka's stature would be trying to censor himself while the official censorship is looking after the general prohibition of his publications. Tatarka rejects such double censorship. If he is going to say just what he wants to say about himself, there is no reason for his sparing others, particularly those who, willingly or unwillingly, hurt him. Thus, after Bartolomej Slzička is ousted from public life, he is no longer published, and he becomes a target of police surveillance; he survives on a state pension and reacts the only way he can: by writing.

In writing he finds the freedom to talk about what had always interested him most, but what he could never say out loud, however audacious he managed to be during his writing career. He can discuss those things with his friends – whether dead or alive; he can have an ideal mistress – young, beautiful, intelligent – the like of whom one can only dream of in reality. He also looks ahead, into eternity, which, true to himself, he sees as being reunited with his grandparents and his mother; that is, being reunited with the source towards which he has always striven, even in his other works: 'Let me be respected by grandparents, children, women . . . Nothingness will not swallow us. We are heading towards our forefathers.'[21]

Tatarka's *Písačky* deserves a wider audience than it has at present. Not only because, among other possible interpretations, it is an example of unusual, audacious literature, but because to the chorus of the great writers who have entered universal acceptance from Central Europe, to writers like the Pole Miłosz, or the Czechs Škvorecký and Kundera, the voice of the Slovak Tatarka might be added as a voice of peculiar authority. Not as a second or third voice, but as a voice of a competent soloist singing his own original tune:

> My mother, in eternity, is my ancestor, my living and present conscience. My mother in me is my Slovak character, a warrior song sung in my language, in Slovak. Certainly, I appeared from the protoplasm of Slovak-Carpathian-Polish-Hungarian-Mongol-Vlach penetration, rape, and love . . . I, a Slovak, Carpathian warrior, am loved by free nations. I magnificently know how to sit down with them to drink and talk . . . Do not lower me into ethnos, nation, mass. I am such and such, whose mother and grandmother ascended to heaven as eternal light. I, too, despite everything will go there with all my friends, for example with the Czech and Polish poet, with Ďuro and Albert, and my sister Žofia.
>
> This self-projection into eternity is beautiful. This is a song about freedom, love and friendship.[22]

However trite this may sound, Tatarka's audacity throughout his career has consisted in trying to sing his song of freedom, love and friendship, audaciously, which means: in his own way, the only way he knew the only way he could. From his early stories and lyrical novel to his most recent works, there is a continuity and a sense that, despite enormous pressures of an extraliterary character, Dominik Tatarka has remained faithful to his most deeply felt undertaking, which was to follow the narrow road to his beginnings, his ultimate source. Few writers in central Europe could boast of more.

NOTES

1. First published as *Démon súhlasu*. (Fantastický traktát z konca jednej epochy,) in *Kultúrny život*, II (1956), nos. 15–17. My (somewhat abridged) translation, 'The Demon of Conformism', appeared in *Cross Currents*, 6 (1987), pp. 285–97. Unless otherwise indicated the translation of other texts is mine.
2. Stanislav Šmatlák, 'Literatúra posledných metamorfóz,' *Slovenské pohľady*, 81 (1965), 9, p. 12.
3. Milan Šútovec, 'Démon sa vracia,' *Slovenské pohľady*, 80 (1964), 5, p. 123.
4. Stanislav Šmatlák, 'Literatúra posledných metamorfóz,' p. 10.
5. Tatarka, 'Niekoľko hlasov o avantgarde,' *Slovenské pohľady*, 81 (1965), 10, pp. 51–2.
6. See my short anthology of Slovak Surrealist poetry in translation, *Prism International*, vol. 15 (1976), 2–3, pp. 146–64, as well as my 'Slovak Surrealist Poetry: The Movement and its Rediscovery', *Canadian Slavonic Papers*, 20 (1978), 2, pp. 237–44, and 'Slovak Surrealism as a Parable of Modern Uprootedness', *Cross Currents: A Yearbook of Central European Culture* (1982), pp. 219–32.
7. For the discussion of this decade, see my 'Modern Slovak Fiction: The Sixties, A Decade of Experimentation', *Slovakia*, 30 (1982–83), 55–6, pp. 153–64.
8. The novel was republished, (Bratislava: 1964).
9. Dominik Tatarka, *Proti démonom* (Bratislava: 1964).
10. Ibid., p. 195.
11. Dominik Tatarka, 'The Demon of Conformism', *Cross Currents*, 6 (1987), p. 286.
12. Most effusively in 'S ústim do nekonečna,' *Slovenské pohľady*, 74 (1958), 12, pp. 1246–1300.
13. *Slovenské pohľady* 81 (1965), 7, pp. 23–4.
14. 'The Demon of Conformism', p. 297.
15. Dominik Tatarka, *Prútené kreslá*, Bratislava, 1963.
16. Tatarka, *Proti démonom*, p. 198.
17. 'Niekoľko hlasov o avantgarde', p. 52.
18. 'Kohútik v agónii', *Slovenské pohľady*, 74 (1958), 7–8, p. 703. The words 'Now you have roasted me, you must eat me as well' refer back to the Romantic Ján Botto's version of the Slovak bandit legend, *Smrť*

Jánošíkova.
19. *Písačky* (Cologne: 1984), *Sám proti noci* (Munich: 1984), *Listy do večnosti* (Toronto: 1988).
20. See Peter Petro, 'Písačky ako literatúra vypovedania', *Premeny*, 1985, no. 3, pp. 298–323.
21. *Sám proti noci*, p. 100.
22. Ibid., pp. 103–4.

4 Literary Tradition in the Satirical Prose of Alfonz Bednár

Halina Sivachenko

We are at present witnessing a powerful revival of the grotesque in connection with the traditions of 'folk ludicrous' culture. The satirical works of the prominent Slovak writer, Alfonz Bednár, *Pri holbách smoly* (Tankards of tar, 1978) and *Za hrsť drobných* present a vivid example of grotesque based on animal mataphor.

The central figure in the *Pri holbách smoly* cycle is a certain Michal . . . ský, a senior research fellow at OVUPVOŽAP (Branch Research Institute for the Organisation of Life and Work), who is engaged at this fictitious institute in looking for a 'scientific basis' to justify his killing time in this fashion. The absurdity of this existence is manifested in a most original form: Bednár's anti-hero Michal . . . ský sinks on and off into unusual dreams in which he sees himself metamorphosed as a dog, a frog, a snail or some other representative of the animal world. Although externally transformed, he still retains his 'human' consciousness: under no conditions does he ever forget his position as a 'senior research fellow', and, therefore, in any situation and in every respect he acts in accordance with the demands of his real self. This allows the author to expose the basest, literally animal, instincts of this 'scientific philistine' for all the sophisticated mimicry to which he resorts.

The next stage in Bednár's exploitation of the resources of realistic grotesque was his burlesque trilogy *Za hrsť drobných*. The very title of this work 'for a handful of coppers' is clearly polysemic. On the one hand, it reveals the mercenary, venal nature of a philistine, the pettiness and meanness of his interests and tastes, while, on the other hand, it indicates a paradoxical development of the trifles of life into serious problems.

The form of the book is quite unusual: the family squabbles and other troubles of Jozef Kamenický are shown through the eyes of a dog. The fantasy plot contains some concrete indications of the present state and evolution of social consciousness. The writer's irony manifests itself both in how he presents certain facts of life and in the grotesque essence of events. The comic aspect of the trilogy is multifarious, embracing all the standard notions of philistines and the stereotypes of their actions and thinking. The fantastic element here serves as their comic negation; in other words, it embraces the whole sphere of a philistine 'spiritual standard'. Stereotypes are also overcome in a comic manner – if there is anything positive about them, that is by no means to be taken seriously.

The story of the Kamenický family may be defined as a ramified family chronicle in which straightforward realistic narration alternates with grotesque scenes of family farce. The narrator is the dog, Flip, who, after a long life among human beings and after his reign on the fantastic planet Tryfé, has found himself back in his old kennels. It is there that he recounts to the other dogs everything he has witnessed. Flip's sombre and oppressive impressions of life among human beings (impressions which he makes extremely vivid and compelling for his listeners) include only a preliminary preventative diagnosis of the problems touched on in the trilogy. But this intellectual dog, this narrator with canine 'outlook and views', discusses those problems quite frankly. Because of all this, 'another world' evolves, Flip's world, a carnival, fairy-tale show in which the morally impeccable narrator, the dog, scourges the narrowmindedness of man, his greed, his pragmatism, his indifference to suffering. It contributes to the development of cosy stories into a profound satirical analysis of the contradictions in modern society.

Bakhtin once noted that 'We usually try to understand the writer and his work from the position of the time he was living in, or from the position of the most recent past [. . .]. We are often afraid to step aside from the period under study. Meanwhile, books are not infrequently rooted in the remoter past'.[1] It is tempting to look into this remoter past and to undertake at least a superficial survey of the mythopoeic literary ancestry of Bednár's Flip. The discussion of even hypothetical sources and comparison with them will help towards a better understanding of the artistic conception and originality of Bednár's *Za hrsť drobných*.

Literary theory has established that there are several layers of meaning in any literary work, which can give rise to more than one interpretation at a time. On the one hand, this plurality of interpretation is the product of a subjective choice of position on the part of the scholar or reader. On the other hand, it is an objective characteristic of literary material which is independent of the perceiving consciousness. Veselovsky stated that comparative studies had revealed an important phenomenon: 'a number of invariable formulae stretching into the sphere of theory, from modern to ancient poetry, to epic, to myth . . .'[2]

The literary interpretation of the image of a dog is organically connected with the earlier folk and mythological tradition. Transform-ation of a man into a dog presents in fairy-tales and folklore the theme of the innocent who suffers, but is later compensated for his suffering. On the other hand, it constitutes a punishment for breaking certain norms of social behaviour. In Czech, for example, one can find the tale of an inhabitant of Prague who in 1674 was turned by God into a black dog for being 'unchaste'.[3]

The dog can be placed not only at the foot, but also at the top of the hierarchy of mythological creatures (cf. Zoroastrianism). One must note, however, that even in cases where dogs (or wolves, recognised in Indo-European culture as mythologically equivalent animals)[4] assume the role of especially valued creatures, they still symbolise detachment, albeit honourable detachment, from society.

To demonstrate this point, we may remember the legend of Cyrus, born of a bitch, or Romulus and Remus, or the themes of the hero's premature death in Charlemagne's prophetic dream in which Roland appears as a hunting dog (*Chanson de Roland*). Then, in the Kiev-Pechersky *paterik* (chronicle) the devil, having assumed the aspect of a black dog, prevents Theodosiy Pechersky from reading psalms. One notes that in Titian's allegorical representation of the three ages the profiles of the young man and the old man are compared with the heads of the dog and the wolf, while the full face of a mature man is compared to the head of the lion.[5] The dog in its mythological aspect is a totemic animal, usually linked with the earth and the next world.[6] In fairy-tale folklore, man in the image of a dog pleases his master with artistic buffoonery, making his guests laugh.[7]

The reconstruction of the pre-Slavonic image of the world[8] indicates that Veles (Volos) – one of the pagan gods – combined the roles of sponsor of the arts and keeper of cattle (this double 'function' is mentioned, in particular, in Cervantes's story of two dogs, Cipion and Berganza, and in the final part of the ballad 'Vavila and the Buffoons', where one finds a merging of the themes of cattle and the hermit world of the 'Sovereign Dog'). These facts obliquely suggest that the connection between the motifs of dog and art might exist in the realm of mythopoeic notions only potentially; its actualisation might take form only in the course of the development of literature.

In the early aesthetic tradition the simultaneous rise of these motifs is attended by a special bizarre, ludicrous atmosphere, which is particularly important when we are considering Bednár.

When we attempt to view the image of the dog in Bednár's *Za hrsť drobných* within the mythopoeic perspective, it should be borne in mind that the writer has annulled the theme of death, which is central to the whole mythopoeic complex. The traditional antinomy of life and death is replaced by another which is extremely important for contemporary fiction, namely, that of life-in-society versus life-outside-society. This replacement is accompanied by an upsetting of the balance between the hero's expulsion from human society and some kind of compensation for the outcast. It is appropriate to recall here the teaching of the Cynics who adhered to the view that the social outcast, compared with dogs, should be regarded as the chosen ones who prophesy the truth. One thinks also of Léon Bloy.

Several stories treat the metamorphosis of man into dog.[9] Among them are the Cervantes tale I have already mentioned and Baudelaire's 'Good Dogs'. In addition, the literary pedigree of Bednár's Flip embraces La Fontaine's fables, Apuleius's *Golden Ass*, Leo Tolstoy's *The Story of a Horse*, E. T. A. Hoffmann's *Kater Murr* and *Ponto, the Poodle*, N. Soseky's 'obedient servant'. Hoffmann, whom Heine called 'a wizard turning people into wild beasts, and turning the latter even into councillors of the Prussian royal court',[10] could not express it in a more insulting form than by making an inseparable couple out of the fashionable sycophant and stupid braggard Alcquiliad von Vhipp and his dog.

Russian literature of the nineteenth century gave the world an important masterpiece in which philistine triviality and pettiness are seen and shown through the eyes of a dog, Gogol's *The Diary of a Madman*. The satirical scope of this work is immensely enlarged with the 'correspondence' of the two lap-dogs, Madge and Fidel. Motivated by Poprischin's psychological disorder, this correspondence (allegedly found by him) exposes the seedy side of the red-tape atmosphere in which the hero lives.

The humanisation of animals is taken by the author to absurdity, and that increases the ludicrous impression. According to Vladimir Propp, 'Gogol's [just like Bednár's] blend of social satire by no means reduces the satirical aspect of his work; on the contrary, consistent satire, not sprinkled with purely comic elements, would have been monotonous, didactic and biased'.[11] The writers in question transfer human relations and customs to the animals' life, and mingle two absolutely different perceptions of reality to create an especially acid satirical effect, a realistic grotesquery which, as one Hungarian writer has remarked, 'challenges the sense of symmetry, breaks the usual order of things, opens other proportions, new laws, and, on top of all this, claims that this cosmic disorder should be recognised as trustworthy, perfect, and quite logical'.[12]

When one considers tradition in literature anywhere in the world, one has to turn to the satirical and grotesque presentation of animals in 'modernist' literature, particularly in Kafka. His *Metamorphosis* can serve as a classic example in this respect. Gregor Samsa, an inconspicuous clerk, finds himself one morning transfigured as obnoxious vermin. Wishing to emphasise the absurdity of human existence, Kafka paradoxically changes the narrative modes. Thus, in some of his stories whose main characters are animals who recount their life, that life is still no more than a variation of human life, or a model by which to assess it. In Kafka's *Letter to the Academy*, written on the behalf of an ape who has managed – after rather poignant tests and trials – to become a human being, that is to say, to acquire the outlook of a man and so, too, to assume the way of life of man, the author's ironical scepticism turns into a cruel satire on humankind.

Bednár is far from Kafkaesque pessimistic 'modernist' aesthetics in his interpretation of a man's metamorphosis into an animal. But in Bednár's use of certain techniques in this allegorical transformation, something like a Kafkaesque touch is palpable. Bednár, however, is rather more drawn to the satirical tradition evident in, say, the Czechs Karel and Josef Čapek who, in *The Insect Play*, became interested in indications of a remote similarity between the animal world and human relations, and who resorted to animal metaphor which highlights 'all that is wrong, meaningless, cruel and anti-human in the "normal" life of people, noting how bitter and discouraging it is to see the analogy of human life in the vain hustle and bustle of butterflies, dung-beetles, ants or crickets'.[13]

In Bednár's laughter one might also hear an echo of the Slovak literary tradition. For example, Ján Chalupka (1791–1871) in his best comedy *Kocourkovo, anebo: Jen abychom v hanbě nezůstali* (Kocourkovo: We don't want to look foolish, 1830), wittily and ruthlessly mocked life in the fictitious town of Kocourkovo, whose name later became a personification of stagnation, complacency and narrow-mindedness.

Another Slovak writer, Jonáš Záborský (1812–76), turned to the imaged of Kocourkovo in his mock-heroic, satirical *Faustiáda* (partly published 1864, complete edition, 1912); here he develops the Renaissance line of realistic fantastic. He finds a parody form for a plot richly loaded with topical problems, and plays ironically with orthodox techniques and the topoi of the fairy-tale and the chivalrous romance. Záborský creates a judgemental and at the same time comic effect by a parody combination of material and conceptual incongruities. He maintains a lofty tone, gives allegedly positive characteristics a negative air, reduces high-flown notions to the ordinary or, vice versa, hyperbolises trifles. All this makes the satire of the work stronger. In Bednár's trilogy more or less similar artistic techniques perform analogous functions.

In his work Bednár has succeeded in making a synthesis of the best traditions of literature. It is worth noting that among the writers whose works Bednár has translated, Mark Twain is of special interest for this chapter because of his *The Story of a Dog*. It is reasonable to suppose that Bednár as a specialist in English and American literature was familiar with the story and that it gave at least some impetus to Bednár to write his novel. Both Twain's story and Bednár's novel do more than merely focus on a dog possessing certain human features and outlook.

Both dogs have alien, comic names: Twain's heroine is called Aileen Mayvorin – the name had once been heard somewhere by her ecstatic mother; Flip's official name is Dagobert zo Šošvičného, that is something like Dagabert von Schoschowitsch; he has papers to prove it. Aileen, just like Flip, lives in the family of a scientist, an experimental physiologist, so there is a visible coincidence in the plots and situations of the two works. Twain's satirical purpose, however, is to show man's cruelty to animals, while Bednár seeks to satirise the weaknesses and limitations of human nature.

'Purity', or rather a lack of preparation in the dog's 'psyche' to perceive certain sides of human existence, becomes for Bednár (and Twain, for that matter), an apparently inexhaustible source of lively, brisk and unexpected reactions. Flip's address to his 'dear colleagues' who faithfully serve humankind is, in fact, the story of the hard life of dogs sacrificed to science (it is quite appropriate to remember here *The Story of a Dog*, in which the 'heroine' selflessly saved her master's child from the fire and then found to her astonishment and despair that this very master, for the sake of some senseless experiment, had taken the sight of her own little puppy).

Bednár's Flip initially loves his master's son Cintľa but then he watches with horror his pop group, the portrait of which is presented by the novelist on a generalised symbolic plane, in the spirit of a lampoon. The members of the group are spiritually bankrupt, without any moral backbone; they have no interest in life, and are thus pictured as faceless in a multifaced fantastic embodiment of the essence of spiritual bankruptcy. In a curious way Cintľa's group reminds us of the gang of *jeunesse dorée*, with the untalented Lee, the future movie star, at its head, in Karel Čapek's *War with the Newts*. Both writers resort to similar satirical devices, which become particularly evident in grotesque, typifying generalisations, and in the way they reduce people to the level of either animals or monsters.

The accumulation of events in Bednár's trilogy is not infrequently taken to an absurd extreme and the absurdity begins to compromise the fictional element. While trying to secure the illusion of verisimilitude, mystifying the reader, the author consistently denies the conventional and reveals his chief concern in parody and game-playing. The reinterpretation of the conventional to expose the seamy side of the hierarchy of values, the atmosphere of base miracles and other forms from the folk culture of the ludicrous, are vividly expressed in the pages of *Za hrsť drobných*.

The work is so crammed with events that it assumes something of the character of drama. In particular, the extensive use of dialogue contributes to this. The reader is faced with a kind of performance, both conventional and unreal. The author more and more frequently reminds us that everything taking place in the Kamenickýs' house is nothing but a theatrical performance. The polysemy of everyday scenes brings the parody of a philistine milieu to the level of pure grotesque. At the same time it is the grotesque effect that raises the problems of the novel to the socio-political level. Bednár creates the atmosphere of relative values, in which a positive idea advocating the prevalence of the natural over everything one-sided or pompous expresses the views of human beings. The author's irony and parody of fantastic images and events explain the double significance of *Za hrsť drobných's* general conception which denies and ridicules primitive, superficial form.

The theme of space travel to a fictitious planet appears in the first part of the trilogy, when Cintľa, talking to his girlfriend Daša, expresses a utopian wish to fly into space, to settle on some planet and from there to improve humankind. Cintľa's dream is later realised by Flip who, after his flight from the Kamenický family, finds himself on the 'developing' planet of Tryfé. There Flip continues to investigate the cause of human suffering and degradation, this time as the planet's ruler, Trifemos XIII.

Bednár's work, like, for example, Swift's *Gulliver's Travels*, differs from other fictional travels by one most important feature: the reader is not shown some unknown lands, but is gradually given the impression that he has been taken from far away to some repulsively familiar places and shown ways and manners he is sick and tired of. Or, rather, the reader has not always understood previously how repulsive these ways are; he has grown used to them and cannot imagine another angle from which to view them – since to do that requires independence of thought, courage and imagination. Both Swift and Bednár skilfully employ alienation, showing the customary, the familiar from an unusual angle, causing it to be recognised as natural, necessary or right. In this Swift's principle is observed: 'Life is not farce, it is some antique tragedy, that is, the worst kind of fiction'.[14]

Alfonz Bednár offers a somewhat different version of this assertion. He is certain that the majority of people has not become accustomed to the flaws and evils of modern society; he believes in the remedial powers of socialism. But the essence of the artistic device remains the same – Bednár, like Swift, at first, as it were changes the lenses through which he views people, and then he turns all customary relations inside out. Thus the reader finds himself in a topsy-turvy world where the reasonable and wise animal rules anti-social and wild people.

The world of the planet Tryfé is graphically presented through all sorts of anomalies. The humour here opposes distorted norms, the hypertrophy of regenerated humanity. A joke, a piece of ridicule, parodies unacceptable ideological concepts and at the same time mocks their simplified representation. This enables quite serious problems to be treated with laughter, but not in the least in any simplified or facile form.

The third part of the trilogy, which has the subtitle *z rozvojové planety Tryfé* (from the developing planet, Tryfé, 1981), is, like *Gulliver's Travels*, a fantasy, but a fantasy of an unusual kind; neither writer in principle resorts to unusual things in his fictitious worlds. They consistently humanise animals, which is the main factor in their fantasy and irony, and that helps them to create a dystopia and to show the degree of degradation to which people can be brought by certain tendencies present in 'civilised' reality and, indeed, in the very nature of a man – when these tendencies prevail.

The story of Flip's becoming the ruler of a fictitious planet helps the author expose in a satirical, symbolic, exaggeratedly farcical way the weaknesses and evils inherent in man. Bednár creates a grotesque of anxiety and posits it as the aptest form to express the folk outlook and the convictions of a writer bound by the European humanist tradition; his form is reinforced by the extensive use of Swiftian artistic techniques.

There are analogous phenomena in Soviet literature. Works which immediately spring to mind include Mayakovsky's poem, 'That is How I Became a Dog', which was written at the time when the poet was working for the journal *Satiricon*, Fedin's early story, 'Dogs' Souls', Ilf and Petrov's story 'Ich bin from Top to Toe' and, Bulgakov's *The Master and Margarita* and *The Dog's Heart*.

Bulgakov's cat Begemot, who functions in the novel as a kind of devil's errand-boy, feels quite at home in the philistine environment of Moscow. He is perfectly likeable in all his actions, small intrigues and minor machinations, being, in the author's view, undoubtedly useful. According to Bulgakov's conception, the cat is indispensable for controlling and limiting the stupidity which people simply cannot be rid of. Begemot the cat plays the role which people have thrust upon him – just as upon the whole of Voland's gang, for that matter. When the situation is more or less normal, they assume the aspect of a baby sparrow or a cat; when things go from bad to worse, the mocking figure of the 'chequered' one comes into sight; and when the situation acquires dire qualities Voland himself turns up. Though these diabolical forces are endowed with a destructive power, they only ruthlessly reform and correct what would not or could not be reformed and corrected without them. Thus these are forces which, according to the epigraph from Goethe's *Faust*, 'eternally look for the evil, and eternally create the good'.

Some interest in the grotesque and satirical uncrowning of a modern 'anti-hero' is to be found in works by contemporary Ukrainian writers, O. Chernoguz, in particular. In his novels *The Aristocrat from Vapnyarka* and *Pretenders to the Sheepskin Hat*, the author skilfully uses satire and irony, which help to demonstrate the complex process of the degradation of a socially irresponsible person to a social conformist. The ideological and aesthetic evolution of Evgraf Sedalka-Sedalkovsky (the main character of one of the books) ends in moral ruin and, to some extent, in depression, which is caused by the realisation of all the hopelessness of his own methods and means of establishing himself in society. Everybody in the fictitious research institution called FINDIPOSH (one cannot but remember here

Bednár's OVUPVOŽAP), like Bednár's Michal . . . ský, represents a definite social and psychological type, a model of sycophancy and social mimicry.

V. Drozd's *A Lonely Wolf* reveals an interest in the aspect of an 'animilistic' solution to the problems touched upon. Its hero gradually loses his own face, 'growing' into the skin or rather, the manners and ways of thinking, of his colleague – a pragmatic cynic. In the long run he turns into a werewolf, thus symbolising the final stage of his self-destruction as a man.

I have made no attempt to discuss all the works in the European literary tradition which belong to the line of realistic grotesque based on the animal metaphor which might have influence or might be compared with Bednár's *Za hrsť drobných*. Certain coincidences in the plot of Bednár's novel with Twain's story, like the definite resemblance between the third volume of the trilogy and *Gulliver's Travels* may derive only from chance. There may be other parallels of interest to students of Slovak literature, for, as Likhachev believes, 'real cultural values develop only in contact with other cultures, grow from a rich cultural soil and take into consideration the aesthetic experience of their neighbours . . . the more "dependent" any culture is, the more independent it is'.[15] Looking at Bednár's trilogy from the point of view of its satire and grotesque places it in the framework of a definite literary tradition, and contributes to a better understanding of its original attitude to reality and to the devices of the contemporary novel. It also clarifies our ideas about the development of conventional forms, and, particularly, of the realistic grotesque in socialist-bloc literature.

NOTES

1. Mikhail M. Bakhtin, *Estetika slovesnogo tvorchestřa* (Moscow: 1979), p. 331.
2. Aleksandr N. Veselovsky, *Istoricheskaya poetika* (Leningrad: 1940), p. 47.
3. Alla M. Panchenko, *Cheshsko-russkie literaturnye svyazi XVII veka* (Leningrad: 1969), p. 114.
4. Evgeny Kaganov, *Kult fetishei, rasteny i zhivotnykh v drevnei Gretsii* (St Petersburg: 1913), p. 218; V. V. Ivanov, *Rekonstruktsiya endoevropeis-kikh slov i tekstov, otrozhayushchikh kuľt volka*, published in the Literature and Language series of the Academy of Sciences publishing house (1975), vol. 34, p. 5; Roman Jakobson with M. Szefter 'The Vseslav Epos', Roman Jakobson, *Selected Writings*, vol. 4 (The Hague

and Paris: 1966), pp. 346–50.
5. This may be linked with the motif of the old man as an anthropomorphic substitute for the wolf in Slavonic mythology, see Vyacheslav V. Ivanov and Veniamin N. Toporov, *Issledovaniya v oblasti slavyanskikh drevnostei* (Moscow: 1974, p. 192).
6. Cf. the Ukrainian legend of the monstrous dog-headed ogres who live underground. See Mikhail Dragomanov, *Malorusskie narodnye predaliya i rasskazy* (Kiev: 1976) pp. 2 and 384–5.
7. L. Mayakov, *Velikorusskie zaklinaniya* (St Petersburg: 1869): p. 39.
8. Roman Jakobson, 'Voprosy sravnitelnoi indaevrocheiskoi mifologii v svete slavyanskikh skazanii', *American Contributions to the Sixth International Congress of Slavists, Prague, 1968*, vol. I (The Hague and Paris: 1968) p. 128.
9. See R. Schambers, 'Artist as Performing Dog', *Comparative Literature*, 23 (Oregon, 1971), p. 4.
10. Quoted from Heinrich Heine (Geine), *Sobr. soch. v. 10-ti tomach*, translated in Russian by X. Malovtakov, vol. 6 (Moscow: 1958), p. 219.
11. Vladimir Ya. Propp, *Problemy komizma i smekha* (Moscow: 1976), p. 50.
12. I. Örkény, 'Razmyshleniya o groteske', *Inostrannaya Literarura*, 4 (1973), p. 205.
13. See 'On Pessimism in the Play *Scenes from the Life of Insects*, an open letter from the Čapek brothers to Owen Davis *New York Herald*, 9 March 1923.
14. *Swift, Modern Judgements* (London: 1968), p. 55.
15. Dmitry Likhachev, 'Chem "nesamostoyatel'nee" lyubaya kul'tura, tem ona "samostoyatel'nee"', *Voprosy literatury*, 12 (1986), p. 111.

5 Transformations of Prose Structure in the '56 Generation
Ludwig Richter

When, at the end of the 1980s, one looks at the development of Slovak prose fiction since 1954, one can say, without exaggeration, that the '56 Generation have made a decisive contribution to the formation of prose. This contribution has been reflected not only at the level of 'programmes' but also in the Generation's own literary production. That is quite apart from historically ineluctable changes in the understanding of the general function of literature and of the particular artistic structure of prose. The influence of the '56 Generation did not always come about in accordance with declared aesthetic postulations, but rather within a dialectic of reaction and counter-reaction to accepted national literary tradition and conventions and to the demands of contemporary currents in world literature. However different the individual manners of writing, the individual poetics, of the writers Vincent Šikula, Peter Jaroš, Ján Johanides, Ján Lenčo, Rudolf Sloboda, Anton Hykisch and Jozef Kot might be, together the representatives of the '56 Generation, have played an essential role in the modernising revival of Slovak prose and thus also in establishing prose as the prime genre in Slovak literature since the 1970s. With hindsight many literary critical judgements on the beginnings of these writers can no longer be upheld, judgements which declared that the joyously experimenting writers of the 1960s, with the odd rare exception, had abandoned the tradition of Slovak literature. Any consistent literary historical treatment of the whole development, not merely small segments, of Slovak fiction since the 1950s, must lead to a re-evaluation, without any *ex-post* smoothing out of inconsistencies of development.

When the '56 Generation entered the literary scene, Slovak literature was in the midst of a dynamic process of change which concerned all genres and writers of all age groups. In a 1981 interview with the periodical, *Weimarer Beiträge*, Jozef Kot formulated what was special about the Generation's contribution as 'the experience of those who had reached maturity in the conditions of postwar society and who had lived through the first rapture of that society', but who had then been forced to realise that 'this idyll had suddenly started to become unstable'.[1] That explains the vehemence with which in the periodical, *Mladá tvorba*, the Generation raised their voice to declare their determination not to be satisifed with the 'criteria and truths' of 'literary historians and aestheticians,' but rather to find a 'more subjective, selective approach' to their 'predecessors' work'. That is to be found in their programme-like 'Miesto manifestu' (In lieu of a manifesto).[2] From this point of view the term '56 Generation should actually cover not only prose writers but also poets, as Vladimír Petrík makes clear when he speaks of the '*Mladá tvorba* Generation'.[3] In their basic intention of renewing, modernising Slovak literature by dismantling the obtaining literary canon, narrative and lyric writers were in agreement. Not all writers, however, linked a belief in a universalist modern literature which avoids vulgarising conceptions of realism with the artist's social task as consistently as Laco Novomeský had done even before the Communist take-over in February 1948.[4] In the article, 'Cesty poézie' (The paths of poetry, 1958), Miroslav Válek did the same. Both were confronting the threat of semantic hermeticality, of autocommunicative 'soul-baring' in which, finally, the lyric subject appears only as a human being alone, far removed from all social bonds.[5]

The most important part of the '56 Generation's programme consisted in questioning the literary *status quo* in the attempt to find a point of departure from which they could develop their own alternative conceptions. In a 1974 interview with the weekly *Nové slovo*, Peter Jaroš expressed this programme thus: 'We wanted to be better than all who had come before us', and: 'we wanted to mark ourselves off from the short period of Slovak schematic prose'.[6] In fact the '56 Generation were turning both against the one-sided assessment of nineteenth and twentieth-century social Realism and against the early 1950s obligatory conception of a firm line of national literary tradition in prose which led from the Romantic Ján Kalinčiak (1822–71) to the Socialist Realists Martin Kukučín (1860–1928), Božena Slančíková Timrava (1867–1951), Jozef Gregor Tajovský (1874–1940), the social critical and ironical novelist Janko Jesenský (1874–1945), and finally to the Socialist Realists, Peter Jilemnický (1901–49) and Fraňo Kráľ (1903–55). With Georg Lukács's preceptive conception of literature in mind, in the 1960s Kot described the attempt to 'build new prose fiction on the aesthetic postulates of the nineteenth century' as a 'mistake which is still palpable today'.[7] He considered the aesthetic models concomitant with that conception to be neither adequate nor appropriate; the narrative writer, he wrote, needed 'a far more varied palette [. . .] for a truthful representation of reality'.[8]

The '56 Generation's insistent call for a modern literature certainly found open doors, but not unconditional agreement; they were bragging of aesthetic novelty that bit too much, and so they were accused of being hostile to tradition. Against that Kot stated that the young prose writers did not want 'to break their links either with the domestic tradition or with the older generation of writers'.[9] He asserted that the artistic differentiation which was now manifesting itself was not the product of 'a generation-gap phenomenon', but of necessity.[10] A 'new, positive, programme of committed art' was to normalise literary life and liberate it from 'dogmatic errors and anti-dogmatic crazes'.[11] It should also 'discuss things' in Slovak literature 'which are self-evident in other literatures'.[12] And indeed the equation of artistic modernity with ideological decay and political reactionariness, an equation which began to be made in the discussions on Formalism and which in the early 1950s had become an obligatory component of literary theory, now came under general attack and, gradually, literary practice itself demonstrated the unviability of the equation. This process naturally brought with it varied, sometimes contradictory, notions about the paths which should be taken to achieve renewal and the limits which should be imposed on a modernisation which was of itself inevitable. A decisive step towards this renewal and modernisation was taken when the Slovaks' own socialist literary heritage in the form of the DAV[13] tradition was restored, together with its universalist conception of literature, which certainly linked artistic and social progress, but did not consider them identical.

As far as the national literary tradition is concerned, writers of the '56 Generation found certain points of contact (and these points differed from writer to writer) primarily in the prose fiction of the inter-war period. Hitherto much of this literature was 'illegal and unobtainable,'[14] and thus formally excluded from the socialist literary heritage. For example, Šikula's style of representation bears a certain resemblance with the artistic methods of the Lyrical Prose school. To be sure, Šikula protested at Slovak critics' calling him that school's immediate successor, however much he valued members of that school, Dobroslav Chrobák's (1907–51) or František Švantner's (1912–

50), 'fine-chiseling' verbal art.[15] Generally speaking, the '56 Generation's relationship with this school was somewhat ambivalent.
Hykisch also recognised the school's linguistic imaginativeness and
its endeavour to create great metaphors. This fact played a central
role before the discussion on Formalism in the debate concerning
Hana Zelinová's novel *Anjelská zem* (Land of angels, 1946). Hykisch,
as an 'urban writer', however, felt 'a certain aversion' to Lyrical
Prose because it sets up the rural as the genuinely Slovak and thus
preserves a consciousness which had been overtaken by history. For
that reason Lyrical Prose did not seem to him to be 'the most
appropriate platform from which to raise questions which interested
the Slovak of today'.[16] From the very start the picture Lyrical Prose
writers present of the Slovak village was always an anachronism for
Kot, 'a belated pursuit of a dream, long after sleep had been
disturbed'.[17] The Lyrical Prose school is naturally not the only part
of the modern national literary tradition which the by no means
homogeneous '56 Generation rediscovered. Hykisch, for example,
sought an equivalent to the endeavours of the painters Benka,
Bazovský, Fulla and Galanda, in whom characteristic Slovak features
and artistic modernity did not run in parallel, but fused. He found
'the germs of an unprovincial view in the short-stories concerning
artists or set in towns written by Ivan Horváth [1904–60]'; he also
found instructive impulses in the stories of Ján Červeň (1919–42),
who did not start writing until after the beginning of World War II
and employed a highly imaginative representative style. In the works
of Tido J. Gašpar (1893–1972) and Gejza Vámoš (1901–56) one could
already see an 'open treatment of the role of sexuality' of the kind
which was being attempted in present-day literature.[18] Finally, in his
Nie Johanides makes some use of the poetics of Surrealism, a trend
which had been strong in Slovak verse during and shortly after World
War II, but which had made only sporadic appearances in prose, for
example in Tatarka's early works. In his use of Surrealist techniques
Johanides was reacting to the 1960s discussions concerning a re-
evaluation of the Avant-Garde in general and Slovak Surrealism
(*nadrealizmus*) in particular. From all this it is evident that, in their
search for alternative aesthetic solutions, the '56 Generation may
have been decidedly anti-traditionalist, but they were not hostile to
tradition. In 1974 Jaroš declared that authors whose main works were
written before, during and just after the war, like Milo Urban (1904–
82; last work, however, published in 1970), Jozef Cíger Hronský
(1896–1960; last work published when the author was an emigré in

Argentina, 1960), Chrobák and Švantner, as well as writers of an older generation who were still writing, Margit Figuli, Alfonz Bednár and Mináč, 'had created modern Slovak prose'.[19] One must admit, however, that this constitutes a somewhat belated act of reverence for the national literary heritage performed by an author who in the 1960s had paid tribute mainly to foreign aesthetic models.

In Slovakia in the second half of the 1950s, attitudes to the heritage of world literature and also to new works in foreign literature began to change, too. This change was a general process concerning all genres, but it was probably most marked in narrative literature, because the need to catch up as well as the interest of the Slovak readership were particularly great. The '56 Generation became actively involved in this change on three levels: in literary criticism, in their own translations and in the processing of foreign artistic impulses in their own writing.

It is symptomatic of the Slovak literary landscape which began to change so fast at the end of the 1950s that the reception of other national literatures now included also those writers who had been indiscriminately excluded from their national literatures by Czechoslovak critics as 'Modernists'. Naturally, this affected not only Western authors, but also, for example, Russian or Soviet literature. Thus the creative reception of Dostoyevsky, which had been interrupted in 1949, could be taken up again only in 1957 and a Soviet writer like Bulgakov could be seriously considered only in the middle of the 1960s.[20] Not only Alfonz Bednár but also the younger Jozef Kot were fully involved in the manifold attempts to open up English and American literature as literary critics, but primarily as translators. As Kot has himself admitted, this 'without any doubt influenced the development of my conception of literature, even though that influence was definitely not as linear as it, perhaps, appeared to many at first sight'.[21] Indeed it was far less a matter of individual poetological borrowings than of the fact that Kot achieved a profounder consciousness of form through his translations of Faulkner, Hemingway, Joyce, Salinger and Updike and thus became ever more convinced that today the novel could no longer be built on the foundations of the classic novel's poetics, and that writers should fully exploit the widest possible range of aesthetic experience. Finally, it was a question first of dispensing with the automatic equation, in their own literature, of social and artistic progressiveness; and secondly of making known the historical state of the art, the level of achievement in the mastering of literary techniques; incidentally, these last two matters were of concern to most literature in European socialist countries at the end of the 1950s and the beginning of the 1960s.[22] A re-evaluation of bourgeois modernism, however, and here I align myself with the view of Robert Weimann, could on no account mean 'that criticism of the self-imposed limits of an author's isolation should be withdrawn; on the contrary, the criticism of bourgeois individualism should be radicalised by examining the modernists' self-perception on the basis of a knowledge of the true ideological and communicational processes'.[23]

Together with the increasing reception of bourgeois modernism there came intense discussion of the *nouveau roman*. Although the fundamental works of this trend, Michel Butor's *L'Emploi du temps*, Alain Robbe-Grillet's *Le Voyeur* or Nathalie Sarraute's *Les Fruits d'or* were not published in Slovak in book form,[24] the *nouveau roman* was extensively discussed under the label 'anti-novel' by critics in Slovak periodicals. The potential for taking artistic impulses from the *nouveau roman* lay not so much in the trend's total negation of traditional narrative schemes as in its use of new narrative techniques. The emphasis on the manner of writing, on the aesthetic structure, in a narrower sense: on the linguistic aspect of the work of literature, as long as that aspect was not made absolute as it could be in the *nouveau roman*, could certainly contribute formative elements for a modernisation of Slovak prose. On the other hand, the unbridled interest in the invention of forms and the concomitant devaluing of subject matter, the conscious renunciation of all object or purpose in literature, the deliberate or consciously accepted isolation from the mass of readers, and the rejection of political commitment were not acceptable in the Slovak literary situation.[25] Because of that, attempts to apply the poetics of the *nouveau roman* as such, without paying any regard to the different social contexts, had to end in a cognitive and artistic cul-de-sac. In the mid 1960s Peter Jaroš belonged among those young Slovak writers who saw a source of artistic inspiration in the *nouveau roman*, but he was himself cautious about its possibilities; he spoke merely of 'some discoveries of the anti-novel' which were necessary for the further development of the novel and which he intended using in his work.[26] In fact, his grappling with the *nouveau roman* was linked with borrowings from the French Existentialists and formed part of a lengthy phase of experimentation, which turned out to be only a period of transition. In Jaroš the uncritical appropriation of foreign elements resulted in his picture of humanity remaining general, abstract, or at least it did not have its roots in the society in which the author himself lived.

One has, however, to ask whether Jaroš had just taken the wrong path. In her structured analysis of the early works of Jaroš, Johanides and Sloboda, in which she compares and contrasts elements of the 'classical' with those of the 'modern' novel, Nora Krausová comes to a thoroughly ambivalent conclusion. Their novels or long short stories are not so much an artistic reflection of social processes as a mirroring of their own pathologically stylised inner selves, which results in a loss of cognition. The fictional figures are depersonalised and the action reduced to a minimum, so that no character development is possible, but, probably, only an alienated angle of vision, a camera-flash-like illumination which can replace the 'parametric' development of 'classical' figures. The narrator lacks 'epic distance'; his chief function is playing with time; events are presented on various time-levels; among other things the flashback is frequently employed.[27]

Thus, if one does not consider the '56 Generation's artistic achievement exclusively from a broadly social standpoint, one will have to see their attempts at innovation not in some crass contrast to their later works, but in causal connection with those works. It is true that in the 1960s a negative attitude to the literary canon of the early 1950s dominated. At the same time, however, a quest for new ways of writing beyond the national tradition and as a result of the exhaustion of the Slovak literary 'modern tradition' was set in motion. From this point of view the members of the '56 Generation may not have been the only writers to do it, but they probably were the writers who, relatively unencumbered by developments hitherto, took the renewal and modernisation of Slovak prose particularly seriously. They took a decisive stand against superficial historicism, against pure empiricism and, above all, against stereotyped conventions. They sought to set authentic statements about their contemporaries up against broad historical frescoes. On the one hand, turning to the individual and his or her everyday life, concealed in itself the danger that socially irrelevant problems of humanity could be elevated to 'eternally' human, existential problems; on the other hand, it offered writers the chance to discover socially significant phenomena 'in the world's tiny little things'.[28]

If one takes into consideration the later, quite different, development of this generation of Slovak writers and tries to sum up their contribution, one may certainly state the following. Their special emphasis on literary fiction did not lead to a separation of literature from life, as was to be feared at the beginning, for fiction was brought into an ever closer relationship with their own experience of socialism. Playful experimenting with forms gradually moved from a state where they were simply copying foreign models to creative work-shop endeavour; thus formal experimentation eventually introduced an intellectual tone into Slovak prose. The retreat from grand epicality did not necessarily result in a noncommital fragmentation of their view of reality; their turning to everyday problems aimed at dealing with important questions of existence, even if these questions were raised more from the 'periphery' than from the 'centre' of socialist social praxis.

NOTES

1. Ludwig Richter, 'Interview mit Jozef Kot,' *Weimarer Beiträge*, 27 (1981), p. 44.
2. *Mladá tvorba*, 1 (1956), p. 1.
3. Vladimír Petrík, *Hodnoty a podnety* (Bratislava: 1980), p. 273ff.
4. On this see Ludwig Richter, *Slowakische Literatur. Entwicklungstrends vom Vormärz bis zur Gegenwart* ([East] Berlin: 1979), p. 157ff.
5. Stanislav Šmatlák, 'Dichter und Politiker. Zur sozialistischen Lyrikkonzeption Miroslav Váleks', *Weimarer Beiträge*, 27 (1981), pp. 37–8.
6. Ľuboš Jurík, *Rozhovory* (Bratislava: 1975), p. 40.
7. Jozef Kot, 'Mezinárodne o próze', *Slovenské pohľady*, 79 (1963), 4, pp. 23–4.
8. Jozef Kot, 'Pravda života a literárna konstrukcia', *Slovenské pohľady*, 77 (1961), 8, p. 100.
9. Jozef Kot, 'Prvé predstavenie', *Slovenské pohľady*, 79 (1963), 10, p. 2.
10. Jozef Kot, 'Marginálie', *Slovenské pohľady*, 80 (1964), 6, p. 3.
11. Ibid., pp. 3–4.
12. Kot, 'Prve predstavenie', p. 2.
13. *Dav* was the periodical of the left-wing Slovak intelligentsia which appeared, 1924–6, then in 1929 and then 1931–7. Its title is taken from the initial letters of the Christian names of three leading members of that intelligentsia who had already published together under the ciphers D+A+V in 1923, Daniel Okáli (1903–88), Andrej Sirácky (b. 1900) and Vladimír Clementis (1902–52). The word *dav* also means 'the masses'. Contributors to the periodical and others who identified themselves with the ideas propagated in the periodical were known as *davisti*. The most important Davist was Ladislav (Laco) Novomeský (1904–76).
14. Interview with Anton Hykisch quoted after Július Vanovič, *Antidialogy so slovenksými spisovateľmi* (Bratislava: 1968), p. 133.
15. Interview with Vincent Šikula, ibid., p. 305.
16. Interview with Hykisch, ibid., p. 133.
17. Richter, 'Interview mit Jozef Kot', p. 50.
18. Interview with Hykisch, Vanovič, *Antidialogy*, p. 134.

19. Jurík, *Rozhovory*, p. 40.
20. Libor Knězek, *Preklady z iných literatúr do slovenčiny 1945–1968*, vol. 2 (Bratislava: 1969), pp. 346–8 and 338.
21. Richter, 'Interview mit Jozef Kot', p. 48.
22. On this see L. Richter, H. Olschowsky, J. W. Bogdanow and S. A. Serlaimowa (eds), *Literatur im Wandel. Entwicklungen in europäischen sozialistischen Ländern 1944/45–1980* ([East] Berlin: 1986).
23. Robert Weimann, 'Literaturwissenschaft und historisch-materialistische Theorie', *Zeitschrift fur Anglistik und Amerikanistik*, 1 (1980), p. 24.
24. None of these titles appears in Knězek's bibliography. See note 20.
25. For a Marxist treatment of the *nouveau roman* see Brigitte Burmeister, *Streit um den Nouveau Roman. Eine andere Literatur und ihre Leser* ([East] Berlin: 1983).
26. Peter Jaroš in the blurb to his *Urob mi more* (Bratislava: 1964).
27. Nora Krausová, *Význam tvaru, tvar významu* (Bratislava: 1984), pp. 277–308.
28. Ladislav Novomeský, 'Báseň', *Básnické dielo*, vol. I (Bratislava, 1971), p. 54.

6 Ján Johanides: The Consistency of Blood

Robert B. Pynsent

Johanides himself gives his readers instructions on how he should be read: 'It is altogether a mistake in intelligent, enthusiastic readers and critics, if in their enthusiasm they forget that only what is down there in black and white, only what is actually written in a work, not what is interpreted into it, is valid. The critic must take the whole text from A to Z, consider each sentence, consider the construction of each sentence. Indeed, a little attention to morphology does no harm'.[1] Those words testify to the author's concern with the mechanisms of social communication, but they also suggest a man who accepts literary scholarship as an exact science. It is not true that he does, as is clear if the reader follows his texts[2] carefully. Johanides is interested in word-magic, which means that he makes the reader work hard in interpreting, and no doubt often inveigles the reader into 'interpreting in' what is not there. The old colonel in *Podstata kameňolomu* becomes fascinated by the acoustic proximity of *zásada* (principle) and *záhada* (enigma) and converts that into semantic proximity.[3] As the main female character says at the beginning of *Nie*, 'If you look properly, everything is enigmatic'.[4] The retired charwoman, Betka, considers the whole of art, not only literature, to contain black magic: 'Artists', he maintains, 'destroy everything that's nice in a person . . . They eat your soul'.[5] Johanides also refers to the Oriental notion that the mouth is the womb of words.[6]

Perhaps Sulík is right when he calls Johanides a *provocateur*.[7] He is a sensitive, undidactic, discursive writer. None of his works has both a straightforward story-line and a strictly chronological narration. Šabík labels his works 'analyses, literary recapitulations of facts, almost essays'; his words and sentences, Šabík continues, 'are not only signs communicating a meaning, but also become *realia* (epic objectiveness) [. . .]; the objectivised word derives from the practice of life, not from the literary tradition'.[8] Truhlář has a similar opinion, but he adds that Johanides primarily depicts 'those forces in the world which destroy man's contact with his fellows'.[9] Johanides's concern is with the individual rather than so-called society. From the beginning his individuals are, however, hardly complete individuals; that is not because they are members of society, but because they are repositories. As repositories they often appear to be little more than ciphers, at least until *Pochovávanie brata*, and possibly *Slony v Mauthausene*. Especially in *Pochovávanie brata* the author uses a more conventional, less modern technique in characterisation. In the modern novel altogether individuals tend to 'dissolve',[10] become fluid. The clearest example of a fluid character is the central figure of *Podstata kameňolomu*, the actor Peter, who sometimes constitutes the *Ich* of the text.

The notion propounded in the standard reference work on Slovak literature, that in the late 1970s, when he starts publishing again, Johanides suddenly begins writing about 'more serious' things, like war, and suddenly becomes 'realistic and ideologically progressive',[11] is untenable. The imagery is consistent. Johanides consistently describes his figures by concentrating on those areas of their anatomy he considers the prime vehicles of communication. I list these areas roughly in order of frequency: hands (or arms), eyes, voices, facial expression, lips (mouth). This order probably also indicates a hierarchy of means of becoming close (negatively or positively) to a fellow human being. Johanides is blessedly unexplicit about sexual relationships, and that is rare in a 1960s writer. He is consistent in this, too. His own, almost ascetic, attitude to erotic desire is expressed when sexual intercourse is repeatedly referred to as eating dust.[12] And two of the five stories in *Súkromie* concern the Slovak partisan war; war does not first become a theme for him with *Balada o vkladnej knižke*. He may write about the harsh violence of today's western society in *Slony v Mauthausene*, but he had written about the heartlessness, indeed utter cruelty of the lower classes in capitalist Slovakia in 'Nerozhodný', and would write about the same lower-class cruelty (except that the workers are more cynical in 1984) in socialist Slovakia in 'Stotisícová prémia'. Johanides's concern about mankind's pollution of his surroundings does not begin with *Nepriznané vrany*; the central landscape of *Nie* is a rubbish dump, the tangible representation of affluent society's moral detritus. Johanides comments on the Slovaks' craving for material goods from his first to his most recent work. The cars they celebrate buying change: in 'Potápača pritahujú pramene mora'. a Škoda Octavia and in *Nepriznané vrany* a Škoda 1000MB. That is an example of what is called progress, an Enlightenment and Victorian concept Johanides clearly rejects. He links living in high-rise blocks with the pursuit of turpitude: 'the people living in the multi-storey greyness of pre-fabricated tower-blocks, far from condemning the debauched life of journalists and actresses, endeavoured to imitate them in their modest one or two-bedroom flats.'[13] Adultery and divorce form the background to most of Johanides's works from *Súkromie* to *Pochovávanie brata*. A superior drives one of his managers, who has a bad heart and ever-ready nitroglycerine tablets, to death in *Súkromie* and in the last work. The old colonel in *Podstata kameňolomu* has the same tablets and the mother, Luca, in *Balada o vkladnej knižke* has angina pectoris. Johanides is also clearly interested in dreams; he enjoys their potential grotesqueness as well as their interpretation. The lengthiest examples are the wild-pig dream in *Podstata kameňolomu* and the cardinal's mole dream in *Marek koniar*. The pig may not be emblematic (gluttony, lechery – and dreaming of a wild pig signified a coming erotic misfortune), but the mole certainly is, because of the historical context. The mole, according to the tradition, was deaf and blind, but it also represented earth as one of the elements and in his *History of Four-Footed Beasts and Serpents* (1607), Topsell informs us that the mole is a magic animal: 'if a man eat the heart of a Mole newly taken out her belly and panting, he shall be able to devine and foretell infallible events'.[14] The cardinal knows that in the Old Testament the mole was considered an unclean animal (Leviticus, 11:30). In the Old Testament the snake is initially creative, phallic, and a civilising influence, as it remains in some symbolism.[15] Johanides usually uses it as a destructive principle because it is chthonic. One of Peter's women in *Podstata kameňolomu* tells him that he is quite capable of living underground like a snake (serpent).[16] The weeping of the woman of *Nie* is compared with the weeping of a snake.[17] That constitutes an inversion of an inversion: the Gorgon or Medusa weeping, something normally unimaginable. More conventionally, in *Marek koniar*, the Devil is 'the old serpent, the father of lies from time immemorial'.[18] A Greek captain links the 'great serpent'[19] in the Garden of Eden both with deceit and with providing scapegoats for men's misdeeds in the figures of the gods. Homer becomes the Devil, because he is the myth-recorder. Homer had escaped from Eden. In 'Ľudský pot' snakes take on an emblematic role which is more or less Johanides's; they represent Czechoslovak wheeling-dealing for the sake of hard currency. The author may also be satirising Slovaks' erstwhile perception of the West as a paradise.

Not only is Johanides a consistent writer,[20] but he is also an interpretable writer. That can cause strong adverse reactions. For example, *Marek koniar* is a psychological study of three or four figures from the beginning of the sixteenth century, and contains little of the conventional historical novel. Valér Mikula is irritated by the work, and thus, it seems, by Johanides as a phenomenon. He asks what the main point of the novel is; then he answers:

> Everything that follows 'like' or 'as', this whole world of comparisons, conceptions, possibilities, assumptions, pseudo-arguments and pseudoanalyses, all this futile rationalising, this excavation of a few flashes of intuitive cognition of the essence, all these revelations of connexions which we cannot see and which we might sometimes consider attractive. It would be poetry if it did not serve the obsessive affirmation of his unclear notion that behind everything there is something which determines and explains it, and behind that something there is something, and so on *ad infinitum*. There is no joy in living in a world one has to excavate thus and no joy in reading a text which burrows so far into the depths [. . .] Johanides's world is uninhabitable and unreadable.[21]

Krausová's criticism of artistic devices in *Súkromie* and *Podstata kameňolomu* is more serious. First, though it is certain that the author did use the *vous*-form in two stories in *Súkromie* under the influence of Butor's *La Modification* (1957), particularly in 'Nerozhodný' the *vous* has a completely different function from Butor's *vous*. In Butor's novel the *vous* includes the reader as actor; in 'Nerozhodný' it does not. Johanides uses the *vous* semi-politically; it aids de-heroisation, perhaps even mythoclasm. He 'speaks to' the physician *vous* as a typical intelligentsia representative of his father's generation. Secondly, Krausová avers that the women are more ciphers than the men in Johanides and that they tend to be banally attractive, vacuous and mysterious – like the woman with green glasses. Men are equally ciphers. Johanides tends to spend more time on men than women (except, perhaps, later in *Balada*) simply because he is a man – and Slovak society is strongly male-dominated anyway. Not only women have green glasses (emblem of material success and of potential coldness); Miro in 'Postoj', for example, wears them. One cannot, however, deny that the author's use of the *vous* form was a trifle trendy at the time, that Johanides was altogether often inspired by the *nouveau roman* and that particularly French Existentialism had and still has an impact on him.[22]

Johanides's determinism perhaps derives from that impact, but also from his apparently Protestant upbringing and from his Marxist environment. The Existentialist will normally believe that he and his destiny are indivisible, that his selfness at least predisposes him to how his life will develop. The narrator of 'Nerozhodný' shows signs of a Tainean determinism: 'You were horrified at the thought that "we are all determined by circumstances and milieu"'.[23] That *vous* conceives of a variety of the Hegelian *Zeitgeist*, a *Jahrhundertsleidenschaft* which constitutes the prime determining factor in one's life. Every individual is the 'witness, hero or victim' of that historical passion and in the past such passions 'usually started as an "idea" and finished as more or less a denial of that "idea"'. The people who end up victims are those who do not understand the passion, but 'march into the attack in just the same way as the creators of the idea'. (The Slovak reader will think of the Communist idea.) Finally, the *vous* becomes a sceptic and 'jokily' declares that 'these "passions" are leading the European to a certain "tameness" – not being afraid of killing himself'.[24] That reminds one of Camus and Sartre – and possibly even of a cultural pessimist of the sort one links with Spengler. Determinism, or at least the presence of a punishing Fate, is evident in Johanides's plots. As the under-chef, Doval, is dying of cancer, his wife persuades him to buy a car; she wants to go on trips with her young lover; they crash and she suffers a heart attack as the car slurs onto the verge ('Potápača pritahujú pramene mora'). The brutal, unfaithful, coarse Alex has filed a petition for divorce, whereupon he is run over by a tram, has both his legs amputated and so does not leave his wife; indeed he changes psychologically and she finds she cannot leave him either ('Kráska a výlet'). The story of *Balada o vkladnej knižke* manifests both biological determinism and a punishing Fate (an ironic Fate, too). A German dancing-girl tries to evade Fate; a palmist tells her she will be killed in an air-raid; she burns off the lines on her palm with acid; she is killed by flying masonry as she opens a shutter-door to save others from an air-raid. One of those saved is Murák, who, in accordance with the dying woman's wishes, also marries such a girl. This second girl's family had been rotten through, had had no sense of shame; she has been rotten until a few moments before her death (ironic Fate); their children are rotten, have no sense of shame. Murák, if anything, has an exaggerated sense of shame, as the woman does in 'Kráska a výlet'. An old basket weaver says concerning the curse of shamelessness of the family of Murák's wife: 'one should not talk out loud about such a curse for, they say, the more you talk about a curse, the greater its force becomes'.[25] Sartre rejected chance firmly in a work which Johanides probably knew, *Existentialisme et Marxisme* (1960, later published as *Questions de méthode*), for example: 'Contre l'idéalisation de la philosophie et de la déshumanisation de l'homme, nous affirmons que la part du hasard peut et doit être reduite au minimum'.[26] Although in *Slony v Mauthausene* he employs the incongruous banality, 'chance is inscrutable',[27] Johanides's view of chance generally concurs with Sartre's. The eponymous hero of *Marek koniar* states that there never had been such a thing as chance,[28] and the central character of *Podstata kameňolomu* realises that 'the so-called cruelty or injustice of chance is statutory', follows rules.[29] He links his notion of a logic of chance with a conception of man himself as a series of determinate variations; 'every event in your life is only a variation on a single theme which repeats itself like night and day, night and day'.[30] One might say that Mikula in the passage I quoted was paraphrasing Johanides himself, for the latter has his *Ich* state: 'I saw a definite natural link between certain circumstances, to which I had hitherto not considered attributing any inner relationship, any relatedness, connexion, interaction.'[31]

Once one begins to consider the regulatedness of chance, the existence of Fate or any other guiding principle, one runs against the notion of authority. In 'Nerozhodný' the *vous* is acutely conscious of his authority and the responsibility it brings with it. Through his authority he refuses an abortion and thus indirectly kills a woman. He dislikes his attractiveness to women because it causes him to interfere in other people's fates. Authority creates fates, or fulfils them. Cardinal Bakócz in *Marek koniar* considers the relationship between secular authority and guilt in a manner which will cause a reader to think of war-crime tribunals and perhaps of the state as sinner and punisher. In other words one might see Johanides expressing here the kernel definition of the adversary state posited by de Jasay as: 'the organization in society which can *inflict sanctions without risk of disavowal* and can disavow sanctions by others'.[32] Bakócz, watching butchers removing swallows' hearts for the ecclesiastical banquet, suggests: 'we have led them into crime and then we accuse them of two crimes: allowing themselves to be led into crime and committing this crime'.[33] At the end of 'Kráska a výlet', Johanides at least suggests the existence of arbitrary authority. The apod Alex's eyes 'resemble those of an uninformed bewildered man who is being chased, but who has nowhere to disappear to; he is no longer able to run and he still does not know why he is being pursued'.[34]

Man against authority suggests man against the gods, the pride of Lucifer, hubris. The ironmonger, Silberstein, in 'Pochovávanie brata' suggests that the type of prayer which asks for divine action is a form of hubris: 'when someone prays, "Dear God, do this", you can stake your life on it [. . .] that that person wants to become God at all costs. [. . .] That sort of person is not praying, but ordering God about like an insurance salesman'.[35] Such hubris is a form of alienation, in Existentialist terms. Hubris creates arid existence and awareness of the role of hubris creates fear. The ending of *Nie* manifests some of Johanides's thoughts:

There have always been many people who wanted to be gods. And some people would always like to believe they were those gods. The only trouble is that they do not then want to have partners among other gods. Suddenly there are no gods. But likewise, there are no people. And that is the worst price: the price of gods. The price of people. The writer [i.e. the main male character] is looking out onto the city [. . .] suddenly he buckles as if he had been kicked in the testicles; he grabs his crotch and it looks as if the whole city has just kicked him in the genitals. He did not fall to the ground. As if his opponents were not a gang of two thousand magic assassins there in the other half of his inexplicable night. [. . .] the worst exile is an excellent memory. [. . .] It is true that experience of people frequently darkens the path leading to people. But still remorse prevails over fear in people. Only night is evil.[36]

Through hubris one will be alienated from the rest of society and from a spiritual understanding of existence, from man and from the divine. The whole of society might rebel against the rebellious individual. That is the tradition. The conscious individual will always rebel against society, if not against the divine, and he will be punished for that. The city may be understood as the adversary state; the city represents civilisation. The Greek captain conceives of Homer as the encourager of hubris: 'he invented the twenty-four-hour exchange office where you can always change people for gods or the other way round and at that exchange rate which is most favourable for your mind or in your mind'.[37] In *Podstata kameňolomu* suicide is seen as a manifestation of hubris, 'the protest of pride against pride',[38] not as an Existentialist assertion of man's freedom to kill himself. In the text's incipit Johanides may be satirising stock Existentialism at the

same time as asserting the wonderfulness of trivia: 'I intended to kill
myself today, but I didn't because I bought myself a nice sweater'.[39]
The dancing girl who burnt away the lines of her palm in *Balada o
vkladnej knižke* was guilty of hubris and was given the traditional
punishment, death. Logically, only those with hubris have to submit
to Fate; 'Fate had never succeeded in bringing Marek to his knees.
[. . .] he knew that, for that, Fate would need his pride as much as
an executioner needs [. . .] his axe.'[40]

Pride and the assertion of self produce conflict, which produces
guilt. (Marek is as sensitive and innocent as Doval in 'Potápača
pritahujú pramene mora' – and innocence implies having an understanding of human frailty and vulgarity combined with an understanding of possible other worlds.) Still, any individual's existence must
limit the freedom of other individuals (which both Marek and Doval
are all too aware of), and that potentially produces guilt. Furthermore,
we remember that in the Heideggerian form of Existentialism,
existence itself is culpable. The woman in *Nie* (named simply L.)[41]
feels a general guilt, albeit she later traces it to a specific source. Still
her general sense of guilt cannot be comprehended by her or by the
reader as anything but Heideggerian culpability. One might add some
esoteric interpretation (for example, the guilt derives from a previous
existence or the astral self and so forth), which is not contrary to
Johanides's way of thinking, but it is not necessary to complicate (or
simplify?) matters in that way. L. says:

> My sensation of guilt is like another persons's sensation of migraine,
> [. . .] It seems ridiculous, but actually it's horrible. I have normal
> feelings of guilt and I don't know what about. [. . .] I've never
> before been [. . .] so entirely innocent as now; I sense clearly, I
> don't only sense, I know that this feeling of guilt has absolutely
> not been brought about by something I've done. It's completely
> unfounded [. . .] this sensation of guilt in me is utterly wild
> [. . .] And it suddenly appears – like cancer. Just like cancer: out
> of the blue.[42]

Culpability can arise from general incompetence in life. One of L.'s
interpretations of her guilt is circular. Because she had always felt
guilty, she had wanted to be 'terribly nice' and so she had done
'whatever I was commanded, even things I could not bear doing . . .
things which . . . actually revolted me'.[43] Because she had been
willing to help out anyone, everyone began to consider her a wimp.
L.'s husband, now dead, had understood her and behaved as if he

had been as much the eternal culprit as she. They had even made love like culprits, had 'tried to bury themselves in each other' and when he had been rough or 'mystical' with her (Johanides's interest in occultism), she had found him the softest, gentlest of 'criminals'.[44] In the figure of the repugnant actor, Peter, Johanides mocks and sympathises with human cruelty and frailty. The passage where he absolves himself from guilt at having knocked out one of his first wife's eyes is grotesque. Over two weeks his guilt grows and grows and so he attempts to gas himself, with the windows open. Then, because he has almost committed suicide, he no longer feels guilty, although he knows he is still guilty: 'My own guilt suddenly stopped being in the way, like a wart or a gold tooth. [. . .] my guilt was no longer painful.'.[45] In *Balada o vkladnej knižke* Murák perhaps tries to absolve himself by marrying the dancing girl, Luca, but in fact he gives himself penance; he is given absolution only when Luca dies and he is able to leave his repulsive family.

The sense of general guilt may be seen as a form of general fear, anxiety. Among those thinkers conventionally labelled Existentialist, the man closest to Johanides, also in his irony, is Kierkegaard, who is particularly interested in anxiety, that 'dangerous affair for the squeamish'.[46] In 'Nerozhodný' guilt appears to follow every act, in a Hinduesque manner, but the result is anxiety, and anxiety which results from guilt imposed by someone outside the individual. It is like the anxiety Abraham derives from his guilt at being willing to sacrifice his son, to use Kierkegaard's example. On his way home from hospital after a suicide attempt, the actor Peter is accosted and threatened by three young thugs who had mistaken him for someone else. Peter, however, is overcome by that form of anxiety which derives from a belief in the visibility of guilt: 'But I had the feeling that they were beating me up just because I had tried to commit suicide'.[47] There one is reminded of the judge's guilt when he is struck by a motorcyclist in Camus's *La Chute*. Johanides returns to anxiety of a similar type in the figure of Osoha in 'Pochovávanie brata', the sense of being threatened which had pervaded his childhood:

> Great events which will or could take place seem to cast their greatest shadows and their greatest light from a state which has not yet come into being; it is as if they had been cast from the future into the present, something like when a pedestrian casts his shadow now before himself, now behind himself. [I was in a state of] barely comprehensible fear, privileged anxiety.[48]

That is as real and unreal as the imposed guilt of 'Nerozhodný'. The *vous* cannot decide whether or not he is actually guilty when his subordinate's wife dies after he has refused an abortion. If he is guilty, that guilt is imposed as a prison, is typical of the guilt society's unanalysed system of principles imposes on the individual:

> First one acquires only the thoughts of a prisoner, but then one's prison becomes real [. . .] people more or less help those who want to make culprits of themselves, and their aid to the imprisoners and future judges lies in that senseless fear and excitability which appears in everyone as soon as someone tells him he has done something wrong [. . .] the accused man begins thinking up reasons, begins defending himself, making excuses, and by that he simply proves that, if he had done what he is accused of, he really would be guilty.[49]

Man's essential prison is his mortality, and Johanides displays a dialectic of guilt on that matter. Instead of Arthur Janov's fashionable Primal Scream, Johanides posits a primal moan; 'the oldest languages of the world' consist in 'moaning',[50] because moaning is concomitant with giving birth. The mother giving birth knows what new pain she is introducing into the world. In *Nie* L. hears a hyena (the author's irony) utter just such a sound: 'a high-pitched, very long moan which had the same tone from beginning to end'.[51] The hyena's moan causes L. to weep. The mother gives birth to a creature who will suffer only pain, but will also inflict pain. All creation is based on the moan:

> The figures of the Communion chalices, the decorative barrels of cannon, the richly embroidered sleeves, the cellars, the casemates, the ramparts, the fortresses and the cathedrals were made first and foremost of moans; moans assembled them from moans, from homogeneous moans as from some fundamental building material. As from some primal matter indicating that they arose from pain. From pain as from some common denominator for all mankind. [. . .] From pain which may be imagined as fluffy clouds in the spring sky or as countless flocks of little white clouds or as white breath hanging in the air, most perceptible and most visible only in the hardest frost, light, warm breaths as uncatchable as the wind, the breaths of people, breaths breathed out into a hard frost.[52]

The hard frost is existence. Anxiety may arise from the awareness of that frost. Anxiety may be the product of the knowledge that one's parents have put one in the world to die. Man is not born for his own will, but forced into the prison of mortality at birth. The *vous* of 'Nerozhodný', who consciously uses his existential freedom not to have children (and even tries to deprive others of that freedom), does not know whether his parents had wanted to conceive him or whether he had not been the product of a more or less coincidental moment of passion. He is repelled and made anxious by the idea that he might have been a mistake: 'your anxiety, which is welling up from you at the mere possibility that your existence might have been caused by chance, by unexpected circumstances, by reasons hidden from you for ever in the unknown, the thought that you began to form as an unwanted, surprising consequence which was not meant to have anything to do with those circumstances'.[53] The woman in 'Kráska a výlet' is conceived before her parents are married, but, she says, 'I don't cry because I was born by chance. Why should that make me cry? After all, we were all born by chance'.[54] No man and woman can decide when[55] to have a child and what child. Since I cannot, except through suicide, change my status as an existing individual in a prison of suffering mortality, I may resign myself to it, reject the Occidental sense of the evil of death. If I accept that death is simply a return to the preconceptual state and that it has the function of giving form to my being, I may live an authentic personal existence. Such an existence may not be understood by my fellows, but I should be able to alleviate their life, a little. Johanides makes comedy out of Doval's complete acceptance of his death. He is a whole man, where his wife, his former boss and others are incomplete, comic, because they cannot accept his attitude to his death. They feel he might have the same attitude to their deaths – which would be offensive. To his fellows he is frivolous about cancer, too – in the early 1960s still very much a taboo sickness. Because he is sensitive, as any authentic human being must be, he finds going on visits to his old place of work difficult: 'I had a feeling of something like shame that I wanted to go there. After all I was out of service'.[56]

Erotic activity with his Monika provides the actor Peter with release from his consciousness of the prison of mortality: 'Sexual excitement changed me into an ignorant tree. This [. . .] relaxation made me dead tired, which is probably why I did not feel mortal'.[57] Peter is as insensitive as Doval is sensitive. He is unaware and probably could not care less that sexual activity may release its agents from the sense of mortality, but that it normally eventually leads to the conception of another victim of mortality. Essentially Johanides is making the

old connection between Eros and Thanatos, which he makes again
with more obvious irony in *Slony v Mauthausene* when he speaks of
'that eternal songstress, death, who needs hundreds of thousands of
strong herds of human hearts, without which she would not be
immortal, she who has always offered marshal's batons and raised
male genitals. At this point death fused with Venus. Venus was
death'.[58] Sexuality is itself a prison. Johanides laughs at that, and by
possibly making his Slovak reader laugh he is ironising the debasement
of sexuality in modern society (the public ownership of privacy) at
the same time as declaring both the vulgarity of sex-centredness and
the way in the past the potential 'mysticality' of sexuality had been
vulgarised. Thus in *Nie* the not entirely uneducated[59] road-sweeper
describes intersexual relationships in what he calls the Rococo age
thus: 'Men were mostly judged by what they had between their legs,
yeah, yes, how good they were between the thighs, yeah, yes! And
women killed off their men with that black stuff . . . black . . . black
magic . . . in massive numbers, you might say, in masses'.[60] That also
satirises the male conception of the vamp. When the Roumanian
foundling Church Reformer Djelefi in *Marek koniar* has had his
hands nailed to the cross he has been condemned to hang on, a
German mummer decides the time has come to put Turkish trousers
on him and so he lifts Djelefi's cassock. Whereupon he exclaims,
'Cor! He's . . .! He's got a little one! . . . just like a skylark! . . .
exactly! . . . he's got a skylark instead of a cock'.[61] This exclamation
sends the womenfolk scurrying away and Djelefi's life is saved. He
had been said to be a prophet, but prophets cannot have small penes.
The women are insulted that they had had faith in someone who had
a small penis. Here Johanides is linking esoteric knowledge with
sexuality, but simultaneously satirising the male-inspired female
mythopoeia of the penis. Right at the beginning of the novel, a gaoler
says that women had made a prophet of Djelefi. 'They didn't know
what they were talking about, but they smelled a cock! A huge hawk
of a cock.'[62]

     The womenfolk's fascination with Djelefi's genitalia manifests not
only the prison of sexuality, but also the prison of society (socially
accepted values) and of the temporal altogether. One thinks of
Gilbert Murray's words in his apology for literary scholarship: 'The
Philistine, the vulgarian, the Great Sophist, the passer of base coin
for true, he is all about us and, worse, he has his outposts inside us,
persecuting our peace, spoiling our sight, confusing our values,
making a man's self seem greater than the race and the present thing

more important than the eternal'.[63] Murák in his marriage with Luca experiences just such a vulgarian social prison. That is all the worse, since he has previously escaped from a German prison camp. The Dutch nobleman van Maase, in *Slony v Mauthausene*, had been liberated from the concentration camp but had then had children who had become just as hard-nosed Philistines as Murák's children. The wife of the company manager, Mecko, Alica ('Súkromie') lacks 'a sense of promising'.[64] She feels excluded, and so has no goals, because she considers only the present realistic; she is incapable of putting any trust in the future. Again one thinks of Murray: 'The material present, the thing that is omnipotent over us [. . .] just because it happens to be here, is the great Jailer and Imprisoner of man's mind; and the only true method of escape from him is the contemplation of things that are not present'.[65] But the individual memory can also be a prison. Usually that is memory as self-myth transposed onto a third party. In 'Nerozhodný' the *vous* sees himself as having an individual sphere (*okres*) to which he is limited. This sphere is determined by his occupation and his experience; for the *vous* communication is possible only with those who can enter his sphere. What makes the *vous* different from many others is that, although everyone has his sphere, the *vous* was aware that he had such a sphere and felt it was too small for him. This particular prison (sphere) includes the desire to influence others as a 'strong individual'.[66] That sphere does not, however, include responsibility. The *vous* feels his sphere threatened when his girlfriend, Viera, becomes pregnant. He refuses to marry her. Having influence is far from having responsibility. Johanides is suggesting in his story that that is typical of a politically immature person. The liberal van Maase warns against just such immaturity: 'a man should be most vigilant when it looks as if his egoism is on the way to becoming *sancto egoismo*'.[67] The actor Peter is just such an egoist; he is concerned about the discrepancy between expectation-of-self and self-fulfilment to a degree which verges on schizophrenia or self-mythopoeia: 'everyone is surprised when he realises that his experience is in contrast with what he had imagined his feelings to be'.[68] In a world where there is neither a God nor any political faith the self is mythicised. Johanides provides us with one example of that where the self-mythicisation is a product of a disturbed mind and a false memory, and where that mythicisation is fundamentally harmless. In the end it acquires a certain grandeur. That is the case of Veronika's brother in 'Postoj'. He will now allow Veronika to divorce her criminal husband because he believes he had rescued him from a burning hut during the war. In fact he had gone out of his mind in the burning hut and had managed to escape from it by himself. When Veronika tells him the truth and gets divorced, her brother casts no judgement. The brother had been to an extent happy in his worship of Veronika's husband, but had remained mentally sick. Veronika had been unhappy in her marriage. The reader knows the scholar, Miro, whom she wants to marry now, is a cad who is very unlikely to marry her. Parallel to that is Murák's memory of the dancing girl to whose dying wishes he devotes most of his emotional and physical, if not intellectual, life. By mythicising the dancing girl he has created self-seeking children, but may have helped lead his wife to salvation just before she dies. Both Veronika's brother and Murák are varieties of Kierkegaard's 'knights of infinite resignation', for whom 'the memory is [. . .] the pain, and yet in his infinite resignation he is reconciled with existence'.[69] That pain may distort, as in 'Pochovávanie brata', where Osoha is convinced a man met by chance is the son of a vicious traitor because, according to his memory, his facial features are exactly the same as that traitor's 40 years earlier. It turns out that Osoha is wrong.

Johanides also conceives of racial and genetic or biological memory. It appears to constitute a metaphysical belief rather than to result from an adherence to a particular school of psychologists or neurologists. On the other hand, his conception does appear to approximate Kierkegaard's notion of 'eternal consciousness'.[70] Marčok has suggested that right from the beginning Johanides had 'led his characters out of Existential aloneness and had them experience sensations of human solidarity'.[71] That is bland, unless one links it with a notion of a shared historical consciousness which binds all humanity or large groups of humanity. The active awareness of tradition constitutes the only tried prophylactic for alienation. It has nothing to do with modern political or social theory. It may take the form of primal consciousness. The narrator-author sees that in the eyes of the crows who are to die in the fumes from the artificial-fertiliser plant: 'the eyes of the crows have a gleam I was incapable as a child of comparing with anything although I did want to compare them with something then, too; I imagined the gleam of the crows' eyes together with the gleam of Peru balsam, the gleam of thick forest honey, with a gleam of the kind which lives in the eyes of ancient peoples'.[72] Biological memory may, however, take the form of something like hereditary instinct: 'like the scenting of a hunting dog's infallible snout, he sensed something; he perceived with the inherited senses of unusually sensitive peasants (and unknown forbears within him), who certainly did not look on a meadow as ordinary cattle fodder'.[73] Instinct may be projected forward, whereby a member of the older generation presumes his hereditary instincts will pass on to his descendents, whereas, actually, part of modern 'civilisation' in Johanides's conception consists in the destruction of instincts, indeed of all eternal consciousness. We are presented with the following picture of the generation gap, when the young Fero was brutally killed while taking part in a bet to see how fast one could skin a mink. Here Johanides puns to diminish sentimentalisation and to emphasise his conception: 'Fero's grandfather had spoken about his grandson with full-blooded admiration, with that admiration which is some sort of instinctive veneration for one's own blood [. . .] His voice had trembled when he had been telling me how young Fero loved animals, and in my mind's eye I again saw young Fero holding that panic-stricken mink'.[74]

That the modern authorities have no respect for tradition or family memory is clear from the way they bulldoze a graveyard in 'Pochavávanie brata' (a scene which, incidentally, strongly reminds the reader of the Czech Bohumil Hrabal's *Harlekýnovy milióny*, 1981). Similarly, in 'Stotisícová prémia', the young labourers have no respect for the elderly people's suffering and fighting in World War II.

Genetic memory becomes evident to individuals in Johanides's works when they notice two or more forces working within them. In a dream the actor Peter has, he sees and feels the one-handed Paula using both her hands when they are having sexual intercourse. The Paula he sees in the dream is also Paula, something like her astral self or a combination of her astral self and her momentary terrestrial self. 'When you were asleep,' Peter tells her, 'your face had an expression . . . it was as if you were actually taking part . . . in some different life . . . some life beyond me . . . a life which is better . . . because it is lived . . . with a better person than me'.[75] That better person is possibly the different Peter he is probably turning into at the end of the text. Since eyes are, with hands, the primary means of communicating self for Johanides, when he describes the presence of more than one self in Tomáš A. in *Nepriznané vrany*, he registers it through the man's eyes: 'for a moment his tense, indifferent eyes did not seem to know what to feel; it was as if they were actually only unconcerned, blind, illegible glass eyes. As if for a second his eyes had lost one identity, and did not yet know what other identity should re-establish his expression with a new, tangible meaning'.[76]

So Tomáš A. is a man in flux, like Peter in *Podstata kameňolomu*, and being in flux could be interpreted as signifying that a series of selves are in confusion and have not yet found a pattern for a composite identity. In the working man, Osoha, the imagery for the plurality of selves is simpler. It is closer to the imagery he could conceivably employ himself to express his sensation of some force momentarily assuming control of his thoughts. 'He became uneasy when he realised that there was some other Osoha inside him, that some cunning dog inside his self, a dog who had not yet introduced himself to him, was assuming the right to solve this "crossword puzzle" of his.'[77] In van Maase's version of Johanides's notion it appears that which of one's many selves is active at a given moment is largely a matter of chance. That necessitates aleatory reactions to situations which might be vital. The plurality of self, then, is a major contributing factor to the sensitive man's existential insecurity; one might go as far as to claim that the Jamesian plurality of self constitutes a major component of Fate. 'A man', van Maase muses, 'only very rarely knows about the second, third or fourth man he "carries" within him, or knows that the most important thing about everyone – for each of us has several people within him – is the reality of which of those people dominates in man at the decisive moment.'[78] The plurality of self in the master of horse, Marek, is explicitly associated with genetic memory; one of a person's selves constitutes genetic memory:

> When he starts laughing in front of Count Zápolya, that reassuring feeling he had had dozens of years ago arose in him again, that feeling that he was not laughing alone, that he was being helped in his laughter not by one Marek, nor by a second Marek, but that some third party had started laughing at the same time as he. That third being is the deepest in him, hidden, and that third being's laughter can never change. It seemed to him that [. . .] that third Marek remembers much more than he himself, more than his memory and that all his blood, all the generations of his forebears, all of his blood handed down from father to son, had started laughing with this laughter. And for the first time in his life he recognised that he had discovered a certain peace in his laughter, a peace which had been accompanying him throughout the years (which were sometimes as painful as whole centuries), a peace which had spoken to him in laughter and told him that everything

that hurts him so much, is only hurting for the first time and that the first time always hurts most.[79]

That peace has often been described or hinted at in previous works; Johanides is speaking of a cosmic, primal peace, that Heideggerian peace Laing refers to in his study of schizophrenia, false selves; Laing quotes Heidegger's description of guilt as the call of *Dasein* for itself in silence.[80]

It is the silence of self-awareness which increases after one of the actor Peter's suicide attempts, a silence which indicates to him 'that I am alive and that I have received the greatest mercy'.[81] Everyone has that quietness buried in him like Marek or Peter; it is part of the primal self, of the eternal consciousness. In *Nie* Johanides writes of 'the other world of omnipresent quietness'[82] and that appears to have the same consistence as the silence which intersperses van Maase's conversation with his Slovak host, Holenyšt (telling name=absolutely nothing). One had 'the feeling, that that surprise silence could be breathed in. Like wet sandstone. But then suddenly it turned out to be a sort of peace [. . .], which no one could disturb, limit, suppress, transfer or surround with walls like property'.[83] In 'Postoj' the narrator realises the near sanctity of such quietness: 'I felt that I had to speak so that the purity of that silence could be fulfilled'.[84]

Johanides's silences, though they may sometimes be conceived in material images, are metaphysical or lead to awareness of the metaphysical. In an atheised world man tends to reject or ignore the metaphysical, and thus he loses faith in everything. He becomes like Isaac in Kierkegaard's essay on the Abraham and Isaac story. Abraham has faith, experiences extreme anxiety as he prepares to sacrifice his son. He survives in his trial of faith, but Isaac loses faith.[85] And for Kierkegaard faith is a passion which is linked with eternal consciousness – as it is for Johanides. For Kierkegaard faith is the 'paradox, that the single individual is higher than the universal [. . .] having been in the universal, the single individual now sets himself apart as the particular above the universal'.[86] Mecko's wife in 'Súkromie' is aware of the importance of faith but she is in the position Kierkegaard finds European thinkers in the 1840s, unwilling or unable to cease doubting everything. She expresses the faithlessness which led to the particularly turbulent ethical chaos of the 1960s and 1970s:

If only I believed in God! You told me that He didn't exist and that everything in this world's our affair, but believe me: nothing's

our affair! [. . .] Everything's just a matter of faith! [. . .] And
if everything's a matter of faith, then everything's somewhere in
the heavens. [. . .] Everything's been moved again . . . do you
realise that? If only I could have faith in something again. But I
don't believe in anything any more.[87]

The actor Peter imagines he will be able to experience normal
gratitude once he 'feels the meaning of supratemporal hope'.[88] In
'Pochovávanie brata' Osoha experiences something like 'mystical'
communication with Nature through pain. Primal physical perception
leads to the metaphysical.

> he had on a few occasions been seized by the feeling [. . .] that
> he was not looking at a bush but at his materialised pain which
> had grown over the limits; because of that he was sometimes
> overcome by a mood (was it a mood?) in which his hands, eyes,
> mind branched out into the trees opposite, but simultaneously also
> into an inexplicable three-dimensional terror which he breathes in
> and which separates the poplar from him and from the low-flowing
> brook and from the school gate.[89]

That is not far from speaking about natural spirits or the aggressiveness
of Nature, but it is also not from the metaphysical terror the reader
knows from Lamartine or Mácha. The roadsweeper of *Nie* may in
his incoherent way be expressing the oral tradition of the renewed
interest in magic in the 1960s or, indeed, simply the most basic faith
in the metaphysical, when he declares that 'there are certainly forces
science still knows very little about, yeah, yes, and if science does
know something, yeah, yes, about these, I'd call them energies, yeah,
yes, that's the way it is; science doesn't know anything at all about
the, yeah, yes, the essence of this energy'.[90] In a writer like Johanides,
then, it is not surprising that one finds examples of the metaphysical
comic of the times, art's compensation for an unspiritual world. In
this world, suggests Guthke, 'metaphysical forces become weird
caricatures of the lost God-image'.[91] Thus at her husband's funeral a
man rouses the widow from her faint by pouring a bottle of soda-
water over her ('Súkromie'). Far clearer than that is the actor Peter's
visit to a cosmetics exhibition, where the label on one of the exhibits
displays a drastic degree of blasphemous bad taste to satirise the
godless consumer society. '*For fast, direct envigorating of the
complexion before a social or cultural occasion it pays to use Golgath*
eau de toilette.'[92]

In a world where nothing appears to be sacred except present pleasures, the possession of goods, a world where the artificial prevails over the natural, including the metaphysical, Johanides consistently returns to primal sensation. The epitome of that sensation is the physical concomitant of the primal moan, the sight or touch of blood. Blood is anti-hedonistic. And 'Blut ist ein ganz besonderer Saft'.[93] Alice Meynell is not as ironic as Goethe, but as forthright; she denies that the colour of blood is the colour of life. 'Red is the colour of violence, or of life broken open, edited, and published [. . .], red is the colour of life violated.' The true colour of life, she goes on, is the mixture of red, brown and white which is the colour of the body, 'the modest colour of unpublished blood'.[94] Mephistopheles's blood is the blood of mythology, Meynell's that of a feminist objector to the harshness of industrialised Anglicanism. Parts of both types of attitude, the conventional religious symbolic (Goethe) and the anti-conventional (Meynell) are to be found in Johanides's treatment of blood. Mainly, however, Johanides combines the anthropological with the psychiatric.

One may trace Johanides's metaphysical thinking by tracing his treatment of blood. I do not think he has any original metaphysical thought; nor do I think he uses blood in any entirely novel manner. On the other hand, that he makes quite so much literary use of blood gives him a special place in modern Slovak literature. One may see in his choice of blood as the foremost vehicle of philosophical metaphor a form of atavism or morbid sensationalism, but one may not deny that it serves the useful function of guiding the reader through his thought. Johanides cannot always avoid the melodramatic, but primal sensation often is melodramatic.

Perhaps the most clichéd use of blood comes in 'Nerozhodný', when Igor calls the *vous* the type of hopeless individualist who could never change the world. Angry, the *vous* replies with the stock phrase of vengefulness, 'blood calls for blood'.[95] That exemplifies Johanides's occasional clumsiness and banality rather than the beginnings of his interest in blood, though actually the entry of the *vous* into the fighting war does cause much unnecessary bloodshed. Again the milliner's hematophobia in *Podstata kameňolomu* appears to consti-tute some stock neurosis; on the other hand, though she is afraid of her own blood, she is not afraid of shedding the actor Peter's. The blood Lojzo shed by hitting his brother in the face, when the latter has been nervously callous about their mother's dead body also has no symbolic meaning (*Balada o vkladnej knižke*). The way the blood begins to flow from the Benedictine's throat in *Marek koniar a uhorský pápež* symbolises nothing; it only makes for part of the depiction of the soldiers' arbitrary violence. It also has a plot motivation, since it makes one of the other characters deny he knows the wretched monk. A cliché may be readjusted into a meaningful allusion and thus regain its original symbolic meaning. Therefore, when the workers and their wives beat the village idiot to death in 'Nerozhodný', the reader hears nothing of his bleeding. On the other hand, 'The sun set and a dark red, almost black, strip the colour of congealed blood moved across the empty, watery sky'.[96] It is likely, given the nature of the preceding events, that this alludes to Revelation 6:12 'and the sun became black as sackcloth of hair, and the moon became as blood'. The colour of the sky expresses the guilt of the villagers as much as or more than the death of the idiot. Blood as a stock emblem of guilt reappears in *Marek koniar a uhorský pápež*, but here it is more complex. Here the blood of butchered swallows elicits a sensation of guilt and some pulpit morality tells this butcher that blood connotes guilt, although he knows empirically it does not. Furthermore, the butcher is working for the benefit of another's hedonism, not his own: 'one of them [. . .] was involuntarily looking even more earnestly at his blood-covered hands and his eyes took on the look of someone who had done something wrong' and Cardinal Bakócz does not like the way the blood evokes in the fellow 'an artificial sense of guilt, which was inappropriate to him anyway'.[97] The blood itself is, so to speak, false.

The biblical curse, 'his blood shall be upon him', is a formula for the penalty of death. The concept blood can denote is punishment. In Leviticus 20 that curse is used to refer to sexual sins. When the milliner stabs the actor Peter's face, she is symbolically punishing him for his sexual sins – and probably for his vanity as well. The figure of Klára in *Nie* bleeds from the corner of her mouth. Because she has attained sexual satisfaction, she is no longer able to write (before her marriage she had been a writer). She has become doubly barren. She is bleeding from her womb of words instead of her uterus. Bleeding at the mouth also suggests mental disorder – and Klára is schizophrenic. A rapist mercenary deliberately crops the gaoler Moczárt's whore mother's hair too closely. Blood punishes sexual sins. After this experience, she goes mad, too:

It was as if [the blade] were passing over the roots of her hair like a running shadow, a spirit, an abstract idea, but still it rid her of her hair. There was a sort of horrifying infallibility in the flashing edge. At that moment his mother fell onto her side. [. . .] she clutched her head with both her hands and shrieked at the top of her voice that she was a man. She did not notice the puddle of gladiolus-red blood around her feet.[98]

Elsewhere Johanides writes of blood's function as a sacrifice or the product of a sacrifice. In her childhood L. (*Nie*) had lived near a slaughter-house. One Friday (Friday is traditionally the day for sacrifices) a calf escapes into her garden; it is killed there among the roses. When God appears to Abraham as three men, he fetched a calf 'tender and good', has it cooked and given to the threefold God to eat (Genesis 18; 1–8). Johanides frequently alludes to woman's sacrificing man to her sexual desires, woman as vampire. This is intertextual irony. The roadsweeper claims, 'I know a woman who literally, but absolutely literally, ate a certain fellow'.[99] The women delight in the blood which flows when Djelefi's hands are nailed to the cross. They seem to be taking revenge on him for their menstruation (it is before they know he has a small penis) as well as indulging in mass hysterical sadism; Djelefi seems to be sacrificed for them: 'the ceremonially red blood, similar to the tough red of cardinals' vestments, the blood which hurried from the centre of the punctured palm of his hand drove innumerabale young adolescent girls and unmarried and married women into a frenzy'.[100] Earlier in the same novel Johanides apparently makes a direct link between female vitality and the ritual drinking of stag's blood. In Ancient symbolism the stag or hart could sniff out snakes and would then trample them to death. Naturally, the stag and the snake might represent rival phallic cults, but Johanides presumably has his women drink this blood in order to confound men's lust (the snake), in order to be able to play with them: 'the old man [. . .] took the empty goblets from the ladies' hands with his own huge hands, which were the same size as his face. He filled them with warm red stag's blood, which had the colour of the shadows in the folds of the Cardinal's cloak, and [. . .] placed them into the graceful, defencelessly slender fingers [of the women].'[101]

In the case of Djelefi's follower, Smíchotár, blood is explicitly linked with self-sacrifice, an almost crazy determination to be a martyr, now that the man finds himself in a Promethean position in his vineyard. The reader sees him through the eyes of young Janko:

A huge pool of harsh red blood surrounding blood-covered, unwashed feet with long toe-nails which had not been cut for a good six months [. . .] A strong copper wire the thickness of an earthworm had been run through the instep of each foot and attached to the stem of a vine [. . .] His wrists were tied with a musket chain [. . .] his long-fingered left hand was nailed [. . .] to a vine with a brand-new wedge-shaped nail. [. . .] 'I'm providing manure – for that prophet', said the man, almost as if only to himself. And the boy looked again at the man's blood flowing down around the stem of the vine into the winter soil.[102]

The martyr's ironisation of his martyrdom is double-edged, since martyrdom should indeed serve to manure the faith, increase the propagation of the faith.

Blood is frequently linked with some rite of passage, as a look into the index, say of *The Golden Bough* will tell us.[103] First I take the unceremonious coming-of-age rite that war may provide. The rite is, here, linked with self-sacrifice. When one's blood (or one's kin's blood) is shed, one's nature changes. Certainly this is history making man, not man making history.[104] The impact of this rite in 'Pochovávanie brata' is somewhat diminished by the fact that the picture of blood in snow is a particularly stale cliché of Slovak partisan-war literature:

When I imagined [. . .] that pool of blood absorbed into the sunken snowdrift after the thaw and [. . .] making the shapes of the snow crystals clearer, I had to stop existing, [. . .] the instinct of self-preservation forced me to start pretending that I was alive. [. . .] I myself, Simon Osoha, have grown accustomed to the fake Simon Osoha who came into being after that night, for a flayed man may not live among people [. . .] when I finally understood that returning from the war was [. . .] a great deal worse for me than becoming a cast-out lump of blood-soaked meat, I started to imitate the person of whom I knew that he had previously probably been me.[105]

The war had deprived him of what he considered his real self and yet the reader knows that self distorts the present for him. Again, Osoha remains somewhat fluid inside. In 'Kráska a výlet' Johanides ironically associates the rite of passage of deflowering (or marriage) with the protection of property. Theoretically at least, the cult of the virginity of women constitutes or constituted the male will to property and male competitiveness; the male theoretically always had to be first. I assume Johanides also considers that a somewhat silly theory. The Beauty's future father had given a cousin a gramophone as a wedding present. Quite accidentally something of a scuffle breaks out at the wedding and the gramophone's well-being is threatened. A girl the future father did not know protects it with her body; she eventually marries the future father. The only harm she comes to in her brave act is that 'a thin trickle of blood flowed from her nose'.[106] The nose-bleed predicts her loss of virginity as well as denoting her sacrifice. Before this event it had been presumed by the locals that she would remain a spinster. The most complex occurrence of blood as part of a rite of passage is L.'s behaviour after the slaughter of the calf among the roses. Straightaway the connection between blood and roses reminds us of St Sebastian. L.'s eventual husband is, however, called Medard, and St Medard was the founder of a festival of roses. L. feels that she is guilty when she sees the calf's blood flowing among the roses. For a moment the carcass lies there; it looks as if it has a halo of hot roses. Since the heat of the animal's blood is transferred to the roses. Then the young L. plucks one of those blood-drenched roses, and she immediately realises she has changed. The rose is traditionally the flower of initiation. She suddenly matures into knowing that 'the only unrealisable thing in life is life itself'. The scene so far may represent first menstruation or sudden sexual awareness; in any case the plucking of the rose may be compared with Osoha's sight of bloody human flesh in the snow. Now, gradually more and more, the female fountain seems to be linked with the phallus. Having plucked the heavy rose:

> I began to kiss it; I pressed it with all my might; I put all my strength into my hands and yet still I did not feel at all that I was holding something; I only felt my own strength and I began kissing that rose hard [. . .] I was full of that rose; I was entirely filled with that rose [. . .] all the tastes of blood filled me and started pouring out of me; I was micturating and I could not stop micturating, I could not stop kissing [. . .] suddenly I felt that all the kissing was something immensely evil; I had the feeling that [. . .] I was committing a mortal sin, a first sin [that is, her first sin and Original Sin], but I could not stop; I did not know how to; I sucked the blood from that rose and I chewed that rose.[107]

Gradually the rose seems to expand in her mouth and it clogs her throat and, eventually, without knowing how she got there, she finds herself in the local church looking at the pictures of the saints. Still unaware of what she is doing, she spits the rose out in front of the picture of St Francis of Assisi. At once the bloody rose becomes an emblem of life, of all living creatures. The slaughter calf becomes a tiny animal in the picture of St Francis of Assisi. As the calf leaves life, for an animal cannot be initiated, L. is initiated into life (or society). Twice during this description of the reasons for her permanent sense of guilt L. refers to the blood as the forbidden fruit, which suggests that the scene may be understood as the individual's re-enactment of the Fall. This hematophagia is also linked with a childish perception of vampirism, for L. begins to believe her father is speaking the truth when he says her mother is eating him alive. The fact that she spits out the chewed rose before a picture of St Francis is linked with her apparent one-time rival in later life, the former writer, Klára, who bleeds from her mouth as if she is also possessed by a blood-rose. According to the legend, St Clare was the beloved of St Francis, before they both took up monastic life. It is no doubt sheer coincidence that one of the esoteric truths Cardinal Bakócz learns in Padua concerns St Francis: 'Jesus did not appear to Francis of Assisi as God of the Central Point, but as a six-winged Sûref'.[108] The six-winged seraphim are connected with the colour red. A seraph puts a live coal on Isaiah's lips, which purges him of sin (Isaiah, 6: 6–7). Seraphim also belong to the red, Martian, area of the Cabalistic tree.

Original Sin, the Fall, is the cause of all the suffering of the world and Johanides also uses blood to represent the pain of existence, the pain which, according to Kierkegaard, cannot be avoided or altered by knowledge.[109] The doctor *vous* of 'Nerozhodný' soon recognises pain's egalitarianism; 'all blood was the same'[110] and signalled pain, a pain which led the *vous* to compose the philosophical notebooks the Communist Igor so condemns. Johanides expands his use of blood as a sign for pain in *Marek koniar* when he describes the eponymous hero's reaction to a pool of blood he sees outside an inn:

> Marek was overcome by the sensation that he was not looking at blood, but at some discarded pain, at fulfilling and fulfilled pain, at pain which had achieved its zenith, but at the same time had gained a new base which no longer hurt [. . .] During his life he had seen a great deal of blood in various hues of red and he was surprised at his own ability to tell human from animal blood.[111]

The Malay van Maase encounters in Indonesia suggests that pain itself purges, like the live coal a seraph places on Isaiah's lips: 'pain sterilises [. . .] but one cannot use another person's pain as a disinfectant'.[112]

Blood itself purifies. As one of the elders tells the narrator in the Apocalypse, 'These [. . .] have washed their robes, and made them white in the blood of the Lamb' (Revelation, 7:14). Johanides's use of blood as a sign of purification persuades me that I have probably under-interpreted him, that I have paid too little attention to the morphology of symbols and their metaphysical content. In *Marek koniar* a greyhound the colour of freshly snapped iron bites off Count Zápolya's index finger, with its ring. And 'blood like a creeping, but still expanding seal with fluid rims was covering the design of the unusual harness which was intended to control a unicorn. It was as if the blood had drunk the design away'.[113] That is the blood of the seal in the Apocalypse. In 'Stotisícová prémia', Slamka, who has the habit of staring at women when he is scared, feels frightened and suddenly receives a blow, presumably from a jealous lover (the setting is France): 'Then he felt the fist, but no pain [. . .] he saw blood spurting from his nose onto the ironed, starched tablecloth before him [. . .] eleven drops of blood began soaking in, as if someone had carefully set them out there in a row'.[114] This blow purges him of the guilt he had felt for having been in prison for something he had not done. By this purging he is also able to feel that he will no longer defile his father's memory. (His father had died on Omaha Beach, on the Allies' side.) Johanides has Slamka shed eleven drops of blood, because eleven is the number of transgression (of the Ten Commandments) and of penance.[115]

Although the external themes of almost every one of Johanides's books are markedly different, the internal themes are markedly similar, and his consistency is sealed by blood – and guilt.

NOTES

1. Ján Johanides, 'Kniha o próze (aj) pre prozaikov', *Romboid* (1986), 9, pp. 76–7.
2. I list now Johanides's works in book form. In all cases the place of publication is Bratislava, the publisher the Association of Writers' house, Slovenský spisovateľ': 1. *Súkromie* 2nd edn, (1964) includes 'Nerozhodný' (A ditherer); 'Potápača pritahujú pramene mora' (The sources of the sea draw the diver); 'Postoj' (A position); 'Súkromie'

(Privacy) and 'Kráska a výlet' (A beauty and her night out). 2. *Podstata kameňolomu* (1965). 3. *Nie* (1966). 4. *Nepriznané vrany* (1976). 5. *Balada o vkladnej knižke* (1979). 6. *Marek koniar a uhorský pápež* (1983). 7. *Slony v Mauthausene* (1985). 8. *Pochovávanie brata* (1987), includes 'Žiarlivosť' s halali' (Jealousy and tally-ho); 'Pochovávanie brata' (Burying my brother); 'L'udský pot' (Human sweat) and 'Stotisícová prémia' (The hundred-thousand-crown bonus).

3. *Podstata kameňolomu*, p. 91.
4. *Nie*, p. 9.
5. *Podstata kameňolomu*, p. 94.
6. *Marek koniar a uhorský pápež*, p. 243.
7. Ivan Sulík, *Kapitoly a súčasnej próze* (Bratislava: 1985), p. 22.
8. Vincent Šabík, *Čítajúcí Titus* (Bratislava: 1982), p. 202.
9. Břetislav Truhlář, *Próza socialistického realizmu, 1945–1980* (Bratislava: 1983), p. 71.
10. Klaus Netzer, *Der Leser des Nouveau Roman* (Frankfurt on Main: 1970), p. 77.
11. Karol Rosenbaum *et al.*, *Encyklopédia slovenských spisovateľov*, vol. 1, (Bratislava: 1984), p. 272.
12. *Nie*, pp. 67–8. Cf. Milton's serpents who 'fondly thinking to allay/Their appetite with gust, instead of fruit/Chewed bitter ashes' (*Paradise Lost*, X, 564–6).
13. *Pochovávanie brata*, p. 106.
14. Quoted from Beryl Rowland, *Animals with Human Faces. A Guide to Animal Symbolism* (London: 1974), p. 126.
15. Cf., for example, Claude Lévi-Strauss, *La Pensée sauvage* [1962], (Paris: 1985), pp. 115–16.
16. *Podstata kameňolomu*, p. 36.
17. *Nie*, p. 57; that reminds us also of Meredith's *Modern Love*.
18. *Marek koniar a uhorský pápež*, p. 220.
19. *Slony v Mauthausene*, p. 100.
20. The *Ich* in *Nepriznané vrany* is explicitly Johanides himself. He disports himself with the cavilling reader and the ideologue who links him with the mythicised 1960s: 'Šano remarked that I should write some song about a savings-book, which even someone like Fero would read, and not just write about these intellectuals, in books like *Súkromie* or *Svedomie* or whatever it was called; he said he had not read it, but that Fero had told him something like that about it.' *Nepriznané vrany*, p. 54. The Czech writer, Jaroslav Putík (b. 1923), wrote a book of fiction called *Svědomí* (Conscience, 1958) about J. Robert Oppenheimer.
21. Valér Mikula, 'Skusmo píše . . .', *Romboid* (1984), 6, p. 94.
22. Nora Krausová, 'Próza nových modelov či rozklad epického tvaru? (Príspevok k žánrovej problematike)', *Slovenská literatura*, 4, XXIII (1976), see particularly pp. 413–18.
23. *Súkromie*, p. 17.
24. Ibid., pp. 17–18.
25. *Balada o vkladnej knižke*, p. 113.
26. Jean-Paul Sartre, *Questions de méthode* (Paris: 1976), pp. 116–17.
27. *Slony v Mauthausene*, p. 98.

28. *Marek koniar a uhorský pápež*, p. 102.
29. *Podstata kameňolomu*, p. 26.
30. Ibid., p. 31.
31. Ibid., p. 26.
32. Anthony de Jasay, *The State* (Oxford and New York: 1985), p. 68.
33. *Marek koniar a uhorský pápež*, pp. 121–2.
34. *Súkromie*, p. 206.
35. *Pochovávanie brata*, p. 66.
36. *Nie*, p. 78.
37. *Slony v Mauthausene*, p. 101.
38. *Podstata kameňolomu*, p. 19.
39. Ibid., p. 7.
40. *Marek koniar a uhorský pápež*, p. 104.
41. 'Žena L.' in Slovak; L. is presumably *Elle*, *the* female.
42. *Nie*, p. 21.
43. Ibid., p. 34.
44. Ibid., p. 36.
45. *Podstata kameňolomu*, pp. 11–12.
46. Søren Kierkegaard, *Fear and Trembling*, translated by Alastair Hannay (Harmondsworth: 1985), p. 58.
47. *Podstata kameňolomu*, p. 20.
48. *Pochovávanie brata*, p. 61.
49. *Súkromie*, p. 26.
50. *Slony v Mauthausene*, p. 65.
51. *Nie*, p. 56.
52. *Marek koniar a uhorský pápež*, p. 137.
53. *Súkromie*, p. 21.
54. Ibid., p. 190.
55. That was before the advent of test-tube babies, etc.
56. *Súkromie*, p. 61.
57. *Podstata kameňolomu*, p. 9. The sun is typical of Johanides.
58. *Slony v Mauthausene*, p. 99.
59. He speaks of Washington, Franklin and Montesquieu's having been freemasons.
60. *Nie*, p. 48.
61. *Marek koniar a uhorský pápež*, p. 223.
62. Ibid., p. 26.
63. Gilbert Murray, *Religio Grammatici. The Religion of a 'Man of Letters'* (London: 1918), p. 47.
64. *Súkromie*, p. 137.
65. Murray, *Religio Grammatici*, p. 22.
66. *Súkromie*, p. 13.
67. *Slony v Mauthausene*, p. 55.
68. *Podstata kameňolomu*, p. 9.
69. Kierkegaard, *Fear and Trembling*, p. 72.
70. Ibid., for example, pp. 49 and 77.
71. Viliam Marčok, 'Literatúra a súčasnosť', *Romboid* (1982), 7, p. 13.
72. *Nepriznané vrany*, p. 23.
73. *Pochovávanie brata*, p. 57.

74. *Nepriznané vrany*, p. 48.
75. *Podstata kameňolomu*, p. 83.
76. *Nepriznané vrany*, p. 48.
77. *Pochovávanie brata*, p. 51.
78. *Slony v Mauthausene*, p. 41–2.
79. *Marek koniar a uhorský pápež*, pp. 60–1.
80. R. D. Laing, *The Divided Self* [1960], (Harmondsworth: 1965), p. 132.
81. *Podstata kameňolomu*, p. 21.
82. *Nie*, p. 77.
83. *Slony v Mauthausene*, p. 35.
84. *Súkromie*, p. 121.
85. Kierkegaard, *Fear and Trembling*, p. 47.
86. Ibid., p. 84. I do not know whether Kierkegaard's perception of faith as a passion might have helped Johanides in formulating his version of Hegelian *Zeitgeist*. (See above.) That would comport with the metaphysical thinking which runs through the Slovak writer's works.
87. *Súkromie*, pp. 141–2.
88. *Podstata kameňolomu*, p. 32. That, as well as other expressions of a desire for spirituality, may show the impact of Wittgenstein, who was immensely fashionable in the 1960s. His *Tractatus logico-philosophicus. Logisch-philosophische Abhandlung* (1921. The edition used here is Frankfurt on Main, 1964) was probably most quoted for two ideas in the preface: 'What may be said at all, may be said clearly, and one must be silent about what one cannot talk about' and 'This book seeks to draw a boundary for thought [. . .] The boundary will only be able to be drawn in language and what lies beyond the boundary will be simply nonsense' (p. 7). In the text itself, however, Wittgenstein states: 'The inexpressible, however, does exist. This manifests itself; this is the mystical' (p. 115).
89. *Pochovávanie brata*, p. 63.
90. *Nie*, p. 46.
91. Karl S. Guthke, *Die Mythologie der entgötterten Welt. Ein literarisches Thema von der Aufklärung bis zur Gegenwart* (Göttingen: 1971), p. 328.
92. *Podstata kameňolumu*, p. 58.
93. 'Blood is a very special juice'. Mephistopheles to Faust in the study scene, *Faust*, Part I. Carl Schuddekopf (ed.), Goethe, *Faust, Der Tragödie erster und zweiter Teil* (Berlin: n.d.), p. 47.
94. Alice Meynell, *The Colour of Life and Other Essays on Things Seen and Heard* (London and Chicago: 1896), p. 1.
95. *Súkromie*, p. 28.
96. Ibid., p. 41.
97. *Marek koniar a uhorský pápež*, p. 121.
98. Ibid., p. 36.
99. *Nie*, p. 45.
100. *Marek koniar a uhorský pápež*, p. 223.
101. Ibid., p. 141.
102. Ibid., pp. 28–9.

103. Sir James George Frazer, *The Golden Bough. A Study in Magic and Religion*, vol. XXII, Bibliography and General Index, 3rd rev. and enlarged edn (London: 1935), pp. 189–90.
104. Cf. Sartre, *Questions de méthode*, p. 119.
105. *Pochovávanie brata*, pp. 53–4.
106. *Súkromie*, p. 189.
107. *Nie*, pp. 24–5.
108. *Marek koniar a uhorský pápež*, p. 16.
109. Cf. Sartre, *Questions de méthode*, p. 19.
110. *Súkromie*, p. 28.
111. *Marek koniar a uhorský pápež*, p. 46.
112. *Slony v Mauthausene*, pp. 114–15.
113. *Marek koniar a uhorský pápež*, p. 196.
114. *Pochovávanie brata*, p. 137.
115. Christopher Butler, *Number Symbolism* (London: 1970), pp. 30 and 75.

7 The Contemporary Slovak Historical Novel and Its Search for the Present
Břetislav Truhlář

Gradually the Slovak historical novel has overcome the period of idealisation and didacticism which dominated the nineteenth century: it has overcome sheer descriptiveness. Those nineteenth-century works which made an attempt at a serious explication of historical events have retained their vigour to this day, for example, the works of Jozef Miloslav Hurban (1817–88), Ján Kalinčiak, and later of Jégé (1866–1940), Terézia Vansová (1857–1942), Jozef Cíger Hronský or Ľudo Zúbek (1907–69). Recently Ján Čajak's novel *V zajatí na Holíčskom hrade* (A prisoner in Holíč castle, 1968) has become a model; it develops the social significance of an historical period and puts Slovak history into its international context. In this novel Čajak fulfilled much of what is now demanded of an historical novel and it has come to be regarded in many ways as the precursory example of the 'historical materialist' approach to an historical theme.

The very fact that the author realises he must begin his literary career with a work which puts historical events into context constitutes a sign of a mature society, and a mature literature within that society. The author like his public, is aware that the depiction of the present (as long as we understand the present as linked with the complex dynamism of society and not as a short-lived today) is unthinkable if he does not link the present with history. That is how works dealing with contemporary society are firmly bound with 'historicising' prose (like Jaroš's *Tisícročná včela*) and historical prose.

Only by seeing this connection between fiction concerned with present-day life, historicising fiction and the historical novel can one gain some idea of what might be done in the future. In his essay 'Historizmus prózy' (Historicism in prose) Vincent Šabík writes, 'All manner of things in today's reality demand an historical dimension. Anyone who avoids the past will neither understand nor gain any true knowledge of the present and, thus, he will limit his chances of understanding the future'.[1] That is more or less an axiom; it has a double application to literature. The acquisition of knowledge about the past always constitutes a social act linked with a consciousness of the present: the cognition of history is determined by today's social situation. Thus the period following the Communist take-over of February 1948 is repeated on a higher level and in different conditions (conditions in which society's independent historicist sense has become particularly accentuated); in the period following the take-over, the nation and the common people were looking for their roots. As Šabík says in his essay, 'The strength of fictional historicism is revealed in its enhancing of the readers' understanding of the world's state(s) of development, that is, in the manner it teaches the reader not to see the world as something given, immutable, as a mere natural accretion or as the product of Fate'.[2] At the same time one must admit that 1970s historical fiction may be divided into popular and mimetic historical fiction. The latter attempts to see humanity with its historical development through the human condition set in history. At the same time the 1970s showed a development of historicising fiction (the term 'historicising fiction/prose' is based on a hypothesis which has not yet been worked out), a type of fiction which takes the present as its starting point (I follow Šabík here) to explain the immediate or more or less distant past.

There is a basic difference between those writers who use historical fiction to illustrate historical facts as well as to pose questions to the present on the basis of the past and those writers who see in the past influences which determine today's consciousness. The first category exploits history as an interesting spectacle. The second is constantly aware that by making the past approachable and explicative they can reveal hidden answers about the dynamism of the world, but also information which will help the reader comprehend contemporaneous psychology. And it does not matter whether the author is dealing with the Great Moravian Empire or the Slovak National Uprising (even the latter is today a matter of history). In contrast to historicising prose, historical prose manifests an awareness that history does not consist only in local colour (different clothes and different customs, different conceptions of honour and so on), but that it has been through history that man has attained, by his own effort, a better understanding of himself and of his race. Knowledge was born in history. What we call the historical consciousness of a people, a nation or an individual was, it stands to reason, born of the past.

The historical novelist need not be an historian. An author does not have to have a detailed knowledge of his whole period to write an historical novel. Nevertheless historiography forms a substantial part of the author's necessary source material, like archaeology and, possibly, palaeography, and so forth. It goes without saying that the basis for fundamental historical cognition has not been formed suddenly over the last few decades. On the other hand, at least a contribution for the bases of historical fiction has been made by non-fiction works by such as Pavel Dvořák and Vladimír Ferko, by the historical essays of Vladimír Mináč or Matúš Kučera, or Ján Dekan's study of Great Moravia.

Anton Hykisch's two-volume *Čas majstrov* (Craft period, 1977) constitutes a significant example of the modern Slovak historical novel. Hykisch bases his novel on the historical painter who signed himself MS and on the possible fate of such a painter at such a time. Hykisch presents a persuasive account of the painter's understanding of his own age, the painter's awareness of the common people's desperate lot, his alignment with the miners' cause and his love for Ulrika. The novelist also goes beyond the central motifs to give his readers an insight into the life of Upper Hungarian mining towns at the end of the fifteenth and beginning of the sixteenth centuries. Generally speaking, he succeeds in fulfilling two intentions: in ascertaining the reasons for the miners' rebellion and in displaying the superior lifestyle the mine-owners and other burghers attained through the exploitation of their employees, which allowed them to give lucrative orders to architects, painters and carvers. Hykisch places the flowering of these Upper Hungarian towns into the broader context of contemporaneous European history. In contrast to his fellow native of Banská Štiavnica, Jozef Horák (in *Smrť kráča k Zlatému mestu*, Death on its way to the Golden City, 1968), Hykisch carefully distinguishes between the German and Slovak elements in the working classes and burghers. Horák lays too much emphasis on conflicts between nationalities. At the same time it is clear that the conflict between nationalities was more pronounced among the rich than among the common miners. Hykisch succeeds in showing that for the Slovak historical novel social relationships are of primary importance. He reveals depths of social relationships which had hitherto not been revealed.

The same thing is shown by Hykisch's later novel, *Milujte kráľovnú!* This novel concerns the reign of Maria Theresa, but also the eighteenth century as a whole, and the changes which took place in Austrian and European society at the time. Again Hykisch shows up history as an important constituent of today's Slovakness. Although the novel is concentrated primarily on the personality of Maria Theresa herself, one is never permitted to forget her personal connections, the world of high politics, the new conception of industrial production, new socio-economic relationships and the Empress's relative progressiveness and her capacity to take new ideas on board. No one anyway doubts Maria Theresa's merits in her rearrangements of the relationship between nobles and serfs, her position towards the Church (the banning of the Society of Jesus), her new general legislation and her new conception of the role of vernaculars in her Latin dominated lands. Perhaps all this is somewhat overemphasised in the activities of Adam F. Kollár, who is eventually ennobled and becomes the Empress's close adviser. But, within the context of the novel, the relationship remains convincing, particularly because it comports with the psychological interest of the novel as a whole. Hykisch's inclusion of various European courts and major contemporaneous figures (for example, Voltaire) testifies to his knowledge of the period as well as to his capacity to synthesise a whole.

Much in Hykisch's novels supports the view Mináč propounds in his 1968 essay 'Kde sú naše hrady' (Where all the Slovak castles are): 'As far as the history of civilisation is the history of work, the history of interrupted, but consistently victorious construction, Slovak history is also a history of work. The Slovaks are a nation of constructors, builders, not only in the metaphorical, but also in the literal sense of the term'.[3] That is a notion which has been given concrete form by Hykisch, but also by other writers, like Jaroš (*Tisícročná včela*).

Jozef A. Tallo's (1924–79) two-part novel, *Ohnivý šarkan* (The fiery dragon, The Veselényi Conspiracy, 1981, and Pika's Orava rebellion, 1982), also characterises the specific development of history in Slovakia. A close study of Slovak and foreign historical sources enabled Tallo to represent the multifarious compacts between Christian nobles and Moslem pashas, the brutality of his period (especially the cruelty with which common man was treated), in such a manner that the life of contemporaneous humanity acquired precise contours which had hitherto been veiled in the mist of a complex interaction of a large number of social interests. Tallo's adumbration of the period is successful because of his sociological conception of the development of history, because of his precise characterisation of social relationships. What Hykisch succeeded in accomplishing deductively in his picture of the painter MS, Tallo succeeds in accomplishing by depicting progressive trends. Both Hykisch and Tallo avoid a superficial interpretation of history, attempt to ascertain the inner conflicts of the period and of the individual living in that period. Their conception of progress does not derive from easy evolution: progress is bought by mistakes, by terrible failures and by unfulfilled hopes.

Ján Lenčo's novels about Classical civilisation constitute a new chapter in the development of the Slovak historical novel. As early as in his novel for children, *Čarodejník z Atén* (A wizard of Athens, 1978), Lenčo's serious consideration of how to interpret Classical legend was evident. In this novel he describes a first-rate sculptor's attempt to create a model of a man in search of freedom, so that he can be sure that true art is what can enable that man to achieve freedom. Lenčo's *Zlaté rúno* (The Golden Fleece, 1979) is a novel of quite a different kind. The author retells an old tale, but adds his own apocrypha from various narratorial angles. Many of the questions he poses in his apocrypha are important for a man of today's society, for example, the sense of sacrifice or the meaning of the often adversarial relationship between rulers and ruled. In the novel, *Odyseus, bronz a krv* (Odysseus, bronze and blood, 1983), Lenčo's ironic apocryphising manner of making the past relevant to today is absolutely blatant. This novel is his new, individual, appendix to Homer's song: his individual composition of ironic glosses on individual situations in the *Iliad* and the *Odyssey*. Lenčo gives potential modern characterisations for the action. His Helen is, on the one hand, a capricious, unfaithful housewife, on the other, in Menelaus's version, a virtuous goddess. Lenčo retains fundamental humour while asking serious questions about things like peace and military ambition.

There is no doubt that Lenčo's novel, *Žena medzi kráľmi* (A woman among kings, 1985), was an important experiment. Its sources were Sparta in the reign of the two Agis kings. In this work, more than in other works which are overladen with facts and descriptions of Classical life and manners, Lenčo tries to depict the progressive endeavour of kings to restore egalitarian society, to remove all privilege, including privilege based on ownership. The novel demonstrates that, although these endeavours failed, a will to justice frequently arises in the history of mankind.

The fact that contemporary Slovak prose exploits Classical themes demonstrates its wish to expand its areas of interest and, perhaps, demonstrates its maturity. Milan Ferko's novel, *Medzi ženou a*

Rímom (Woman and Rome, 1980) supports my contention. This novel is a spiritual narration about Marcus Aurelius, in whose reign legionaries carved their words on a rock by Trenčín, the Slovak town then apparently known as Laugaricio. Even if Ferko, because of his own character as a storyteller, tends to melodramatise history, no one could argue that his stories were not based on careful research – on papers published in the academic world. One might say the same about his more or less popular lengthy novel, *Svätopluk* (1975), which is by no means without literary interest, or about his novel concerning the fifteenth-century Queen Elizabeth and her chambermaid, *Krádež svätoštefanskej koruny* (The theft of the Crown of St Stephen, 1970).

From the few historical novels I have taken it is clear that such works aim at finding national roots as well as social consciousness; they look for justifications of 'Czechoslovakness' and for a European dimension to their themes. The treatment of Classical themes demonstrates that Slovak writers are attempting to treat basic existential problems. One can, then, expect only fruitful developments in the Slovak historical novel.

NOTES

1. Vincent Šabík, 'Historizmus prozy', *Romboid*, 10 (1981), p. 2.
2. Ibid., p. 6.
3. Vladimír Mináč, *Tu žije národ* (Bratislava: 1982), p. 63.

8 The Use and Abuse of History in Recent Slovak and Georgian Fiction

Donald Rayfield

If the historical novel is to be a literary, not a sub-literary genre, it has to transcend its material. It should not abuse history by processing reality through the minds of invented eye witnesses for the sake of easy digestion; nor should it colour stereotypical characters and plots in pretty period tints. Whether the novel deals with a past recent enough for readers' memories or remote enough to require the invention of a neutral language for dialogue, an historical setting must have as its purpose either the expression of perceptions that historians themselves baulk at or an allegorical presentation of the present which can only be seen when encapsulated in time, that is, science fiction in reverse.

The historical novel has other, more incidental functions: for the reader it creates (or records the creation) of national identity, as did *Vanity Fair* and *War and Peace* when they showed simultaneously the defeat of Napoleon and the liberation of the hero and heroine from false, alien values: national identity and national ethics, English or Russian, are reinstated by the historical novelist. The historical novel defines national character and ethnic affiliation, if only in defiance of the views of that nation's neighbours. For the writer, in turn, the historical novel makes a broader philosophical scope possible: it can create a theoretical framework for interpreting history – as a cycle, as chaos, as a progression from barbarity to the Kingdom of Heaven on Earth. Above all, the author is freed from his or her egocentric lyrical *persona* and can enjoy the illusion of creating a factual, objective work of art.

In more literary terms, an historical approach can give the novel a place in an *oeuvre*: a stretch of time that can become a link in a sequence, a *roman fleuve*, where each stretch of the water has arbitrary cut-off points in a continuous writing process: a stockpile of character and theme on which the novelist can repeatedly draw. In those literatures whose status is not yet firmly established, at least

114

in the eyes of the world, the historical novel has sometimes a linguistic function, defining the language as it does ethnic affiliation, since its diapason in time, space and social range can be far wider than a novel of contemporary times.

But the problems of the genre are severe. First one has to ask how real and functional events and characters can be merged. If the real are effaced, we have only a fancy-dress novel. If the fictional are omitted, we have only stage-managed chronology. As Marshall Keitl's diary and Cardinal Bakócz's itinerary have well attested, a novelist's invention may only pervert the truth. Secondly, we have the problem of a structure. History is a flux; the novel should be a tautly wrought and finite entity. (The evolution of *War and Peace* shows how hard even Tolstoy found it to establish cut-in and cut-off points for his work.) Thirdly, one has to decide how narrator and protagonists can be inter-related, for it is equally hard to be an invisible God or an interactive narrator in a world that has already happened. Fourthly, one has to consider in what language people speak, for the more remote the period, the less convincing the dialogue: the best philologist cannot write dialogue in sixteenth-century Slovak or eighteenth-century Georgian without being absurd or incomprehensible, but a neutral language avoiding anachronistic modernism is likely to be pallid. Lastly, ways have to be devised to engineer surprise and suspense although we know the outcome of the great wars and no fictional personage can upstage historical figures in the final outcome. Modern Slovak novelists tackle or ignore these questions in interestingly unlike ways.

Ladislav Ťažký's trilogy, *Amenmária (samí dobrí vojaci)* (Amen-Mary [all good soldiers])[1] appears to break all the rules, but its importance becomes clear when we admit its defects. It is swamped by the novelty of its material, a subject hitherto taboo, the Slovak troops fighting in Hitler's armies. Like Solzhenitsyn, Ťažký has heroes who say aloud what everyone knew – the essence of scandal; he places the revelations of the 1960s in the 1940s. 'What camps, camps in the Soviet Union? Father would have burst into tears if I'd told him that.'[2] The effort of breaking new ground exhausts the author: like Solzhenitsyn's first full-length novels, *Amenmária* is also overdocumented, with cardboard characters and a tram-line plot-motor, heavily dependent on the Russian classics (Solzhenitsyn on Tolstoy, Ťažký on Dostoyevsky) for patterns, incidents and a morality. Some of the defects are remediable: in a larger literature, competent editing and commercial publishing would have cut down the rebarbative incidents, characters and commentary and disinterred a fine novel from an inflated trilogy. Other faults are more radical: the choice of an *ingénu*, Matúš Zraz, as a narrator-hero makes it hard to deal with a morally complex situation, when the protagonist cannot even hint at answers to the questions he repeatedly puts. Zraz, presumably unintentionally, becomes irritating, even antipathetic: he muddles incidents, places and *personae*; he is too good to commit evil, too feckless to intervene; his appeal to the civilian women on whom he is billetted becomes steadily less plausible. The scenes of violence are especially poor in perspective: could Zraz really witness the fate of the Viera at the hands of Vlasov's cavalry while his convoy is avoiding a Russian air raid? *Amenmária* is a conceit that Ťažký's technical resources are too weak to sustain, as the slickly antiphonic promises of the chapter titles worthy of Norman Mailer, suggest: 'The dead live for the living, Forgive me, Ukraine'.[3]

But the reader who would hang himself in despair at the plot should cut the rope. Ťažký's moral boldness gives the novel its impetus: through Zraz's constant queries, the novel redefines the Slovaks: a question that is urgent for a nation so hemmed in, yet so ill-defined politically and linguistically. Using the peasant ethics of Čierny Hron as a point of departure, Zraz's sensitivity as a Slovak then becomes measured in almost acoustic terms: his reactions to Czechisms in the earlier pages, to '*záhorácky*' and eastern dialects, to Slovak spoken by *Volksdeutsche* and by Magyar-speakers. Zraz's insecurity in his monolingualism: his failure to cross over to the other side is not just the moral flaw in his character or the crisis in the plot, but a stubborn Slovak refusal to submerge. The query and assertion, 'Slovaks are pretty well Russians?',[4] is negated.

Particularly bold is the last chapter, 'The death of the lost division',[5] whose background is the Slovak Uprising, about which today's Slovak historians are so oddly reluctant to speak: Zraz is disarmed by his German officers, buries his map-making equipment in the dungheap at his billet and goes on writing until the SS physically stop him. Ťažký's assertion, in the mouth of an SS man, that writing is another artillery, is a familiar quotation, but it lends great power to the last paragraphs in which the narrator dies and the narrative survives. 'That's a weapon? . . . Editor? Writer?'[6] merges narrator and author, the 1940s and the 1960s; it also demonstrates that Ťažký has taught himself how and why to write and has gained the self-confidence he finally accords to his much loved Matúš Zraz.

Clearly Ťažký knew his weaknesses: characters, even the eponymous Amenmária and the heroines, vanish and resurface before the puzzled reader's eyes. Ťažký compensates these weakenesses by reinforcement from other novelists. The historic retreat across the Carpathians is not a complex enough structure to be self-supporting. Dostoyevsky's *Idiot* is used as scaffolding. Dostoyevsky is included in Zraz's scanty education and *The Idiot* provides a quadrangular pattern, so that Zraz corresponds to the Idiot, Knieža to the magnetically murderous character of Rogozhin and the two women, aroused and ill-served by the Idiot, Ťažký's Aglaja and Viera are parallel to Dostoyevsky's Aglaya and Nastasya. But scaffolding is meant to provide access, not to prop up a ruined building.

Altogether, *Amenmária* is a heroic failure. But it provides space – full, unbowdlerised vocabulary, honesty with facts – for later novelists to build on. It is a pity that so much of the development of the 1970s in Slovak historical fiction has been shoddy. The quantity of historical prose, in numbers of titles, pages and copies printed, is great. But if Peter Jaroš's *Nemé ucho, hluché oko*[7] can achieve 23 000 copies in 1984, compared to *Amenmária*'s 8000 in 1964, some law of inverse ratio is at work. (Though the role of official recognition as well as market forces has to be considered). Jaroš, in fact, has a place in the sociology, rather than the critique, of literature. If he cannot quite be said to be a socialist Jeffrey Archer, his Pichanda family novels – *Tisícročná včela*,[8] as well as *Nemé ucho, hluché oko* – have the slick assurance of soap opera. The generation cycles from the 1870s to the 1920s, broken at 31 October 1918, are skilfully paced: the patchwork of historical landmarks on the fringes of the action and imaginary family events in the centre is even. Mildly lascivious and cinematically violent scenes are discreetly interspersed. Where Ťažký has his sheep cheeses (*oštiepok*), Jaroš has beehives to contrast an idealised peasant and highland ethos with shoddy metropolitan and cosmopolitan values. Perhaps Jaroš's talent for action scenes is sharper than Ťažký's: the fishbone removed with scissors from Samo Pinchanda's throat (*Tisícročná včela*)[9] or the notary dumped in axle grease[10] (*Nemé ucho, hluché oko*) are effectively grotesque.

But Jaroš's action cries out for illustration, as his characters for acting: these are books of unmade television series. The characters are rooted only shallowly in time, and the past is visualised only too blatantly as a prelude to modern times. Jaroš's Pichandas have improbable clairvoyance: Fero Viliš hears of Lenin every day in the Ukraine,[11] whereas Ťažký's Zraz comes across only the unexpected and the senseless. Ťažký may insist too much that Slovaks are much the same as Ukrainians, but he precludes so many false answers that Slovaks are forced to look at their history and search for their own explanations. Jaroš provides not so much a protagonist as a propagandist in Peter Pichanda: his rhetoric, 'What sort of nation are we Slovaks? . . . We've Germanised or Hungarianised ourselves . . .'[12] is only more of his predecessor's verbiage. 'We're here to change the world' only repeats 'Let the world change then; that's how it has to be'.[13]

The ideological context debases the mystique of the beehive scenes which otherwise seem to match Jaroš with Thomas Hardy and D. H. Lawrence: they are decorative incidents in a forced processing of history which turns the Pichandas and Višeses into cardboard cut-outs in an historical puppet show. The novel does not confront, but flatters its readers with a prospect of an indefatigable process by which priest and notary are transcended by peasant. Given the fertility of the Pichandas, we can expect new instalments every five years until, by the end of the century, Jaroš has caught up with a present that cannot be as easily reinvented as the past.

Bad novels have their purpose: their corpses fossilise and accrete into a reef of narrative prose on which later and better novelists can build. They stabilise readership, narrative language and a thematic base for development or demolition. The popularity of such work as *Tisícročná včela* may stimulate the most unlikely rivalry. The publication of Ján Johanides's *Marek koniar a uhorský pápež*[14] in 1983 is just such a development, quite unexpected even for a writer as innovative, unpredictable and silent as Johanides can be.

Johanides may be the only living Slovak novelist whose claim to European stature, and on posterity, is convincing. Not only does he exploit every nuance of Slovak, colloquial, poetic and narrative, but he has turned it into an expressive medium and overcome its inferiority complex: paradoxically he is the most translatable of Slovak writers (as the Hungarian reception of his work shows). But to a reader of *Súkromie*[15] and *Podstata kameňolomu*[16] with their metropolitan irony and laconicism, the virtuoso flow, rich imagery and dream-like strangeness of *Marek koniar* are amazing. Like his initial teacher, Albert Camus, Johanides has turned to history, but in a new way: the past is a field as remote from and as close to the present as a nightmare and forces us to interpret an historical nightmare, the kingdoms of Bohemia and Hungary in 1514 on the eve of devastation, in terms of our present; but it leaves us to compile our own dictionary for this interpretation. It is a novel that makes demands, but not impositions. Many of the levels on which *Marek koniar* operates may not be apparent to the reader, even to the author, but the novel has to be read and re-read polysemantically.

Marek koniar is not wholly disconnected from Johanides's prose of the 1960s: the Camusian irony, 'I'm incapable of distinguishing my own wrongdoing from other people's'[17], and the paradoxes 'deciding doesn't lead to the goal for which you made the decision'[18] are now more explicitly moral. Johanides could always be classified as an Existentialist: *Marek koniar* has a religious, if not quite Christian, Existentialism whose core is in the remark, 'That age-old sentence, "Understand me: I have a family" is the most important, fundamental cog in the torture chamber'.[19] This is the moral centre of *Marek koniar*; it articulates what Ladislav Ťažký's narrator could not quite formulate. Mikhail Bulgakov has superseded Camus as the reigning influence of Johanides.[20] The Christian attitude to Caesar is as well expressed in Marek's attitude to the Hungarian Pope, Cardinal Bakócz, as in the Pontius Pilate sections of *The Master and Margarita*; the construction of both novels around a meeting between the naive custodian of creative forces (the groom, the novelist or Jesus Christ) and the cynical ruling sophist (Cardinal Bakócz or Pontius Pilate) is identical. Above all, the linguistic acrobatics and atmospherics, whole sentences spinning out to whole pages, saturated in sensuous imagery and yet still narrative, rivals Bulgakov's *Master*.

The plot's irony, by which all plots are undone, leaving the characters' universe in disintegration, while some essential binding force – the horse Hašemen – goes free, is also consistent with Johanides's earlier patterns. It is the requirements of the genre that are different, and Johanides's exploitation of history deserves close study.

First, history is not for Johanides primarily a source to which the present can be traced; nor is it a mystery to be explained or glorified. On finishing the book, the sixteenth century is even stranger to us: it resembles the future more than the past. *Marek koniar* is an allegory, one of whose meanings is that Marek is the poet; the horse that he has introduced, cherished and set free is inspiration – a Pegasus or Hippokrene symbol – while Moczárt, the quintessential secret policeman and Cardinal Bakócz, the decrepit but mighty politician, equivocate like Pontius Pilate between ultimate truth and short-term interest. The work's ending is an apocalypse: Hungary is in ruins and Dózsa, the last hope against the Turkish threat, is executed on his *tüzes tron*, his throne of fire. It would be wrong to dismiss the disintegration of Johanides's last pages as constructional failure. All his prose is about disintegration of personality, private worlds and – here – of history. The scattering of horse, groom and historical figures is a calculated effect.

Like Bulgakov with his *Master*, Johanides uses a strict chronology – here, from 26 January 1512 to the capture of Dózsa in 1514, to give urgency, rather than a timetable, to the plot. The binding elements lie in the imagery, above all a set of animal images that link Bakócz and Marek long before their confrontation. Badger-skin clouds like a white horse's fur lead to Marek's own 'badger-like caution'; Marek's dream of beaver and hedgehog builds up to a haunting, if absurd, lyrical list of the 'desolation of amazed animal eyes', until the chain of images culminates in Bakócz's realisation that Marek is the mole he dreamed of in his clairvoyant nightmares.[21] At the top of this system of animal images is Hašemen, the horse whose sacrifice is demanded by the powers that be. But the animal images also belong to the biblical subtext of the novel. Marek, the hairy mole compared with the smooth Bakócz, declares himself to be 'hairy as Esau',[22] a division of poet and ruler, as hairy and smooth, like Esau and Jacob ('Behold, Esau my brother is a hairy man, and I am a smooth man', Genesis 27, 3), which is only one of the religious patterns linking the two main actors. While Johanides is very skilful in merging excremental with sacramental, the ultimate effect is a stream of clairvoyance, rather than mere intelligence, that makes the novel's meaning far wider than its historical setting.

Johanides approaches the pitfalls of the historical novel warily. He reduces dialogue to a minimum, compared with the confessional or adversarial language of his earlier, often first- or second-person prose: he rarely palliates or emphasises archaism. Characters think, rather than speak, and do so in contemporary Slovak, hardly ever venturing into idiolect. Reality is separated from fiction in a set of notes appended for the worried reader. For all the apparent uninvolvement, the novel is intensely personal: dedicated to Johanides's dead father, it is illustrated by Oľga Johanidesová with drawings half-Blakean, half-Magyar, that give a powerful extraliterary reinforcement to the text. Overall, the novel transcends the problems of ethnic and linguistic identity so crucial to Ťažký and Jaroš: in the kingdom of Vladislav, ethnic affiliation, the distinction of Czech, Slovak and Hungarian was as unimportant in the face of the struggle between papacy and Ottomans as it should be in the face of today's global conflicts. An apocalyptic vision lets Johanides incorporate into his work Magyar themes of the horse and the crucified rebel which are traditionally outside Slovak spheres.

Johanides's success in singlehandedly rescuing the historical novel from a sunken culture is curiously mirrored in contemporary Georgian prose. The Georgian novel has some elements in common with the Slovak, which accounts for the similarities between writers: a population of only four million speakers, barely enough to create and sustain a demand and a climate for the novel: the threat of a larger literary language to which most readers and many writers can readily switch (Russian for Georgian, as Czech for Slovak); above all, a flood of world literature in translation often more professional than the local original writing and more attractive, both formally and materially, to readers and writers. Georgians, however, have some advantages: their literary language has no inferiority complex to overcome: within its republic it is a majority language and 1500 years of history give confidence. Fazil Iskander may not write in Abkhaz and Chingiz Aitmatov no longer writes Kirghiz, but few Georgian writers have turned to Russian, or any other *lingua franca*. Yet the Georgian novel of the last 30 years is poorer than the Slovak. The novelist who sees his work misprinted with worn type on absorbent paper, bound so as never to survive a second reading, with atrocious artwork, knows that his prestige must be lower than that of Slovak novelists whose books are so beautifully produced in Bratislava.

Georgian novelists are weighed down more by a surfeit than a deficiency in history: glorifying the age of Tamara and David the Builder has reduced such major talent as Konstantine Gamsakhurdia to rhetorical pulp. Traditions of improvised panegyric leave the Georgian novelist short on critical insight and linguistic innovation: the creative impulse seems to have settled on Gabriadze's puppet theatre, Abuladze's films, or at best in daring translations such as Qiasašvili's *Ulysses*.

One work of this decade, however, heralds an upsurge: Otar (not Tamaz) Čiladze's *qovelman čemman mpovnelman* (Everyone that findeth me).[23] (The title is Biblical, Genesis IV: 14 and implies, to the few readers that know the quotation, 'shall slay me'.) Hitherto known as a lyric poet, perhaps more widely in Russian translation,[24] Otar Čiladze is entranced by Orphic themes of rescue from Hades, which he now applies to a grotesque family saga that encompasses the whole of the nineteenth century and makes for an original, if strangely awkward, world.

Čiladze has taken a provincial moral quagmire – the typical

setting of such classics of nineteenth-century Georgian fiction as Ilia Čavčavadze's *Kacia-adamiani* (Is he human?) and placed it at a century's distance, further from the civic intent and satirical, Saltyko-vian techniques of the founders of Georgian prose: he has muffled that sense of the present as the purpose of the past which cheapens so much fiction. Although the last two chapters of *Everyone that findeth me* are cautiously affirmative, Čiladze's vision, at its sharpest, has the ghoulish self-sufficiency of Johanides.

The structure, however, is conventional: Uruki, a backwater in eastern Georgia, which the Cain-like soldier, Kaixosro – an orphan after the sacking of Tiflis by the Persians – claims as his adopted home. He marries a widow, turns her stepson into a dumb beast of burden and spawns a dynasty benighted by his bullying cowardice and his wife's resigned stupor. Long pages of brooding analysis are punctuated by horrible catastrophes: the Tatar whom Kaixosro ousted and shot returns to stab his stepson to death; his grandsons try to rape the *dukhobor* servant, then blow up Kaixosro's pigsty. One of them, Aleksandre, becomes the hero of the last third of the novel, a crippled symbol of an alienated Georgia and a second 'fugitive and a vagabond in the earth'; the other, Niko, dies a helpless rebel in Siberia. Women hang themselves, are raped by gravediggers, die of consumption or turn violently but uselessly on their oppressors, but the repressive Cain, Kaixosro, whom all wish to slay has an invisible mark and senile dementia takes the slowest course ever mapped in a novel. Čiladze ends his work with the very Chekhovian device of Aleksandre rescuing his orphaned niece, a hint of redemption matched by the gradual coming of the railway (another Chekhovian device).[25]

These relatively conventional lines are bisected by stranger lines. One is the Orphic theme of burial and resurrection, usually illusory. Kaixosro rescues Ana from the Tatar only to plunge her into deeper hell. The Tatar rises to kill after two generations' absence. Aleksandre rescues the coffin-maker's daughter from her Hades, only to throw her back again. The railway engineer rescues Anetta, Aleksandre and Niko's sister, only to leave her at the mercy of a rapist. Only the trudge through Siberia in the penultimate chapter to rescue Marta, Niko's daughter, is a quest not explicitly doomed to fail, although she is brought back to the ill-starred family house. The village of Uruki is itself entombed in snow; the starving deer taken in for the winter by the Makabeli womenfolk is shot on release and buried in the same yard as the suicidal servant. Aleksandre sees his home as a hell that God has already created, a Golgotha tailored for each individual.[26]

The vision of Golgotha reminds us of Johanides, just as the fugitive deer, the only free agent in the novel, recalls Johanides's Hašemen, the horse that runs free. An apocalyptic fate is uppermost in Čiladze's mind: he assigns Voltairean views to Iaghora, the philosophical rapist gravedigger, who decides that man is to Fate as mouse is to man.[27] Like Johanides, Čiladze sets his fatalism in a Christian context. Čiladze uses Biblical brothers – Cain and Abel, Simon and Levi – as Johanides uses Esau and Jacob – to build the plot. But, again a Chekhovian device, Čiladze uses the professional classes as angels: the priest, Zosima, for all his smug bibulousness, is a repository of Christian wisdom: it is he who defines Kaixosro's senile anguish as the agony of Cain and puzzles him by cryptically uttering the novel's title, 'Everyone that findeth me shall slay me'.[28] Like the railway engineer who intervenes too late or the doctor who can only act as a herald of death, the priest has a wholly Chekhovian role as an inadequate but unique redeemer, bringing the only compassion or freedom available to a captive world.

Like Ťažký, Čiladze leans on Russian literature and learns his art as he writes, with no editorial instinct to curb the flow of synonyms and recapitulation. But he has a more idiosyncratic vision that makes his recent novel, *Marṭis mamali* (The March cockerel),[29] more assured. Like Johanides, Čiladze sees character as bonded to Fate, not ethos, and he challenges ethnic clichés. He refuses to draw consolation from such universally respected bonding elements as the Georgian *supra*, the unity of hosts and guests that is meant to heal families, communities and strangers in a ritualised affirmation of ideals and human brotherhood. Čiladze calls it insanity, when Aleksandre hijacks a party of strangers and forces them with his warring family into a *supra* where all drink to ideas and persons utterly alien to them.

Čiladze, like Johanides, is unlikely to do the same thing twice. Their historical novels are, however, no accident, but ways of learning to grapple with the present. As Čiladze's railway engineer says, 'the devil takes over an abandoned church'[30] – one more reason why novelists by vocation should not abandon history to purveyors of pomp and soap.

NOTES

1. Ladislav Ťažký, *Amenmária* (Bratislava: 1964).
2. Ibid. p. 359.
3. Ibid. pp. 96 and 364.
4. Ibid. p. 381 *et passim*.
5. Ibid. p. 575, 'Zánik stratenej divizie'.
6. Ibid. p. 596, 'To je zbraň? – . . Redaktor? Schriftsteller?'.
7. Peter Jaroš, *Nemé ucho, hluché oko* (Bratislava: 1984).
8. *Tisícročná včela* (Bratislava: 1979).
9. Ibid. p. 17.
10. *Nemé ucho, hluché oko*, p. 8.
11. *Tisícročná včela*, p. 479.
12. *Nemé ucho, hluché oko*, p. 410.
13. *Tisíčročna včela*, p. 501.
14. *Marek koniar a uhorský pápež* (Bratislava: 1983).
15. *Súkromie* (Bratislava: 1963).
16. *Podstata kameňolomu* (Bratislava: 1965).
17. Ibid. p. 14.
18. *Súkromie*: 'Nerozhodný', p. 7.
19. *Marek koniar a uhorský pápež*, p. 75.
20. But Bulgakov's worship of women does not affect Johanides, whose male world, in his *Marek koniar*, remains Camusian in this respect.
21. Ibid., pp. 13, 55, 110, 141, 150 and 160.
22. Ibid., p. 160. Constructing a novel around a bond between a 'hairy' and a 'smooth' man is essentially a Tolstoyan device.
23. *Sabčota sakartvelo* (Tbilisi: 1981).
24. A retrospective selection of Otar Čiladze's verse in Georgian can be found in *Mnatobi* (1982), VII. The best Russian version and selection is *Stikhi* (Moscow: 1977).
25. For example, Chekhov's *Rasskaz neizvestnogo cheloveka, Moya zhizn'*, *Ogni*. Cf. the clumsy use of the railway in Jaroš's *Tisícročná včela*.
26. *qovelman čemman mpovnelman*, pp. 376 and 417.
27. Ibid., p. 400.
28. Ibid., p. 287.
29. *Mnatobi* (1987), I–III.
30. *qovelman čemman mpovnelman*, p. 421.

9 Innovation in Vincent Šikula's Prose
Manfred Jähnichen

Šikula's prose fiction may serve as an example of cultural continuity in a period where, apparently, the end of the 1960s and the beginning of the 1970s constituted a caesura in Czechoslovak culture.

As he has himself frequently emphasised, Šikula's great theme is 'home'. And 'home' means a precisely defined region, as it does for other major contemporary Slovak writers whose subject is 'home', for example Ladislav Ballek, Ivan Habaj or Peter Jaroš. For Šikula 'home' means a West Slovak village situated between Modra and Trnava. This geographical area forms the primary structure for Šikula's prose. As a story-teller Šikula performs in this area, just as he has his characters assume their forms there. His characters are predominantly ordinary people doing ordinary things, usually in a period through which Šikula himself has lived or, at least, about which he could learn from the lips of ordinary people who had lived then.

Outside any specific regional point of view, however, these people simultaneously represent a development of Slovak history which goes beyond the area concerned and has numerous points of contact with European history as a whole. That is clearest in the results of both World Wars whose manifold consequences came to a head in the Slovak National Uprising. Thus the geographical area as narrative structure becomes a decisive social and historical factor. The social experience of the ordinary individual becomes the historical experience of the whole community. Šikula has permanently registered that in different ways in the first two volumes of his 'Majstri' trilogy, *Majstri* and *Muškát*, and in *Vlha* and *Vojak*.

In his works of the 1970s and 1980s Šikula records for the most part ordinary everyday people – and often from the viewpoint of a child or a maturing young man – where in the 1960s his ordinary people were often outsiders or eccentrics. That viewpoint is radical because it is not distorted; it is a viewpoint in which historical time is reflected first and foremost as human time. It is, however, also a viewpoint which enables the author/narrator to present reality through a lens of childlike naivety or youthful trust and, thus, to suggest to the reader that the representation of reality is authentically evaluated.

Making this viewpoint the narrator constantly leads the reader to consider the way people actually lived in a particular social environment. Thus narrating (and this is an important principle of Šikula's poetics and, at least for the 1960s, in a generalised Slovak model, also a principle of innovation) always becomes the declaration of a personal approach to the world concerned, its people and their inner selves.

But then narrating means (and this is a serious consequence of Šikula's basic standpoint) identifying oneself as narrator with one's characters, even in circumstances where the narrator's standpoint, for example in *Majstri*, introduces fundamentally critical remarks. One could hardly claim that that would encourage a narrator's critical *distance* to his characters. He is far more likely to leave such criticism to his characters in the dialogic or monologic expression or evaluation of his fiction.

Thus Šikula designs his prose as fictive narrative from a point of view which is undeniably marked by his own life experience. Therefore his narration acquires a special authenticity which has an almost documentary quality. The frequently physiologically, and always psychologically, young narrator with his particularly acute visual and acoustic sense of characteristic detail can display his villagers in their spontaneous behaviour if the author employs such a narratorial point of view. Their thoughts, actions and emotions are conceived authentically and the motives for their action derive from the firmly established value system of the Slovak village. Given all the hardship of everyday pre-Communist times, this motivation is based on general ethical principles which Šikula concretises by means of his characters: as, for example, in their spontaneous helping of each other in times of need (for example, the 'beggars' in *Nebýva na každom vŕšku hostinec*, There's not a pub on every hill, 1966), in their creative activity and the unalienated mutual communication which exists between his characters. That constituted consecration of an important idealist principle in 1960s Slovak prose, a principle which, for a time, functioned as polemical innovation, but it also constituted an ethical appeal to the writer's audience.

In spite of everyday hardship Šikula's characters are capable of maintaining, first and foremost, a constructively optimistic approach, which can be creatively exploited. That appears to be for Šikula a central quality of the Slovak villager and, therefore, of a principle which hallmarks Slovak history altogether. Thus he comes conceptually close to Vladimir Mináč's oft-quoted words in *Dúchanie do pahrieb* (Blowing into the embers, 1970): 'We're a nation of builders, not only in the metaphorical sense of the word, but also in the real sense of the word . . . We are not a nation of pacific doves; we are a nation of plebs'.[1]

In his first period, the 1960s, Šikula mainly gave only hints of his favourite principle of the reflective lyrical mosaic. Later, primarily in the novel *Majstri*, he gave wide-ranging expression to that principle, particularly in the manner in which that principle could exploit a multi-layered reality. Such exploitation characterises his best fictions: the picture of country people represented by Guldan and his three sons, constitutes a socially precise painting of everyday life in the countryside, circumscribed by a series of details. At the same time, this picture becomes a permanent emblem of Slovak history. It becomes a metaphor of the positive content of Slovak history, which existed within what has become conceived of as the Slovaks' thousand years of national and political dependence. Šikula's picture, thus, also expresses the 'democratic' continuity of the history and value-system of the Slovaks. That is particularly important for Šikula as moral philosopher.

Šikula's depiction of Slovak village life constitutes, then, a fundamental denial of everything which implies destruction – and, above all else, destruction means the war which was apparently imposed on the Slovaks. Šikula's main character, Guldan's youngest son, Imro, represents that denial by his joining the Uprising, even if that joining is brought about by incidental circumstances and his actual participation is not all that heroic and ends 'tragically' in the second and third parts of the trilogy. Still, Šikula by no means relativises the creative activity of the everyday individual or the everyday community or the individual or community's reaction under the test of war, here: the Slovak National Uprising.

In the third part of this trilogy, *Vilma*, beyond the 'tragic' relationship between the dying Imro and self-sacrificing wife, Vilma, Šikula appears to be monumentalising the individual act. That is his way of showing the universal human dimensions of a specifically Slovak fate. Šikula describes the constantly recurring heroism of everyday life through the narratorial point of view of the young Rudo/Rudko – as the fundamental point of view which will make the utterance of an individual constitute a truly documentary account. Thus he can emphasise what he in his stories can often only hint at through allusions or subtext: that only the high moral values of the common people can give the individual the power not to submit when he is threatened. Thus the spiritual culture of the common people constitutes the prime source of strength for the individual and so helps him in his every act. In spite of a centuries-long primarily patriarchally structured village community (and all the coincidental attributes such a community incurred) which survived until the Communist Party took over, the ethics of the common people did not by any means, as Šikula himself shows, manifest a conservatism of any sort. The peasant system of values could apply to socialist society just as well.

It is *via* his characters that Šikula transmits this active approach to tradition, which forms an essential ideal component of his work and which (as, perhaps, in the verse of Milan Rúfus), in the 1960s, also signified innovation. In their physical and mental activity Šikula's characters represent the power of this positive tradition, a tradition which, whenever necessary, gives them the strength to play their own part in the so-called great movements of history and, thus, as in the Slovak National Uprising, to help to achieve their own socio-political fulfilment, in a 'progressive direction'. This is the way the individual integrates himself into history.

A precondition for that (and Šikula as story-teller manifests this precondition primarily in its consequences) is that such creative activity should be consonant with everyday experience. Šikula exemplifies that in the most varied interpersonal relationships, relationships which are usually intact and thus contribute to the fact that, in spite of all difficulties, everyday life remains amicable and harmonious. As a story-teller he demonstrates this primarily through his sensitive depictions of erotic relationships. Particularly in the first period of his writing he used bland plots or 'undramatic' situations. He concentrated on the inner world of his characters and indicated that world (initially rather close to the Slovak Lyrical Prose tradition of the late 1930s and the 1940s) particularly through lyrical reflexion. Within his method he was capable of producing a multifarious range of 'poetic' situations.

Other characteristic stories of his first period, like 'Mandula' in his second book, *Možno si postavím bungalow* (Perhaps I'll build myself a bungalow, 1964) or *S Rozarkou*, constitute paradigms of the way Šikula could penetrate deeply into the inner selves even of mentally underdeveloped figures. Such figures' childishly naive perception becomes manifest in lengthy revelatory, monologically conceived reflexion. Because Šikula places the everyday perception of reality into a broader field of poetic associations, real events often fuse with the imaginary. In this way he manages to elevate the simple, but fundamental, life values of his characters and thus simultaneously to show those characters' inner dignity. As early as in the story 'Tancuj' (Dance), in *Možno si postavím bungalow*, Šikula formulated his aim as far as what he wanted to express with his Slovak villagers was concerned – and this applies to his whole *oeuvre*: 'I like people who say nasty things without hurting. I can't bear people who are full of pleasant words but don't move a finger to help someone in need, even if they needed to make only a tiny sacrifice'.[2]

Šikula's figures act within or without the realm of such basic human activity, an activity where just a kind word can help. Even in such a difficult situation as Filomenka finds herself in *Vlha*, a kind word can function as a bridge between individual human beings. The often gently ironic, teasing repartee in which Šikula has his characters indulge is simultaneously 'realistically' coarse and poetic and it reflects their affirmitive attitude to life (*Lebensbejahung*).

For a story-teller like Šikula, however, the word itself has a comprehensive, if you like, primal, function. The word constitutes the expression and emblem of all human activity and creativity. When in *Vilma* Imro becomes dumb, life itself is endangered; the incurability of his sickness, his death, acquires allegorical dimensions. That reflects how important for Šikula spontaneous communication and, thus, story-telling is. Communicating is for him the principle of life or, as Šabík rightly remarks, altogether the most important human activity. The logic of Šikula's artistic idea and of his personal poetics lies in the fact that his villagers realise themselves beyond their narration, whatever class or social grouping they belong to. One of the most active villagers in the 'Majstri' trilogy is the narrator, who is often designated as the experiencing author, first Vinco (hypocoristic form of Vincent [Šikula]), then later as Rudko or Rudo. The narrator is, then, one of the villagers, is set up with the villagers' mentality, understands what name or value to give to the objects which form part of their cognitive system.

The narrative models for the dialogues and monologues largely abide by the rules of village folklore; they are immediate, graphic, coarse, judgemental and stylistically loaded. The narrator also introduces definite action-bearing events beyond such monolgues or dialogues, to create necessary links in the action (that is particularly clear in *Majstri* and *Muškát*). These links serve to dynamise the narration, even if that narration must always remain episodical.

Taking all this into consideration, Šikula is clearly concerned to bring the reader into the narration as an active partner, to make contact with him, to create a sense of trust, to render narrator and reader equals. One might call such a narratorial position that of a democratic story-teller. At the same time it becomes clear that the initially apparent spontaneity of the narration becomes ever more strongly marked by self-consciously demonstrative formulation. Šikula's narratorial point of view, which is often expressly stated during the second period of his writing, acquires a definite sharp edge in *Majstri*. That sharp edge consists in a perceptive narrator's commenting or polemically digressing and appealing directly to the reader or the critic, with the latter's assumed reservations.

Even if such a treatment of the narrator had been far from rare in European literature before, narratorial divagation to the extent to which it occurs in *Majstri* was something special for 1970s Slovak literature – if you like, an innovation of Šikula's. This exploitation of the narrator led to numerous 'discussions' in Slovak periodicals in 1977 and 1978. Šikula, however, no doubt employed this form of immediate communication with due consideration, as becomes clear from Okáli's or Kochoľ's objections to *Majstri*; Šikula, no doubt, wrote in full awareness of what critics would say.

Šikula's representation of the Slovak National Uprising was something far more restricted than that offered by the standard model, Vladimír Mináč's *Generácia* trilogy. Šikula's trilogy did not pretend to present the same all-embracing historical and sociological analysis as *Generácia*. On the contrary, Šikula's trilogy consciously presented a subjective standpoint and that subjectivity necessarily entailed a more limited, ideologically less determined, world view. Instead of attempting like Mináč a broadly conceived social analysis, Šikula tries to depict historical events at a time of vital consequence for the Slovaks through a personal lens, through the limited vision of a growing boy or a young man, whose vision is further limited by the region in which he lives. In so doing Šikula was aiming at a totality of authenticity in which concrete everyday details acquired central significance.

Since its publication Šikula's 'model' has been acknowledged in Slovakia as complementary to the models of Mináč, Alfonz Bednár or Rudolf Jašík. In the second half of the 1970s, however, it was so new that it justified itself.

What I have here designated as specific to the trilogy actually indicates a characteristic tendency in the whole of Šikula's fiction, the notion that story-telling constitutes the most essential of all human activities. I return to Šabík's conception of Šikula. Story-telling itself becomes a myth, but the principle of story-telling can run through manifold variations. What is characteristic for Šikula is that his characters have an ever greater possibility to acquire traits from beyond their capacity as participants in a dialogue. That is as true of Simon as it is of Janko, of the conservative Guldan as of the Marxist tinker Karčimarčik. At the same time action-bearers like Guldan receive a constant chain of opportunities for loquacious expression of self and judgement of the world.

That is important for the authenticity of the narration; and Šikula strives for such authenticity. To a degree the world of values inherent in the Slovak village is represented from the perspective of such figures, from the perspective of everyday living. Normally that needs no additional commentary from the author. At the same time it serves as a form of narratorial authenticity.

The unity of the authorial narrator, Šikula, and the narratorial point of view of his western Slovak villagers, the concurrence of their moral norms, is particularly characteristic of Šikula's fiction. That concurrence probably also constitutes one of his innovations – in the context of the two periods of his writing. Even if these villagers, with the possible exception of Karčimarčik, act with no real social awareness, they act in accord with human 'progress'. That is true, under the Populist Slovak State, when they act out of a spontaneous sense of justice and pay for that action with their lives as in the case of the blacksmith Onofrej or the verger Jakub.

Šikula always tries to broaden or deepen the Slovak experience into a general human experience. One cannot read Šikula as some sort of narrowly Slovak national writer. His characters and episodes are realistically presented, but, at the same time, often contain some broader connotation. Often they have a metaphorical significance. I mentioned earlier building as a metaphor of Slovak history and the Guldan family as representatives of that creative activity.

One might establish many attempts at the metaphorical elevation of the ordinary. That may concern characters as well as the spheres of life in which they are involved. An example of that is the author's series of mentally powerful women. Particularly with his women, however, one might say that Šikula was innovative, in that he as narrator, shows the weight of responsibility which women normally still have to bear in the twentieth century.

Šikula is, however, far from slow in distinguishing between the lots
of various types of women, from Mandula *via* Rozarka to Vilma or
Filomenka. The fates of all of them are different. The reasons
for their fates range from individual intellectual limits to socially
engendered condemnation. In his attitude to these women, however,
Šikula remains a *Lebensbejaher*, retains a creative attitude to the
man or woman on the Clapham (Modra) omnibus, and has always
succeeded in documenting the ordinary life of the ordinary human
being.

If we look at Šikula's works chronologically we shall find different
narratorial approaches. Near his beginnings, for example, with
'Mandula', he shows a predilection for lyrical allusion. Later, in the
cases of *Vilma* or *Vlha*, he gives a complex interpretation of
everyday characters. Now he attempts some sort of synthesising
characterisation. His previous dominantly lyrical representation of
characters has been replaced or outshone by epic representation. The
principle of lyrical association (which is often conditioned even by
the theme, as in *Liesky* or of musicification or internal rhythmatising)
is still retained, even when Šikula's prime genre is epic. That is
particularly true of Imro's 'anabasis' during the Uprising and subsequent partisan war and his encounter with the dead German soldier,
Hans Wassermann. The suffering of the Slovaks in the war becomes
a metaphor for the suffering of all men in all wars.

Šikula succeeds in achieving a particular intensity in his narrations.
One might speak of a compromise between the lyric and the epic
where the tendency to the epic is clearly gaining the upper hand.
The rococo love story concerning the (blatantly autobiographical)
student of music and the grammar-school girl, Adrika, in *Liesky* does
nothing to contradict the notion of such a compromise in Šikula. The
principle of polyphony, which results from the compromise between
the lyric and epic, is just particularly clear in *Liesky*. Thus an
especially sensitive and sophisticated text comes into being.

Šikula's village world, the world he comes from and the world to
which he to this day belongs emotionally, is realistically depicted
and, at the same time, elevated to lyrical status. Thus this world
attains a broader metaphorical significance: it is a world in which the
basic rules of society have survived, like the rule of mutual aid, as
well as the creative actions of the individual in everyday life. That is
reflected in the apparently spontaneous activity of the narrator. As
long as the existence of this world is not threatened or disturbed by
hostile intrusions like war, it will evolve into a kind world. That will

not, of course, save the individual life from the experience of 'tragedy', as Šikula clearly displays in the exemplary case of his Vilma.

The sense of kindness means that the individual, in spite of all suffering, feels himself to be indebted to some community and is also aware of that community's spontaneous participation in his own suffering. From that derives Šikula's optimistic view of life. At the same time these circumstances make for the fact that Šikula's characters are unbroken; they retain their wholeness as subjects and personalities and, in so doing, they, mostly unconsciously, gain sustenance from the spiritual culture of the common people.

In this way one can see that Šikula's prose in its fundamental *Tendenz* represents an important line in the development not only of Slovak fiction of the 1960s and 1970s, but of socialist-bloc fiction altogether. Šikula's fiction concerns a set of values which are particularly important in the present world, dominated as it is by the consumer mentality. Šikula's prose concerns more general values, values which have nothing to do with consumerism. Thus it represents a literature of active 'humanism'.

In the Slovak literary tradition Šikula's works comprise both continuity and innovation.

NOTES

1. Vladimír Mináč, *Dúchanie do pahrieb* (Bratislava: 1970), p. 63.
2. Vincent Šikula, *Možno si postavim bungalow* (Bratislava: 1964), p. 72.

10 Morality Novels: Alfonz Bednár, Rudolf Sloboda, Ivan Hudec
Ján Števček

Right at the beginning I should like to make it clear that neither Bednár nor Sloboda, nor Hudec has as yet been made part of the Slovak literary canon. Nor have they yet met with any general critical judgement as to whether they are 'good' writers or not. The reasons for that are characteristic of Slovak literary development since the mid 1950s, and are of general validity for any interpretative theory of works of fiction. In this chapter I wish, then, to concentrate both on the problem of the critical evaluation of Bednár, Sloboda and Hudec and on the question of the morality as a subgenre of prose fiction.

At the time of its writing a literary work's primary impact is thematic – and that is understandable. First reviews usually concentrate on the problems the work throws up and tries to solve. Bednár published his first prose work in 1954, Sloboda in 1965 and Hudec in 1979, and from the 1950s to the present day these authors' works have provoked discussions primarily about their contents, their interpretations of reality, the social values presented in them, but not about their literary value, their poetics. None of these three authors was a pleasing, harmonious writer for either the critics or the reading public. On the contrary, the picture of reality presented in their texts aroused conflict and challenges. What these authors' works constituted on the aesthetic level was often felt not to comport with the poetics of a morality, and essentially the works are morality novels. Today the Czechoslovak readership is more mature than it was in the 1950s; in other words, the type of fiction I call morality prose has achieved recognition in the Slovak literary consciousness by virtue of its artistic specificness.

As recently as 1986 when there was public literary discussion of Ivan Hudec's novel, *Pangharty* (Bastards, 1985), one heard opinions like, for example: the author's conception of emotional love is inappropriately callous and incomprehensibly disillusionist. By stating this I intend suggesting that the morality as a subgenre, even if it has been generally accepted, still functions as something special in the present situation of the Slovak novel, even if it is clear that even the most harmonious of novels (like, for example, Ballek's *Agáty*) contains a certain degree of moralistic exposure in the theme.

A contradiction between elevated moral intention and the base realities of life which refute the intention may be considered the primary sign of a morality. Hegel in his *Phenomenologie des Geistes* was perhaps the first to point out the essential antimony between the moral standpoint, which he considers sheer appearance, and the moral reality. In the chapter of the *Phenomenologie* entitled 'The Spirit Sure of Itself: Morality' we find the following formulations: 'there is no morally perfect real self-confidence'; 'there exists no moral reality'; moral reality 'is only imagined', 'is nothing but pure thought'. Finally, Hegel has to express himself in paradoxical statements like: 'moral self-confidence exists, but that is linked with another [proposition], that there is no such thing as moral consciousness'.[1] Morality of itself embodies the opposition between opinion and reality, which, according to Hegel, may manifest itself in two ways: first, in the realisation of the actual contradiction between moral ideal and sensuous reality (Nature) and, second, in the awareness of that state which Hegel labels 'transitional'.

I hope I shall not confuse the reader with my use of both meanings of the world 'morality' when I suggest a third category which is valid in a literary morality and that is the attempt to understand the antimony between the moral and the immoral through an immoral lens – and that has a great deal to do with the grotesque.

I would not have begun by alluding to a philosopher's notion of a 'spirit sure of itself', in other words, a moralist's notion, if the Slovak morality novel were not, at least basically, responding to the thinker's theories. Ivan Hudec and writers like Jozef Kot represent this third, playful, and in its own way the most consistent, type of morality (that is, more consistent than the two manifestations of morality/moral consciousness/moral system posited by Hegel), morálity in the form of grotesquery. This gives the contemporary Slovak novel a special place in the culture of literary narration.

Alfonz Bednár stands at the beginning of this trend; from the 1950s to the present his work has constituted latent morality prose. His is the first serious type of morality prose. Bednár's moralities are thematic. He sets up against each other ideal and reality, that is a moral ideal and an amoral reality as something given, something whose existence cannot be denied. It is certainly no coincidence that, when his novel, *Hromový zub* (The thunderbolt, 1964), one of the profoundest prose works in Slovak literature, was published, the first literary critical discussion of the novel to appear spoke of Bednár's harsh way of modelling his characters and of the contradiction between the objective determinants of life and the illusion of life. (The critics involved in the 1986 discussion of Hudec's *Pangharty* saw in the author's conception of love an antimony between the erotic and the emotional; in fact we must seek in that motif a morality model). In one of the most characteristic scenes of *Hromový zub* Bednár builds a symptomatic morality situation on the motif of the mental state of a girl who, after her first sexual experience, abandons for a time her emotional attachment to another man whom she actually loves. This episode resulted in a critic's stating that Bednár was an author of harsh objectivity and psychological determinism. In fact what we have here is the determinism of a moralist who perceives the contradictions in intimate, social, history-making life in a harsh light but who also adds the semantic ingredient of pathos. Pathos is Bednár's expression of unease at the moral state of a world which is objectively contradictory, although these contradictions are not experienced in their full force subjectively. That has serious consequences for the poetics of a Bednár morality. First, Bednár writes typifying iconic prose in which the characters are independent units, and the most important semantic units in the work's structure. Secondly, he selects an objective narrator who does not comment on the characters' situations, but lets them act directly on the reader. Thirdly, he prefers traditional prose forms, for example, the psychological analytical short story (in the collection, *Hodiny a minúty*) and the large historical novel (*Hromový zub*); then he has intermediate genre forms where the moralist is more evident in the content than the form (the long short story, *Cudzí*); finally, he may veil the moral *Tendenz* of his writing in allegorical grotesquery (the trilogy, *Za hrsť drobných*) where the author retains the objective narrative tone, but, in accordance with the poetics of the allegorical grotesquery, he chooses as his narrator the intimate animal companion of a contemporary family, a dog.

Bednár's 'harshness' or 'cruelty' may, then, be understood as thematic and personal and as motivated by the times in which the author lives and by his psychological inclinations. At the same time, however, from an historical point of view, it may be understood as an objective element in the development of literature, in particular an element which one might call the intellectualisation of prose.

The intellectual element in Bednár is first and foremost a rational element, in which individual emotion and social morality are evaluated by *ratio* and the antinomies of moral ideal and moral reality are revealed as the relationship between a concept and the natural amorality of life. It is thus that we are able to explain the monolithic thematic unity, as well as the multiplicity of genres, in Bednár's prose. The author's *ratio* constitutes the authorial point of view and, therefore, the basic problem of his works. On the one hand, we have a pointedly moralistic long short-story and an historical novel which is marked by full epic iconicity, monumental dimensions, and on the other, we have the functional allegoricality of his grotesquery novels.

The two types of stylisation in Bednár's fundamental approach to his writing, the creation of rounded images and the predilection for the grotesque are symptomatic of the literary situation of the morality, which belongs genetically to the 1950s. In the 1950s he was drawing complete outlines of moral questions affecting the individual and society as a whole; he was depicting whole general moral problems, not nuances of those problems. Today Bednár's morality prose unconcerned with nuances is, paradoxically, aesthetically more effective in works where the epic is strong (*Hodiny a minúty*, *Cudzí*, *Hromový zub*) than in works which are closer to the actual subgenre of the morality (*Za hrsť drobných*). Today, nearly 40 years after Bednár began publishing original prose, the reader values primarily its epic quality (particularly in *Hromový zub*), although it is clear that without the moralist tone which, consonant with Hegel's conception of morality, exposes the real ('amoral') nature of life, even Bednár's prose would lack the aesthetic and semantic expressiveness necessary to serious literature.[2] The possibility cannot be excluded that consideration of Bednár's work from the point of view merely of its epicality will in time change in conjunction with the development of morality prose in Slovak literature and with mature critical responses to that development.

The work of Rudolf Sloboda forms a link in the chain of that development. The attempt once made at an analysis of Sloboda's works on the basis of the opposition of 'higher' and 'lower' poles of life and their value systems was possibly the right path to take critically to appreciate Sloboda's prose. But it is necessary to go further and what I write here will constitute a critical commentary on my own essay on this author.[3] Within the system of Hegel's theory of morality Sloboda's prose represents the 'transitional state', an oscillating between ideal and reality.

A particularly typical work of Sloboda's has the title *Rozum*. The author's basic concern is to express scepticism about the possibility of rational cognition and the rational comprehension of reality – and thus Sloboda's conception is the opposite of Bednár's. Sloboda's intention is to demonstrate that, faced with reality, reason is helpless because the individual as bearer of rational qualities is inconsistent and does not have the capacity to give direction even to his own life. The intellectual schizophrenia in the form used by Sloboda to stylise his characters suggests that these characters also embody the author himself and makes it impossible for Sloboda or his narrator to assume an intellectually clear-cut attitude to reality. Such an attitude is possible only in the framework of a 'situation' not dissimilar to Sartre's notion of '*être en situation*'. That is why Sloboda's characters move in a circle, in the circle or captivity of their own personalities which are incapable of development. Personalities are so disturbed, however, that they perceive the practice of life as something alien, involuntary. The 'transitional state' of the psyches and moral worlds of Sloboda's characters, particularly in what constitutes perhaps his best work, *Druhý človek* (Another, 1981), is a state issuing from an insurmountable disproportion between the ideal and the practice of life, between the moral ideal and the triviality of life. From the point of view of poetics we see here the resurrection of two cultural traditions, the sensibility of the Renaissance and the world of Slovak folk-tales (sometimes corruptions of medieval or Baroque literary forms). The 'higher' intention is here set against the 'lower', the *exemplum* against the jest. In Sloboda's interpretation the *exemplum* constitutes a definite spiritual state of the world not dissimilar to certain passages in Joyce's *Portrait of the Artist as a Young Man*, a state which does not comport with sensuous reality, for example, with the erotic. Sloboda's hero rejects the natural erotic impulse because his conception of the world is strictly determined by instructions received. He is concerned not with love, but with the consciousness of love, not with jealousy (in the novel, *Narcis*, Narcissus, 1965), but with the consciousness of jealousy. Natural human emotions are reproduced within the limits of an ascetic spiritual consciousness, the limits of *exempla*. In contrast to that the actual substance of the spontaneous, the instinctual, the human is trivial, becomes the object of mockery, of jests. The concepts '*exemplum*' and 'jest' are organic to Sloboda's poetics and express the aesthetic intention of his works. Historical poetics, drawing our attention as it does to literariness, the literary culture of texts, can, however, be only an auxiliary element in critical interpretations, which by nature actualises texts. I shall, then, treat the topicality of Sloboda's prose on the background of categories employed by historical poetics.

Because, unlike Bednár, Sloboda does not create rounded, epically 'pure' characters, but instead schizoid characters, where the conflict passes through the character, in fact only through his or her consciousness, that actualises the attitudes of a transitional moral state which we might call 'deciding' or 'selection'. Sloboda's works are capable of interesting an intellectually and morally sensitive reader as long as the 'exemplary' world (in Sloboda often an ascetic world) and triviality are balanced out as poles of the *sujet*. When he retains that balance in his texts, Sloboda's artistic stature grows. It diminishes when the trivial descriptive side of the life depicted is not, so to speak, transcended by the spiritual pole of the *exemplum* (for example, his hardly successful novel, *Stratený raj*).

The *sujet*, the action structure, of Sloboda's text is, thus, very demanding; it is 'vertical', metaphorical, not 'horizontal', metonymical. As far as their genre is concerned, Sloboda's works are something like improvised essays or tracts on the behaviour of a human being situated between the 'higher' and 'lower' poles of life. Sloboda's narrator is grammatically objective (normally the *Er-Form* is used), but semantically extremely subjective, since he is the author's more or less stylised *alter ego*. One might come to the following conclusions if one compared the morality prose of Bednár and Sloboda. First, in contrast to Bednár's iconicity and epicality, Sloboda is functional, non-iconic and non-epic. Secondly, in his themes Sloboda, unlike Bednár, constantly emphasises elements of motivation (the anxiety or, say, the spiritual aspirations of a character); thus there is less room for epic variation than in Bednár. Thirdly, Sloboda's texts are for the most part essays, non-epic formations (they have a 'vertical' *sujet*).

According to Hegel, the morality of the 'transitional state' between the moral idea (ideal) and the 'amorality' of life tends towards 'the suspension of morality and of the consciousness of morality'.[4] That thought suggests the point to which Sloboda's prose has developed. In the same passage Hegel avers that moral consciousness tends towards ever greater perfection and therefore to its own destruction. Moral consciousness is, then, ever less adequate in dealing with reality. According to Hegel, the main thing about morality is 'pure duty', in other words, morality itself. The world which we depict in narratives is, however, 'sinful'. One must find means to give shape to the contradictory moral reality by which the consciousness of the ideal would not be described but only hinted at, while reality as it is would be, in the foreground and, thus, in accordance with Hegel's dialectic, amoral, that is: real, living.

Ivan Hudec has tried to treat this second apsect of moralness. At the moment Hudec may be less well-known than Bednár or Sloboda, but at least in the eyes of the critics and the reading public he is an author with a future. To avoid characterising Hudec's method purely theoretically I shall relate something of the action of one of Hudec's earliest short stories (from *Hriešne lásky osamotených mužov*. The sinful loves of lonely men, 1979). Three lonely husbands meet a woman in a bar. They start talking frivolously with her as if she were a prostitute. They only pretend their repartee is serious; it is a mask consisting of typical social conversation. In fact it is what the author here and elsewhere calls fun. This method of epic fun manifests cynicism, a sort of picaresqueness. The wife of the protagonist is strapped into a wheelchair. Because of this the three husbands sometimes start quarrels which are cruel from the point of view of the protagonist. His arguments may often be 'mad', but there is 'method' in them. The point is that if one is an invalid, one must adapt to one's circumstances. The protagonist publicly defames his wife:

'Have you any idea what sort of life she has? How rich it is? Yes, rich. She's liberated from the duty of walking. Present company has gained lots of time for thinking,' and he pointed at Júlia. She smiled sociably, for she expected some joke at her expense. But Dominik is not joking, and he continues, 'No, no, be quiet! Let her find some philosophy of life and she'll be satisfied. Something like, I'm born; I wake up and my first thought is, what shall I do? No, that's not a good example. I'll try again: I've got two arms, two legs, everything. What would happen if I lost my right arm.'[5]

The protagonist 'performs' his cynicism as a theory concerning the necessity of surmounting a given insurmountable state, an idea Sloboda had already introduced into Slovak fiction. In Hudec's works, however, particularly in *Čierne diery*, but also in the historical novel, *Pangharty*, this method is transformed. Hudec is concerned only with producing a view from below, from the trivial aspect of life and triviality is conceived of as the sum of lost opportunities. The *exemplum* is missing and we are left with only the jest. But the jest acquires tragic dimensions; it is also of itself a thematically blurred but semantically clear appeal for morality, for a moral approach to life.

Hudec's own attitude is masked by the epic point of view; this is also the point of view of the narrator. His prose plays at amorality, but this game sounds probable to the reader. What we have is a masked iconicity in a story which has a strong moral appeal as its background. Thus Hudec's method of narration as fun, as something light containing a moderate dose of cynicism, may illuminate Bednár and Sloboda's methods of epic morality. One cannot understand that morality as a mere exposing of certain facts of life; it must be seen as the symbolic expression of a moral situation and the expression of an appeal to change 'evil' into 'good'. Hudec has given strong expression to this method of prose morality in his conceptions of story lines and particularly in his narrations, where one thing is said and something else is thought, where the sensitive is replaced by the coarse and the moral sense by verbal cynicism. Hudec has perfected this method and developed it in an entirely original manner. In his works it is artistically natural, even if it presents the moral unnatural-ness of life.

We do not find morality only in moralities. The reader of Ballek's *Agáty* might be surprised how many cynical motifs of amorality appear in the novel, although the work has as a whole an expressly harmonious mood. The moral convulsions of Ballek's characters and the insolubility of their situations are balanced out by the calm tone of the narration. The broadness of the narration also helps, for it evokes a true epic atmosphere where everything in the chaos of the epic world appears to be smoothed out and put in its proper place. In this novel the narrator plays the decisive role. He wants to draw all contradictions and moral conflicts into his all-harmonising world and solve them by overcoming them. Ballek and the world of his novel may be seen as the outcome of the tendency of the Slovak novel, and not only the contemporary novel, to bring everything into harmony. In the case of *Agáty* we have a modern stylistic instrumentation, where harmony constitutes the main tool for the ordering of disharmonious elements.

We would find a similar tendency in Peter Jaroš's novels, where the world of the spirit, of ideas, morality, history as abstracts is counterbalanced by that of the body, laughter and the senses. To be sure, Jaroš carnivalises the spiritual problems he treats – which is another way of balancing the inconsistencies in the epic material of history.

The common denominator of the two poetics of the contemporary Slovak novel, the morality novel and the novel of harmoniousness, is the intellectualisation of the otherwise vitalist, naive substance of Slovak novel writing.

NOTES

1. G. W. F. Hegel, *Fenomenologie ducha*, translated into Czech by Jan Patočka (Prague: 1960), p. 367 ff.
2. I have developed this idea in detail in Ján Števček, *Súčasný slovenský román* (Bratislava: 1987).
3. Ibid.
4. Hegel, *Fenomenologie ducha*, p. 389.
5. Ivan Hudec, *Hriešne lásky osamotených mužov* (Bratislava: 1979), p. 10.

11 Mythological Aspects in Peter Jaroš's *Tisícročná včela* and Chabua Amiradjibi's *Data Tutashkia*

Giuli Lezhava

The epic genre is one of the oldest genres in literature the world over, but one which acquires new contexts and peculiarities in each age according to the problems to which the age brings mankind's attention. In this respect the 1960s and 1970s are considered a period of return to the epic genre in many countries. The new problems of the century seem to have given an impetus to the broader epic view. It is, then, worthwhile establishing what the characteristic features of the contemporary epic are, at least in general outline.

In the first place, it is a synthesis of different creative traditions and methods. We note that it has its own special poetics, combining myth and reality, fact and fantasy, social assessments and philosophical and political principles. Although when speaking of the peculiarities of the contemporary epic novel, it is Latin American literature that most readily comes to mind, the same tendencies can be observed in the literatures of other countries, as, for example, in Slovak and Georgian literature. It must be appreciated, however, that Latin American literature has become so well known in the world at large because Spanish is a widely known language. Slovak literature on the other hand, in spite of its successes of the last 15 to 20 years, is far less well known outside the socialist countries. Much the same applies to Georgian literature. Although it, too, has achieved new successes during the last 20 years, and although it is one of the sophisticated literatures of the USSR and is more or less well known in socialist countries, it still remains unknown outside the Bloc. Both these literatures deserve closer attention.

When speaking of 'el boom' in the Latin American literature of the 1960s we think that the distinguished translator of many Hispanic

writers, Gregory Rabassa, is absolutely right in saying it would be
more precise to qualify this process as 'fomento' – that is, gradual
development.[1] The same may be said concerning contemporary
Slovak and Georgian prose, which the critics have often described in
the same terms. The historical fate of a nation is the precondition
that gives periodic boosts to and 'explosions' in literature and art,
and in other spheres of human intellectual activity. The history of all
nations is full of drama, but the boundaries of drama are relative . . .

In the gradual development of Latin American literature a great
role is played by its contradictory history: the rise and fall of the
great pre-Columbian culture, Spanish colonialism, wars of liberation,
provincialism, political oppression and foreign influences that endangered native voices; so too, in the shaping of Slovak literature the
main role has been played by the Slovaks' history: Slovaks see
themselves as having suffered for a thousand years as a colony of
Hungary. No less determining for contemporary Georgian literature
is its history full of the hard, and for a small nation, painful, struggle
to preserve its originality and its 1500-year-old literary tradition.

Despite geographical distance, the differences between the two
literatures and between the cultural and historical traditions, some
common traits can be observed in Slovak and Georgian literature of
the 1970s. Their characteristic features are epicity, a synthesis of
mythology and reality (in the so-called 'synthetic novel'), psychologis-
ation and the philosophical quest, the foregrounding of ethical
problems and so on. To bring mythological elements into the
relationships of general time and space is not new in literature. We
speak of the mode of thinking in the category of myth, as for example,
the 'real world of unreality' in the contemporary Latin American
novel, or of myth as a necessary element to give a text a new
structure. These two methods are characteristic of Slovak and
Georgian epic novels in the 1970s.

Slovak literature of the 1970s achieved a high level of figurative
expression. Its themes are rich and varied. Many novels and collec-
tions of short stories concern contemporary city life, for example
Bednár's *Blok 4/B*. We find caustically humorous works concerning
the past. Thus Šikula wrote his trilogy *Majstri, Muškát, Vilma*; the
young Ballek published his *Pomocník* and *Agáty*, and Jaroš proffered
readers his *Tisícročná včela* and *Nemé ucho, hluché oko*.

I intend to make a typological comparison of the mythological
aspect in Peter Jaroš's *Tisícročná včela* and *Data Tukashkia* by
Chabua Amiradjibi, so I shall keep mainly to these two works.

Peter Jaroš is one of the most distinguished and talented Slovak writers; his works have won recognition abroad as well as in Czechoslovakia. He began publishing books in the 1960s, with *Popoludnie na terase* (Afternoon on the terrace, 1963), later we have *Menuet* (Minuet, 1967) and *Putovanie k nehybnosti* (Pilgrimage to immobility, 1967). In the 1970s and 1980s these were followed by *Krvaviny, Až dobehneš psa* (When you catch the dog up, 1971), and then *Tisícročná včela* and *Nemé ucho, hluché oko*. All these works reveal the author as a writer of great complexity.

Tisícročná včela is his most talked-about work. He was awarded a State Prize for it, and a highly successful film was based on it. It is an epic novel of a social historical nature. In it the writer is seeking the meaning of past and present. He describes the historical fate of the Slovaks, taking as his example three generations of a village family from the end of the nineteenth and beginning of the twentieth centuries. The novel is multifaceted, covering almost every aspect of man's life: there is strong love and hate, the urge to fight and passive contemplation, philosophical brooding, romanticism and cruel realism. Using legends and folklore, blending reality with fantasy, the grotesque is characteristic of the writer's style. All these elements and methods enter the plot quite naturally, which makes it attractive to read. The main *Tendenz* of the novel is to show Slovaks as hard-working people striving for national cultural freedom.

First, I must discuss the place the mythological aspect occupies in Jaroš's novel and its purposes. It must be noted here that by 'mythological aspect' I do not only mean the use of purely mythological plots or *motifs*, but the totality of mythological, unreal and fantastic elements. I shall attempt to define its function in the given work.

The characters of the novel are of themselves realistic and down-to-earth. They undergo an inner evolution; their attitude to reality is depicted convincingly by the author. That is why even the fantastic, unreal, stories that are included in the plot seem natural; they serve to hint at the uniqueness of human life.

Among the unreal images we would single out the metaphorical image of the Bee and its symbolism, which forms a sort of dome over the novel. The title indicates that. The Thousand-year-old Bee is a generalised, symbolic image for the Slovaks, who for a thousand years have been working hard like bees. We meet the image several times in the course of the novel. Some unreal episodes are connected with the Bee in the work; elsewhere the Bee is personified. Sometimes

it represents a (female) bee with whom the main hero of the
novel, Samo Pichanda, gets into a dispute. His attitude to the Bee is
ambivalent: on the one hand he admits his and the nation's
resemblance to the Bee, as its main point of life lies in endless work;
but at the same time a feeling of protest awakens in him from time
to time, a protest against the mute obedience of his people. This
comes out well in the novel through Samo Pichanda's behaviour –
his unjustified desire to kill the Queen-Bee and destroy the apiary.
'I am just the Thousand-year-old Queen-Bee, the only one who never
dies and remains alive for ever in the hive. I know everything about
your ancestors, about you, about everyone, and shall know everything
about your children, your grandchildren and great-grandchildren',
says the Queen-Bee to Samo Pichanda, 'not dying, but continuing
its eternal life'.[2] In the image of the Queen-Bee the author skilfully
expresses the unifying idea of the nation, its everlasting energy, its
main purpose, to which many people, like worker bees, sacrifice their
lives, but the Queen-Bee always remains alive, as the successor of a
generation and as the eternal bearer of its burden.

The stylisation of a mythological theme can be seen in Martin
Pichanda's dream, when Martin's meeting with his former mistress,
Zela Matlochová, in the belly of a whale is described. The topos of a
man's being swallowed by a whale is well known in the world's
mythology; scholars believe it goes back to the third millenium BC;
the topos arises in the epos of Amirani. Peter Jaroš gives it his own
interpretation. With great emotion and humour he describes Martin
and Zela's having a good time in the belly of the whale, Martin's
fear and his amorousness. The story ends with the sawing in two of
the whale by the people outside. Martin and his mistress find
themselves in the middle of their home town's square. After a row
with his wife, Martin gets half the whale, sells its meat and pays his
debts. This is the end of the dream story.

In the Old Testament, to punish the prophet Jonah, God orders a
whale to swallow him. After Jonah's confession God orders the whale
to disgorge the prophet. As to Georgian mythology, the whale, like
the dragon, is a fierce enemy of humankind. In the epos of Amirani,
the cultural hero and demi-god Amirani (an analogy is often drawn
with Prometheus), fighting with the whale, is swallowed by it, but
with the help of his golden knife he cuts the belly of the whale and
comes out of it safe. So as we see in both cases, in the Bible and in
the folk epos, the image of the whale represents action and even
aggression. In Martin Pichanda's dream, however, the whale is an

almost harmless, passive, nearly lifeless body. The whale, which was cast down to earth by indeterminate forces, was borne away by the melted snows of the Tatras and was carried to the little town of Hybe. Having appeared mysteriously, the whale does not harm anyone; it is an incomprehensible, strange phenomenon for the people who have never in their lives seen the sea, let alone a whale. The whale does not fight; on the contrary it brings benefit to people: they divide it up, sell and eat its meat. Thus the author demythologises the well-known plot and carries it to absurdity.

Jaroš is a skilful teller of fantastic tales. They are merged with the plot masterfully. The heroes of the novel often acquire an unreal tragic nuance, which is, as a rule, accompanied by humour. I take as an example the life of the bricklayer Benedikt Viliš, whose nickname is 'suicide'. When Viliš's love for the cook was rejected, he shouted that he would kill himself and began to drink a pool in the river Štrb! When he had drunk it his belly became so big that it almost reached the Tatras. The woman was delighted, but he did not care for her anymore – he was expecting to die. When he saw that death was not coming, the man released his belly. The village of Vaša was flooded with so much water that the villagers created a story about a new Flood. Thus too, the tragi-comic life of the thief Oškara is unreal and fantastic. He either starves – he is sure that he does not have a stomach – or eats so much that he accretes enormous proportions, cannot liberate himself from food and becomes its victim. The flavour of folk tales brings the old tinker into the novel. He knows countless unbelievable stories. Samo Pichanda and his wife, of course, do not believe them, but then a strange thing happens. After he had gone they found wine instead of water in the pitchers he had repaired. The story of old Pirčik and his ear is told with sad humour. The old man, who was deaf in one ear, wanted his son to take him to America with him. But the son refused and said he would shout to his father as he crossed the border and the father would hear him with his healthy ear. Every day the old man stood for hours with his good ear towards the border, but he could not hear his son. His ear began to grow and grow, until it filled a whole room. The tired father cut his ear off one night, bled profusely and died. His relatives and neighbours buried him with great ceremony and wrote on the tombstone: 'Beneath this stone lies the biggest ear in the world'.[3]

This kind of hyperbole, tales and 'grand fables' give a peculiar attractiveness to the novel and enhance its readability. It may be that the roots of some of these tales lie in folk legends and that some are the fruit of the writer's own imagination, but, as spontaneous as the origin of them may be, in the thinking of the writer they still have a definite literary aim in the novel – by putting the real and unreal elements on one plane, a specific literary effect is achieved. The plot and characters do not become fantastic or unreal; on the contrary, they become more real and expressive. In this way the 'real world of unreality' is created by the author.

The 1970s and 1980s are also characterised by the creation of grand epic works in Georgian literature. Worthy of mention are philosophical, mythologising novels by such well-known Georgian writers as Otar Chiladze, *Gzaze erti kaci midioda* (There walked a man on the road), *Qovelman chemman mpovnelman* (Everyone that findeth me), *Maradisobis kanoni* (The Law of Eternity) by Nodar Dumbadze, and *Data Tutashkia* by Chabua Amiradjibi (born 1921), all of which have been translated into Slovak.

From the typological point of view it will be of great interest to compare *Tisícročná včela* with the multifaceted philosophico-historial synthetic novel *Data Tutashkia* which appeared in 1973 in Tbilisi. It was a great success and has been translated into Slovak, Czech, English (in the USSR) and other languages. The television film based on the novel was also successful. The writer won the Soviet State Prize for the script. Despite the great differences, the two novels still have many points of contact, since both authors take one and the same historical period; both novels have a distinct national and social character.

The novels' heroes have similar attitudes to reality, tradition and the present. The main characters of the novels are thinking men absorbed in themselves; they experience the evolution and transformation of their feelings towards the outer world. Both novels also share the trends in contemporary literature worldwide which I have mentioned above. The mythological aspect in *Data Tutashkia*, which is what I am here primarily concerned with, is important to the structure of the novel. Here, too, it forms a kind of a dome over it, uniting its parts and at the same time acting as a beacon leading to the inner aim of the work. The novel consists in four chapters and each chapter has an epigraph a part of a myth, stylised by the author and then demythologised by the hero of the myth being reconstrued as the actual hero of the novel; the real world of the work provides us with a stimulus to generalise it in its empirical aspect, and it also enables us to transfer all into the spiritual aspect of humanity. So the novel has the following multiple pattern: myth – reality – the empirical – the spiritual. At the same time it has a complex monolithic unity. The epigraph of each chapter points to the next direction in which the novel is going to move.

The title of the novel, *Data Tutashkia*, is just as symbolic as the title of *Tisícročná včela*. The Georgian writer's tale is the name and surname of a man, but 'Tutashkha' also means 'the day of the moon' and 'Monday' in Georgian (Mengrelian dialect). It should be mentioned that Georgian pagan names for the days shared with other languages the names of seven widespread pagan celestial gods. The Moon was the chief god in the Georgian pagan pantheon. He was the man-god, the protector and helper of the Georgians.

The epigraph to Part II introduces us to the mythological Tutashkha: 'judge over the people and their ruler was Tutashkha, a beautiful and splendid youth. Not a human being of his flesh, he was, however, the human spirit which dwelt in the depths of the soul and entered all its components'.[4] After the epigraph the novel follows with its realistic earthly problems. The mythological hero Tutashkha is converted into his earthly double Data Tutashkia, who is chosen for his appearance and his characteristic features, but his image is not schematic at all; on the contrary, the novel is executed masterfully. It has certain elements of the detective novel, which lends it added dynamism.

Two characters are set up in opposition to each other in the novel: Data Tutashkia, the outlaw, the positive hero, kind and brave (his being an outlaw symbolically points also the spiritual state of the hero who is constantly searching and battling for something), and Mushni Zarandia, who is Data's cousin, a police agent. During the narration he develops into a satanic, evil force and is Data's enemy, but at the same time he and Data are identical both in appearance and in some features of their characters. It is this likeness which enables us to transfer the tragedy played out in the novel into the tragedy that takes place in the spiritual sphere of man – the everlasting struggle between Good and Evil.

The epigraph to the third part informs us how the people deteriorate gradually and loses their moral criteria and how faint-heartedness makes its way into the souls of men. Evil triumphs over Good and the Dragon becomes the ruler of the world. But Tutashkha rises against the dragon: 'And the warrior mounted his white steed, raised his lance to the sun, and swore from now on to trample and punish evil only with strength . . .'[5]

The warrior on his white steed fighting against the Dragon can be immediately associated with St George. How is this mythological passage to be interpreted? Is Tutashkha an embodiment of the god of the Moon, or is he St George? The case is interesting in the history of Georgian paganism: St George does take the place of the chief pagan god, the Moon. This is demonstrated by the religious rituals which were first devoted to the Moon and then, unaltered, to St George. St George occupied the place of highest esteem among the saints in Georgia, and he was recognised as Patron of Georgia. First in the Moon and then in the image of St George the old Georgians united their ideals and wishes. In standard versions, St George was a hero-martyr who struggled to enlighten mankind and exterminate evil. The same image is represented by the hero of the novel, Data Tutashkia: his way to the truth is through martyrdom.

Mythical Tutashkha failed to exterminate evil and he understood that – 'no one will save the human race except man himself, and then Tutashkha decided to turn from an all-embracing and universal spirit into a man, and in his intentions and goals he was already a god.' He loved mankind and only after sacrificing himself could he defeat the dragon, and 'then Tutashkha's flesh remained on earth and his soul rose into heaven and sat there as the Moon and changed from man into god'.[6] We see that in this passage the image of the Moon and St George are again identified.

Data Tutashkia, like his mythical double, is always in search of true ways to expel evil from man. He is often defeated in his search; often he loses hope and even suspects that he does not understand people, but he loves humanity and his strivings are noble; he always returns to the people. And though he himself (Good) dies an awful death, at the hands of his son, he is not defeated spiritually, and after the death of Data, Mushni Zarandia (Evil), loses all interest in life: deprived of his 'bedrock', he dies.

The hero's complex philosophical musings and his dramatic passions, common to all men who are in close touch with the times, together with the skilfully executed narrative gives the novel its aesthetic impact.

Slovak and Georgian writers use myths and the mythic in different ways and with different aims. In Jaroš's novel, mythological elements intensify reality and develop the 'real world of unrealities'[7], while Chabua Amiradjibi styles a myth and uses it as a structural guide through the inner evolution of the work.

NOTES

1. R. Z. Shepherd: 'Real depiction is *fantastica*', 'Gregory Rabassa', *Time*, 7 March, 1983, p. 52.
2. Peter Jaroš, *Tisícročná včela* (Bratislava: 1979), p. 17.
3. Ibid., p. 398.
4. Chabua Amiradjibi, *Data Tutashkia*, translated into English in two volumes by Antonia W. Bouis (Moscow: 1985), vol. I, p. 150.
5. Ibid., vol. III, p. 3.
6. Ibid., vol. II, p. 183 (epigraph to Part IV).
7. Cf. Raisa Kuznetsova (Kuzněcovová), 'Cesta epopeje', *Literárni měsíčník*, I (1987), p. 110–11.

12 Social Cognition in the Novels of Ballek, Habaj, Jaroš and Šikula
Dušan Slobodník

The shape of the novel has been changing fast, particularly over the last few decades. Naturally, that applies to the situation not only of Slovak novels. An analogical development, always with specific features resulting from a concrete social situation, is to be seen in fiction in both East and West. The essential starting point to these changes is formed by social circumstances, trends in social development. Fiction, and particularly the novel, mirrors that development, aims at giving an individual a definite place in the social process, in a changing life, and compares the potential of an individual with the potential of society, with what society has 'on offer'.

Social development has many forms and it is not possible to reduce it only to relationships of production or to a reflection of class relations. Social development is a complex, wide-ranging category. At the same time, however, a 'limiting condition' applies in literature: social movement has its clear epicentre – the individual human being who documents the moving forward of society by his fate, testifies to the inconsistencies of development, tries to solve his or her universal but personal problems which are linked with a concrete period or moment.

In connection with social development as the essential starting-point of changes in the novel one must emphasise the importance of scholarship and science for the construction of modern forms in literature, particularly in fiction. From this point of view the situation of the Slovak novel is by no means exceptional; it reflects the general world situation of the last revolutionary, inconsistent decades of the twentieth century.

In connection with science it sounds attractive to try to trace what impulses have found concrete realisation in the Slovak novel of the last few decades. At least since the publication of Mináč's trilogy, *Generácia*, the technique of stream of consciousness has been significantly creative in Slovak fiction. This narrative device comes, so to

152

speak, from the beginnings of the contacts between modern science and modern literature, where a concrete concept arose in both in the 1880s. The Pragmatist William James formulated the notion of a stream of consciousness in psychological studies, and in literature the birth of the stream of consciousness, the interior monologue is linked with Dujardin's novel, *Les Lauriers sont coupés*, and with the works of Tolstoy and Dostoyevsky.

In the contemporary Slovak novel it is possible to identify other elements inspired or conditioned by silence: the limiting of the extent of the narrator's omniscience, temporary and spiritual changes like the distancing of narrator from a linear time of narration, montage technique in narration, which is connected with film as an artistic product of scientific, technological development.

Two other literary classes make for a completely independent category, that is science fiction and literary non-fiction both of whose development is directly linked with science and scholarship. In Slovak literature the greatest contributions to science fiction have been made by Ján Fekete, Hykisch, Ivan Izakovič, Jozef Repko and Alta Vášová. The development of Slovak non-fiction is equally successful and particularly worthy of mention are the works of Vladimír Ferko, Vladimír Krupo and Vojtech Zamarovský.

In this chapter I should, however, like to concentrate primarily on an aspect of Slovak fiction linked with scholarship and its cognitive epicentre: the growth of the socially cognitive function of the contemporary novel, the conscious incorporation of concrete historical facts into the fabric of fiction, and the attempt of a considerable number of Slovak prose writers to outline the real historical lot of the nation within the structure of a novel.

The attempt to delve into history to find a point of departure for the present has several and various causes and connections which are certainly not linked exclusively with the expansion of knowledge which has been made possible by scholarship. First of all, one has to bear in mind that the post-war development of Slovak fiction began with depictions of the Slovak National Uprising. The Uprising constituted a starting point for modern Slovak history as well as modern Slovak prose, and it could not be described as anything but a positive act, or series of actions. It demonstrated the Slovak nation's desire to live in a joint state with their 'fraternal nation', the Czechs, as well as their wish to make their contribution to the war against Germany.

Slovak *belles lettres* reacted to the Uprising in various fashions, for example, with pure memoir literature, or with an attempt to generalise the Uprising experience as a disruption of the unsavoury conditions prevailing in the so-called Slovak State, to show the human being's duty not to compromise with evil or social injustice. The clearest example of that is *Generácia*, where the Uprising is understood within real historical connections and dispositions of social forces, even though the author does not make use of concrete facts, events.

Mináč and writers like Jilemnický, Jašík and Alfonz Bednár introduced the dimension of concrete historical time into modern Slovak literature; they filled a space between the war years and the present. One might call the Uprising the first historical dimension of modern Slovak prose; works concerning the Uprising constituted a socially important contribution to the knowledge of Slovak history.

The writings of authors who came into the forefront of Slovak literary development in the 1970s and the 1980s are linked with this Uprising fiction. One line, which earned the respect of both critics and ordinary readers, extended the retrospective time-scope covered and assumed comparison or contrast with the present. In this line the time covered could stretch back well before the creation of the Slovak State and thus even further before the Uprising, but also forward into the years which followed World War II. Naturally enough, that did not mean that the Uprising as an historical reality had been pushed into the background. Šikula's 'Majstri' trilogy represents an example of a work where the time-scope is greatly extended in comparison with, say, Mináč's *Generácia*, but where the Uprising still holds the central position.

In this line, writers tried to find reasons for the historical connections in the development of Slovak society, for the struggle for social justice and, at the same time, these writers exposed the inconsistency which held back development and the forces which were in harmony with the social endeavours of the age. Thus history became involved in the living social process. Social cognition was accurately represented in literary works which used aesthetic standards to complete the picture of the times. I am thinking particularly of Ballek's *Pomocník* and *Agáty*, Habaj's *Kolonisti* trilogy, Jaroš's *Tisícročná včela* and *Nemé ucho, hluché oko* and, again, Šikula's trilogy. Each of these four writers created a connecting rod between 'his' past and the present, and through his fictitious characters, usually in one family, each tries to fill in parts of the ground-plan of history that were missing and to bring the past alive in the present.

The one to go furthest back into the past was Jaroš in his *Tisícročná včela*. The continuation of this novel, *Nemé ucho, hluché oko*, which is set in the period after the establishment of Czechoslovakia in 1918 shows that *Tisícročná včela* had been a systematic attempt to map out the links in the chain of history and, on the basis of his native Liptau village of Hybe, to sketch in one of the paths leading from history into today. Habaj wrote about events in southern Slovakia from the beginning of the 1920s to the flooding of the Danube in 1965. The climax of his epic novel is 1938 the year that marks the beginnings of the expansion of Germany and some of her allies after the Munich Agreement and the subsequent 'arbitration'.

Ballek also set his *Pomocník* and *Agáty* in southern Slovakia and in these novels he calls his native Šahy 'Palánk'. The action takes place mainly in he years immediately following World War II, before the Communist take-over in 1948. The novels' atmosphere evokes inconsistent social relations marked by petty bourgeois values. Šikula's trilogy begins during the Slovak State and ends at some time during the early 1950s, after the setting up of cooperatives.

The documentary nature and level of historical authenticity vary in each of these works. Jaroš uses historical props like the reproduction of actual documents or descriptions of events which really did take place. On the other hand, the centre of his attention is the general historical situation as represented in his story, the dominant atmosphere of the period. Ballek, Habaj and Šikula depend on concrete historical facts far less. Historical social circumstances and range of character and tendencies in social development are as accurately depicted by these three as by Jaroš. Their novels' social importance is aided by their temporal and spatial localisation, and that is where the strengths of a realistic depiction of society lie.

The authors were not interested in vague pictures of social relations, but in situations precisely delimited by their historical and geographical settings. Another symptomatic quality all these epic novels share is that their authors did not rely only on their own impressions and experiences, that the period in which they set their works did not correspond to the time of their own maturity of perception. The action of *Tisícročná včela* and even of *Nemé ucho, hluché oko* begins long before the author's birth. The beginning of the *Kolonisti* trilogy also falls before Habaj's birth. Ballek and Šikula depict their adult heroes living in a time when their creators were children.

What retrospective writing means for them is conditioned by the endeavour objectively to transmit a picture of a particular time in history in which those social conflicts which suited their artistic intentions were at their most pronounced. In other words, the authors chose a time in which they could demonstrate important stages in the development process of Slovak society.

All the works I have mentioned have precise locations, even when some towns or villages receive invented names and, with the exception of Habaj's *Kolonisti*, all the works' settings are the author's native regions, in other words, areas with which they are intimately acquainted. Something that links Ballek, Habaj and Jaroš is that, although in these works two ethnic groups, the Slovaks and Magyars, often came into conflict, which, after all, reflects the actual course of history, these writers do not elevate the national above the social problem. On the contrary, the struggle for a juster life which is embodied in all their works, has primarily, almost exclusively, social parameters.

What is happening in Slovak literature is that prose is now, a long time later, taking over the model for the depiction of society which had previously been used by poetry. The Romantic poets of the Štúr[1] generation began by concentrating on nationality but their movement ended, during the period of Magyarisation with the Symbolist Ivan Krasko (1876–1958), in the hierarchisation of their view of society.

The prose works of Ballek, Habaj, Jaroš and Šikula present social cognition, which is not just some retrospective assessment and nor does it constitute an endeavour to demonstrate the axiomatic, what has already been well demonstrated before: that the history of the Slovaks has always been a struggle for the realisation of humanist ideals and that the Slovak people had overcome difficult living conditions by their industry, tenacity and enterprise. In particular Jaroš and Habaj come to mind, as far as the depiction of Slovak living conditions under Magyars are concerned.

The importance of these novels is that they demonstrate the lasting continuity of ethnic values, that the present socialist society in which the authors were writing served as the starting point for their conception of history and thus this socialist society acquires the quality of an historical necessity, a society for which the down-to-earth heroes of the novels about which I have been writing were preparing the way. It appears that these heroes were acting in the name of the socialist future.

That does not mean that these writers (and, indeed other leading Slovak writers, who are not primarily interested in the links between history and the present) were defending the view that values are immutable, that an attempt to extend man's spiritual and material horizons was absent in the novels or that Slovak fiction as a whole was beginning to be concerned about the level of social analysis it had achieved hitherto. Only a literary work that tries to anticipate social developments and does not hesitate to expose the conflicts of a given stage of development, that is: of the period of time to which the writer has undertaken to give artistic form, may hope to retain a position in the history of literature and society. In other words, the purpose of literature will always lie in its conquering of space for the realisation of the human, its showing up of the discrepancy between ideal and reality and its urgent furthering of the future of mankind. If I may put it in yet other words, in prose fiction the dimension of history (distant or recent) must be present, but so must the dimension of the present and of the future which has been prepared. This is true even in a work set in the relatively distant past like Jaroš's *Tisícročná včela.* The author introduces the dimensions of present and future with his mental attitudes, his own hidden activities in the novel, with the transplating of spiritual values which are now, and thus in the future, rare. All this is what constitutes the ethical, ideological and cognitive testimony of leading Slovak fiction writers. The Slovak novel is an open dialogue with the times.

It is because of its complex testimony which is proffered through the prism of artistic generalisation, together with the broad register of narrative devices it has developed particularly over the last few decades, that the Slovak novel has achieved its present position in the structure of literature and society.

NOTE

1. Ľudovít Štúr (1815–56) was the first successful codifier of a Slovak literary language; he received permission to publish a Slovak newspaper, *Slovenskje národnje novini* at the beginning of 1845. This paper, together with its cultural supplement, *Orol tatranski*, began appearing on 1 August 1845. The leading Slovak Romantic poets Janko Kráľ (1822–76), Andrej Sládkovič (1820–72) and Ján Botto (1829–81). The first of these certainly counts among the dozen most important European Romantic poets.

13 The Sensual and the Rational in Ballek's Fiction

Vladimír Petrík

Since the middle of the 1970s the novel has been the dominant vehicle of development in Slovak literature. Previously, for many, many years verse and the short story had dominated. Full-length social novels were now being written by representatives of the 'middle generation' of fiction writers, Ballek, Habaj, Jaroš, Vincent Šikula, and others who had in the 1960s been grouped around the periodical, *Mladá tvorba*. They bore within them the characteristic traits of 1960s poetics and a 1960s approach to reality, but at the same time they reacted to the changes Slovak society had passed through at the end of the 1960s and the beginning of the 1970s. They reacted to change or discontinuity by a return to the past and thus made links between past ages and the present. They decided to express in fiction their own experience, but to distribute or spread it over a broader base of historical development. They sought out new geographical or historical areas which they could incorporate into the Slovak cultural and social consciousness. They tried to show the fate of the individual within the movement of history without allowing him to be swallowed up by history. Their starting point was the particular and from that they moved to the social, the generally applicable. They worked towards the concepts 'nation' or 'mother country' via the notion of 'home' (*domov*), a notion which rings insistently in their works. That is not surprising since the *sujet* of every novel is constructed around a return to where the authors had lived through their own childhood, a return home. In the novels, the notion of 'home' as a firm ideological point is linked with the notion of work as a constitutive force of the national character, given the absence of some great, clearly visible national history. The hero of such a novel will be a simple man (or woman) of the people, a craftsman, a farm labourer or smallholder, who makes his impact on history only through creative work (in other words, in a manner opposite to that of the fighter or conqueror) and in the process of his work he acquires certain characteristic features.

158

Every author emphasised in his hero, apart from stock features like skill, industry, peaceability and so forth, at least one other, one that he himself found closest to his conception of humanity. Thus Vincent Šikula chooses humaneness, Jaroš self-confidence, Habaj prudence and Ballek dignity. The heroes of these authors' novels thus represent something more than just individual personalities; they are emblematic, but that emblematic quality is (usually) not to the detriment of their psychological persuasiveness, verisimilitude or authenticity. Different authors achieve this authenticity (of character, but also of milieu, story line and so on) in different ways. I shall concentrate on how Ballek achieves authenticity in *Pomocník* and, particularly, *Agáty*.

In his essay, 'Intelektuálny román' (The intellectual novel) Ján Števček writes concerning the characters of the second novel: 'Ballek's epic narrative consists of the interplay of character and environment' and 'every character in *Agáty* is more or less affected by the historical situation or is trying to come to terms with it'. This bipolarity of Ballek's characters (bound as they are on the one hand by environment, on the other by history) has its equivalent in Števček's recognition of 'a certain two-sidedness' in Ballek's 'epic imagination', that is conceptuality and its opposite, spontaneous imagination, resting on the warm materiality of life. 'The concept liberates the imagination; the imagination is evoked by the concept; that is how one might describe the logic of Ballek's artistic thought processes'.[1] When we use these terms about Ballek, we must refer not only to the novel's own 'conceptuality' but also to the author's conception of history as it is displayed in the novel; that most frequently consists in a rational discussion put into the mouth of one of the characters. Spontaneous imagination, as, indeed, Števček states, almost always takes the form of sensuality. That sensuality may be built into a character or, and this is the norm in both novels, it may again take the form of an individual's reflection, particularly on Nature, or a discussion of the environment in which Ballek's heroes move (that is, the town of Palánk and its surroundings).

No doubt I am oversimplifying when I maintain that, in considering the relationship between the sensual and the rational in Ballek's works, it may be most completely revealed in terms of the spatial and the temporal. The sensual is linked with space in his books, as the rational is linked primarily with historical time. Ballek introduced themes from a completely new geographical, not social, environment into the Slovak novel. He has carried out a literary appropriation of the southern border areas of Slovakia, a fertile plain with an abundance of 'mediterranean' fruits and smells, an area which contrasts sharply with the hilly, central European countryside of central and northern Slovakia, which had over the years become the more or less stock background to literary depictions of Slovak life. Central and northern Slovakia had come to be considered typical. The luxuriant southern plain fascinated Ballek and he has attempted to transfer that fascination onto his readership. Concrete sensual pictures hold the readers' attention and stimulate their imagination. The following will serve as an example of Ballek's sensualist perception:

> In the light of the setting sun which was as red as a fresh wound, so cruelly large and close that it cut into your eyes, the horse cast an even longer and even darker shadow; it tugged up little clumps of grass and glowed like a pitch torch. Around the spot where they were lying now, they used to take the horse into the water and do a little fishing and then bake the little fish over a campfire, as many people did, actually, over the summer and the holidays. The river was warm, slow, greenish and its sandy banks were always hot from the sun. The willow leaves, the grass, the sandy banks and the backs of the larger fish glistened in the red light of the sunset. These fish started swimming up to the surface. The time had come to try to catch them; they were casting themselves up onto the surface, ruffling it, beating it with their tails. A little further downriver a herd of almost white cattle was passing across the ford and by the edge they sank into the blue-tinged mud and water right up to their great horns. From various directions came the croaking of frogs. A southern evening, moments spent just outside the quietening town of Palánk. Its walls bathed in the red like an ancient Oriental city. The scent of sun-warmed greenness, of water, sand, the crickets, the frogs, the sunset, the slow plod of the cattle as white as a cloud of dust. The quietness was ever greater in the town and all around, on this side and that side of the River Ipel', in the wood, the meadows, the fields, the tracks, the air, the soil, the soul, the acacias.[2]

This is something more than a mood-setting picture, because Nature here, the climate, the plain with its slow, meandering river, inevitably influences human character, and social life, as the author repeatedly points out:

> We people from here know all about eating, drinking, wearing out

our shoes, dancing into the morning, gambling, charming women, fighting, slapping hundred-crown notes on gipsies' foreheads [in historic Hungary it was customary to lick banknotes and then stick them on gipsy musicians' foreheads when one paid for a tune or two]. It was as if the countryside here wanted it that way. This southern clime. Marvellous nights with their secret sounds, lights, this town. And our rich food. Rich scents in the air force a man to drink and sing, to fight and weep.[3]

Nature and the milieu of the southern town lost in the warmth of maize fields influence not only people's characters but also their fates. The environment seeps into them, dulls their judgement and awakens passion and sin. All the lots Ballek describes in his novels, tragically unfulfilled, passionate or lyrical (these three types may serve as illustrations of a sensuous perception of reality), are marked by their milieu, grow out of it absolutely organically. The titular hero of *Pomocník*, Volent Lančarič, is a typical product of this hectic milieu; he is a sensuous, sensual type, uninhibited, a representative of Nature herself. His foil, the butcher Riečan, is anxious, indecisive, a man with a conscience. Riečan had been formed by a different milieu, northern Slovakia. In the characterisation of these two men – but also elsewhere – sharply contrasting between North and South as two qualitatively distinct entities has enabled the author to clarify what he considers special about southern Slovakia. Ballek suggests it is an exceptional area, exceptional particularly as far as the literary tradition is concerned, for Slovak writers had previously avoided the whole region as something alien, unSlovak. Ballek proffered it to the Slovak readership and they accepted it.

In his numerous characterisations of the Southern milieu Ballek shows a preference for that season which provides the basic tone for the events described in the novels: summer. The sunny summer, when Nature is a profusion of colour and narcotic perfumes, has a specific function in the novel: it constitutes its fundamental position. The author reveals his viewpoint in the introductory passages of *Agáty*: 'Men, women and children, we spend these summer weeks at a position from which we were able to see into the hearts of all things, into all the labyrinths of our own spirits, into our unexpected mazes, even into our own inner ears; that is the sort of special vision we have, summer vision'.[4] And if anything awakens the melancholy of the townspeople of Palánk (behind which the author's own melancholy is concealed), it is the fact that summer ends at all, that

it does not go on forever. ('The end of summer, the end of summer
. . . It is always leaving us here. And why? And where does it actually
go? Why is it not here forever, and why are we not eternal, too?'[5])
The eternal summer which focuses the author's vision so that he can
see inside things certainly symbolises Ballek's childhood, the lost
paradise of childhood drenched in the sun of carefreeness and the
sheer joy of living. Here we see the taproot of Ballek's sensuality;
this sensuality flows from memory which is then registered in a form
where facts from the past mingle with creative imagination. Childhood
forms also the taproot of his melancholy, which originates in the
consciousness that everything pleasant has to end, that the only real
immortality is the immortality of the moment. The metaphysical
discussion of Ballek's sensualism lies in the fact that it binds Nature
and humanity with the inevitable, natural fate of every human being.

It is because it is derived from memory that Ballek's sensuality has
its particular character. In his essay, Števček formulates this thus:
'One might say that in Ballek sensual impression is a conscious
arrangement of sensuality'.[6] Ballek recalls the past by means of his
senses, but this past is something finished, does not reach into the
present. Everything has gone; nothing of what happened, what
stimulated our senses, will ever return. The finishedness of all actions
is consistently expressed by the use of the past tense. Thus one may
now see Ballek's sensuality as a record of past sensuality. And so the
sensuality in the texts has more to do with the author's reason than
with immediate perception.

The town, Palánk (actually Šahy where Ballek grew up), in which
the action of *Pomocník* and *Agáty* takes place, is not just a southern
town full of sun, perfumes and flowers. It is also a frontier town. It
lies on the frontier between two states, Czechoslovakia and Hungary,
and two ethnic groups, the Magyars and the Slovaks. The state
frontier simultaneously represents historical time which affected the
inhabitants of Palánk dramatically. And, incidentally, Ballek's father
was a customs and excise man on this frontier. In the twentieth
century this frontier moved northwards and then southwards, so that
Palánk was now in Hungary and now in Czechoslovakia. A change
of frontier or citizenship always affected the one or the other
nationality tragically; it produced hatred and the desire for revenge.
The twisting course of history, which bears some resemblance to the
meandering flow of the Ipeľ, has seeped into the consciousness of
the Palánk townspeople just as deeply as the southern climate. Ballek
conceives of history, the past as a time of tension and human tragedy,

as a counterpoint to abundant, generous Nature, to the 'eternal' summer of the southern plain drenched in the sun of youthfulness and love. Both history and Nature have penetrated his characters and they play their definite role in them. The author is not content with registering how history has determined social consciousness (social determinants are, naturally enough, not negligible here); he desires to give direct expression to his conception of history as a problem. For that he uses the device of having two of the novels' characters utter 'confessions' (the pharmacist Filadelfi's and the postmaster Havrila's) which transmit his own opinions and knowledge. Through them he formulates his relationship to historicosocial matters from the beginning of the twentieth century (including the odd excursion into the nineteenth) up to nearly the present. Ballek does not present his reader with abstract essays but with analyses of concrete aspects of history which influence his characters and the fate of the whole of Slovakia through the actions of politicians. He does not intend merely recapitulating; he is attempting a new interpretation (like his fellows in the same 'generation'), trying to express a standpoint which could lead to a rational conception of historical development. Ballek's attempt at evaluating historical development is just as important as his attempt at evoking a past age in a rich composition of concrete sensual pictures. Without a hint of nationalism or chauvinism, he thus discusses important aspects of Slovak-Magyar or Slovak-Czech relations, but he also considers, for example, questions of democracy, statehood, and changes in social awareness. We come across a similar spectrum of problems in the novels of Habaj, Jaroš and Šikula. The reason why all four authors treat the same problems in the same period lies in the federalisation of Czechoslovakia on 1 January 1969, which increased the self-confidence of the Slovaks. The first writer to begin to think in a manner similar to these four was actually Vladimír Mináč, in his essays, *Dúchanie do pahrieb*. The new self-confidence was projected by writers like Ballek, Habaj, Jaroš and Šikula far into the past. Each in his own way, they came with new ideas about historical events; they rehabilitated some aspects of national history and reincorporated them into the picture of national development.

As I have tried to show, Ballek's sensuality is linked with his own experiences as a child. His rationalism, however, is linked with the considered perception of an adult, of a responsible, mature individual who senses the necessity of 'coming to terms' with the past so that he can find his way in the present, indeed so that he can influence the present, at least in the sense that he can impress a new historical dimension on it. Ballek's intention of strengthening or provoking historical awareness in the national collective is clear, and historical awareness had always been very weak, indeed was traditionally inadequate, among Slovaks.

That is all true, but one may not fail to comment on the relationship between narrative time and historical time, which can consign a whole age to oblivion, or may 'dramatise' the fates of men and women in novels or provoke an author to express his own view of the history of his nation. In *Agáty* there is a certain tension between the two times. *Agáty* is composed on the basis of a concatenation of individual stories each of which has its own hero, but the social background, including all the characters, remains the same. Narrative time moves forward in every story, but, at the same time, in each story it starts from the beginning again, or moves backwards. Thus it happens that in one story we meet characters who had died in previous chapters. The result of this is that one has the impression that narrative time is standing still, repeating itself, returning, going in a circle, fusing with a 'stationary' environment, with the immobility of a sensually perceived world of colours, smells and sounds. As Zajac has said, 'In *Agáty* time serves to create space, to juxtapose events'.[7]

The principle of repetition in the narrative time increases the breadth of the world Ballek evolves. That is also helped by the fact that in each case the author changes the register of the story so that he can describe life at a variety of levels. At one time the register is elevated, at another comic, or cynical, lyrical, passionate or rational, wise-sounding or eccentric, ethically pure or immoral. Ballek's aim was to give a comprehensive view of life, to produce life in its individual, social, natural and historical totality. The sensual Nature level and the 'stationary' narrative time with its emphasis on the lastingness of actions and of individual human fates has, in *Agáty*, less so in *Pomocník*, 'squeezed' historical time to the margins of its own *sujet*, that is: into the 'confessions', and thus it has given historical time the features of reportage. That does not mean that its importance in the novel has diminished. The significance Ballek attributes to history and historical time may be seen from the fact that the 'confession' chapters are in an exposed position in the novel: they constitute the last section of each of its two parts. In the stories Ballek is concerned with the (negligible, often unfulfilled) fates of individuals, but in historical time he is concerned with the fate of the whole national collective. Ballek's stories charm the reader with their sensuality, but over each story arches the consciousness of historicity which forms the ideological superstructure. In him reason is superior to the senses, rules them.

Ballek's contribution to the development of the Slovak novel lies in the fact that he has overcome the traditional, largely emotional, approach of Slovak authors to reality and replaced it with an intellectual approach. He left his children's paradise and walked off to confront adulthood. With him the Slovak novel has also reached the age of maturity.

NOTES

1. Ján Števček, 'Intelektuálny román', *Slovenská literatúra*, xxxiv (1987), pp. 137, 139 and 133.
2. Ladislav Ballek, *Agáty. Druhá kniha o Palánku* (Bratislava: 1980), p. 26.
3. Ibid., p. 74.
4. Ibid., p. 301.
5. Ibid., p. 85.
6. Števček, 'Intelektuálny román', pp. 133–4.
7. Peter Zajac, 'Koncepcia Ballekových Agátov', *Slovenská literatúra*, xxix (1982), p. 512.

14 Ballek's *Lesné divadlo* as a Political Statement

Rudolf Chmel

More than 60 years ago the Czech writer, Karel Čapek, wrote that 'one loves one's native region and serves the state'.[1] These words, which serve as the motto to the second part of the Ladislav Ballek's latest novel, *Lesné divadlo*, were not chosen by the author coincidentally. The nub of Čapek's idea, that it really would not be commendable if Slovak self-confidence ended with the Little Carpathians, is also not without substance. Čapek writes that the boundaries of this self-confidence 'are in Cheb and Sluknov'. And these words do indeed constitute a certain key to the resolution of Ballek's epic conception, in which the native region and that narrow region's history not only love each other incestuously, but also bind them with public, even important, affairs of state. In *Lesné divadlo* service to the state on its southern frontier is linked with service on its western frontier; the gaiety of Palánk is linked with the contemplative sobriety of the Bohemian Forest. The main character does his national service as a border-guard in the Bohemian Forest and his father had been an excise man in southern Slovakia. The relationship between these two men's activities, a relationship which makes for a path to national synthesis, is neither simple nor unambiguous. Nevertheless, it does mark something like a zenith in Ballek's epic conception of the world, of the lot of the Slovaks from a broad national and international point of view, in his conception of man as a part of complex, often contradictory, individual and socio-historical or political systems. Within this conception of man he considers today's attitudes in an historical context which comprises not only individual psychological but also constitutional and historico-political elements. These ingredients are, naturally enough, dissolved and brought as close to the author's epic conception as possible. That is why Ballek's work has nothing in common with the conventional historical, let alone political, novel.

I am not suggesting Ballek does not work with political categories, but he works with them as a composer of epics, not as a politician or ideologist. Those categories fuse into the text, which is not communicated in political or ideological language, although Ballek is fully aware that literature has its own independent ambitions as far as evaluating and, most of all, altering, the world are concerned. In the case of *Lesné divadlo* the world is the Czechoslovak historical, national and state identity. Ballek reaffirms the historical status of the Czechoslovak entity primarily aesthetically, but that has extra-aesthetic, even political, consequences.

Over the last few decades Slovak fiction has made several attempts at asserting Slovak society's self-confidence; and that was particularly clear at the end of the 1950s and beginning of the 1960s in works concerning the Slovak National Uprising. At the end of the 1950s it was necessary to ascertain the significance of the Uprising (literature often went further in that than historiography) first and foremost on account of its historical authenticity as the basic starting point for the development of Slovakia within a liberated Czechoslovakia.

The Uprising Generation in Slovak literature (mainly prose), a generation of authors who wrote chiefly on the basis of their personal experience of the fighting, founded their narratives of the Uprising largely on the historical individuality of the Slovak nation. The new generation had to expand this notion of collective individuality by lending far greater emphasis to personal individuality. It is true that that was sometimes to the detriment of statements about the individual's place in society. In the second half of the 1960s that was particularly the case in short stories (for example, those of Vincent Šikula or Peter Jaroš). An epic synthesis, in other words, the novel of the kind critics were demanding at the beginning of the 1970s, could not avoid presenting a social and, even more clearly, a socio-historical position. The questions an author had to ask himself were what social position should one give the individual, the 'hero', and how should one integrate the social and the historical with the individual.

Several paths may be taken to produce an adequate artistic reflection of reality. They vary from the private, intimate interpretation to the complex socio-historical interpretation, and then to an interpretation which entirely ignores the epicality of fiction. Ladislav Ballek's epic conception is more or less a middle path, which is clear from all his works, but particularly those he has published since the cycle of stories, *Južná pošta*. According to Peter Zajac, characteristic of Ballek's conception (other authors who come to mind are Vincent Šikula, Habaj and Jaroš) is the 'intimatisation' of the historical process within the context of actual political events,[2] particularly the law introducing federalisation of Czechoslovakia. One might say that Uprising fiction had, to some extent, prepared the way, but from the mid-1970s the Slovak novel began to hint at both the historical inconsistencies and the potential contained in the whole complex Slovak cultural development which culminated in the new constitution – and there is no point in trying to conceal the fact that this new constitution had been for a long time an unrealised dream, at least in the Slovak part of Czechoslovakia. And in Slovak literature as well. Theoretically the idea was present among National Awakeners like Ľudovít Štúr and Jozef Miloslav Hurban or, later, in Svetozar Hurban Vajanský (1847–1916), Jozef Škultéty (1853–1948) or Štefan Krčméry (1892–1955). The theory began to attain practical dimensions in figures like Ladislav Novomeský and Vladimír Clementis. The crisis and then turning point for Slovak narrative prose came in the 1970s. Slovak writers appear to have arrived at a crossroads where they perceived the necessity to decide how to combine the aesthetic ideal with the political or, to use a synonym which might sound paradoxical, the moral ideal. This crossroads is the point in the development of the new Slovak novel of the historical, political brand which decides on the kind of artistic conceptions, what approaches to the world and the individual are to be taken up; it is the point where an acute need is either satisfied or not. This need consisted in Slovak writers' apparent sense that they lacked a wide-ranging, thoughtful social philosophical novel which reflected the present at the point where past and future meet, where the historical perspective would be self-evident.

Although I have, perhaps, put them a little too briefly and schematically, these were the starting points for the new situation of the Slovak novel. The situation itself was given by the genre's own development as well as by, broadly speaking, social considerations. According to Mikhail Bakhtin a novel must present 'all the social and ideological voices of the period, in other words: all the more significant period languages'.[3] In his typology, the novel of trials, the *Bildungsroman* or *Erziehungsroman*, Bakhtin suggests a way of thinking about the contemporary Slovak novel and about its connections with politics and 'historicity'. In its main developmental line the contemporary Slovak novel, as represented not only by Ballek, but also, for example by Jaroš (*Tisícročná včela*), Vincent Šikula (*Majstri*), Habaj (*Kolonisti*), authors are not concerned only with the maturation or growing up of their characters, but also with their trials. (I admit, there is nothing specifically Slovak about that.) In the case of Ballek, the maturation and trials of individuals are linked with the maturation and trials of the collective, the nation. Bakhtin created a broad conception of the *Erziehungsroman*, essentially of the modern novel, which is not *expressis verbis* an *Erziehungsroman*, but which necessarily depicts a search, the problem of maturation, that is of the establishment of identity.

Rudolf Sloboda (I think particularly of *Rozum*) discusses from the point of view of an individual the same problem as Ballek, Jaroš and Šikula discuss from the point of view of a society. Once, however, a maturation is individual, it is also social and historical. In contrast to the previous generation, the generation involved in National Uprising prose, the Vladimír Mináč generation, for whom the novel form was taken for granted, only the form of the novel was offered to the writers I have mentioned from the 1970s, not the content; the conception of that content has to come from below, is suggested by life itself. Even the politics come from real life (in contrast to the case of Mináč). Because the politics come from below it is aesthetically more persuasive than the politics displayed in Mináč's Uprising trilogy. That also constitutes a change from the conception of content in Peter Jilemnický's *Kronika* (A chronicle, 1947) or Dominik Tatarka's *Farská republika*, a change which had to a degree been prepared by the original manners of conception practised by Alfonz Bednár and Rudolf Jašík in the second half of the 1950s. Both those authors' conceptions had also come 'from below' rather than 'from above'.

Ballek is not alone, but he is probably one of the most significant of the novelists to have taken the new line. His last three novels (*Pomocník*, *Agáty*, and *Lesné divadlo*), concern times of birth, transitional periods, but also key moments in the historical political development of Slovak society. The emphases of individual writers' novels, however, lie in varied aspects of that development. Ballek concentrates on the flow of time in which the social and the private mingle even in individual relationships. Jaroš concentrates on carnivalisation (if I may use Bakhtin's term) and ironisation. Sloboda concentrates on individual asceticism (a particularly potent possibility for the individual who lives in central and eastern Europe). In Ballek, and not only in Ballek, by overcoming the limits of the Uprising generation's epic narratives, where, as Ján Števček says, 'the ideological intention often went beyond the characters or the characters adapted themselves to it',[4] the 1970s writers laid their emphasis elsewhere; the ideas 'from below' become 'a character in his or her own right; through his or her individual epic existence he or she embodies the social existence'.[5] Though Števček is here speaking of *Agáty*, his words apply equally well to *Lesné divadlo*. The latter is concerned with the history and politics of the 1960s not only in Slovakia, but in the whole of Czechoslovakia; it primarily, however, deals with the border zones in the West and the South. The element linking Ballek's narrative in *Lesné divadlo* is, even more firmly than in his previous works, frontier, state, statehood. As the young observer of *Južná pošta*, Ján Jurkovič, is aware of the central questions more or less by virtue only of child's intuition; now in *Lesné divadlo* as a fully grown man, he is aware of them not so much emotionally as rationally; now he finds himself comparing and contrasting illusion and reality throughout the novel. The two sides which constitute the novel's conflict are not the South, the plain, versus North, the uplands, but the destructive, dislocative, inhuman versus the constructive, collocative, human. This makes for an internally more differentiated division into sides. Everything is reflected in it, not only history and geography, but also what binds history and geography: internally (individual psychology) and externally (politics). This combination constitutes the essential subject-matter of the novel.

Total reality forms epic reality and the novel's point of departure, its principle. Thus *Lesné divadlo* is to a great extent the confession of a generation and a polemic directed at both predecessors and contemporaries who had not had a constructive approach to the past or the present, particularly to the political aspect of the past and the present; thus they had been incapable of exploiting the past and the present for the future. *Lesné divadlo* is, then, not only an aesthetic, but also an ideological and conceptual, polemic concerning past destructiveness from the point of view of the potential constructiveness of today's world. Art is not here only to analyse and destroy, but also, perhaps most of all, to construct, to rehumanise a world which is so frequently dehumanised.

I conclude this chapter with the quotation I took as my starting point. In his 1925 essay, 'My a oni' (Us and them), Karel Čapek wrote the following words, which Ladislav Ballek carefully chose as the motto to one section of his *Lesné divadlo*: 'a man does not live in a land but in his village or region. All local patriotism enhances the value of day-to-day life; all regional specificness enlivens it. Only if, however, regionalism means fullness of life and state means greatness; one loves one's native region, but one serves one's state. A Scot is a Scot for himself and for the Englishman; for the world he is a Briton. It is no misfortune that the Slovaks bear a lively grudge against us Czechs. That inspires and enriches life. But it would be a misfortune if the frontiers of their self-awareness were the Little Carpathians. The Slovaks' frontiers are by Cheb and Sluknov. Ireland is an island. Scotland is mountains. Slovakia is mountains. People do not lock themselves up in mountains; they come down from them. Follow that example, you Slovak highlanders.'[6]

It appears that, in contrast to their predecessors, Slovak fiction writers of the 1970s and 1980s, have come down from the mountains. Perhaps that is why they have had a greater understanding of the recent past and, particularly, of today. That is no small thing – certainly for the novel, but possibly also for politics.

NOTES

1. Karel Čapek, 'My a oni', *Lidové noviny*, 33 (1925), 539, p. 2.
2. Peter Zajac, 'Koncepcia Ballekových Agátov', *Slovenská literatúra* xxix (1982), 6, p. 501.
3. Michail M. Bachtin, *Román jako dialog*, translated into Czech by Daniela Hodrová (Prague: 1980), p. 140.
4. Ján Števček, 'Intelektuálny román', *Slovenská literatúra* xxxiv, (1987), 2, p. 133.
5. Ibid.
6. Čapek, 'My a oni', p. 2.

15 The Humanist Concern of Jozef Puškáš
Yuri Bogdanov

In the complex body of contemporary Slovak prose the works of Jozef Puškáš have won themselves a unique position for both their aesthetic and their extra-aesthetic significance. The period of Puškáš's growth to creative maturity coincided with the general 'face-lift' undertaken by Ballek, Habaj, Jaroš, Šikula and others. Set against the grand epic canvases which constitute the major achievement of Slovak prose in the 1970s and 1980s, and a literature of growing national historical self-awareness, the Puškáš line looks modest, yet, it is no less productive.

Puškáš published his first collection of short stories under the arresting title *Hra na život a na smrť* (Playing at life and death, 1972), just as the general fascination with 'model prose' was beginning to fledge, and in it he managed, with a success rare in a beginner, to demonstrate his command of both of the specific features of that sub-genre and of literary technique generally. With all the enthusiasm of youth the author launched unwaveringly into an explanation of the global problems of being: the fate of civilisation in a world menaced by nuclear catastrophe, the mysteries of man's psyche, reason, and the absurdity of death. The author's then modest experience of life was fully compensated for by an inventive imagination and a skilled use of literary echoes.

It has to be said that the critics of the time, a not particularly fruitful period, were not spoilt for choice by having a large number of works of quality to consider, and they generally looked in favour upon the ambitious young writer. Stanislav Šmatlák complains about his obvious inclination towards 'rationalist contrivedness' with a whiff of 'tedious' model prose, but he did not deny that the literary trio had 'considerable reserves of creativity'.[1] Dušan Slobodník, appreciating Puškáš's extraordinary, though, as he thought, occasionally 'over-gloomy' imagination, was convinced that Slovak literature had acquired a writer whose subsequent works could be eagerly awaited. 'They will probably be more personal and individual than *Hra na život a na smrť*, but, mainly, more firmly rooted in reality'.[2]

The critics must be given their due for accurately recognising in these first attempts of the young author the promise of things to come. Rereading the book today, we see clearly not only what the author owes to those from whom he learned his craft, but also the germ of the subjects that develop later, eventually to dominate the author's work. Let us recall, for example, the story 'The Honest Fish'. It has the clearly defined contours of ordinary, everyday existence, in which thoroughly real and right-thinking characters act with stereotypical purpose until this measured, well-balanced life is rudely interrupted by an event which exposes and questions the automatism of human behaviour.

The hero of the story, Martin Sopko, honestly believed in the power of truth and was constantly 'seeking it in himself and others'. A conscientious statistician, he drove himself to exhaustion, because for him fatigue was the yardstick of a duty honourably fulfilled. In short, as the author tells us with a grin, Sopko was an idealist. Then suddenly, over next to nothing, a total misunderstanding, the hero's entire life collapsed. Thanks to a friend, he has acquired a passion for fishing, and once, having caught his longed-for chub, he became so excited that he lost the fish when it was already half in the landing net. No one can insure himself against that sort of mishap. The next thing proved worse: when the unhappy Sopko began to tell his wife about his mishap, he suddenly felt she did not believe him; that is, just to please him, she pretended she believed, although in fact she was sure that, as in the past, he had caught nothing. There remained the hope that his friend – eye-witness to the triumph, and to the defeat – would testify to the truth of his story. Unfortunately, however, unlike the idealist Sopko, Barnabáš was an out-and-out pragmatist. Having made up his mind that it was better for Sopko to stand before his family as proud but unlucky, than as clumsy and stupid, he feigned amazement at this friend's imagination and modestly confessed that neither had had so much as a bite all day. A lie looked more dignified than the truth and Barnabáš lied without blinking. What mattered to him was not reality, but the appearance of reality; important was not what had actually happened, but how it was interpreted. 'Obtaining the maximum at minimal expense' was the principle to which Barnabáš had grown accustomed. But for Sopko that logic was unacceptable. The peaceable, meek, acquiescent man revolted . . .

Through the wrappings of an uncontrived, almost anecdotal tale of everyday life we see the contours of the genuine conflict which from now on is to excite the writer's attention more and more. Sopko, the idealising seeker after truth, will become the prototype of many Puškáš characters right down to the eccentric insouciant teacher Rotarides of *Štvrtý rozmer*; while Barnabáš, as if broken down in the interests of painstaking research into his component parts, will, in various hypostases, assert his 'legal right' to his own niche, and will, with increasing guile, manipulate truth to his own best advantage, for the sake of peace and quiet and general well-being.

The principle of paradox upon which the story is founded is gradually developed in the collection that followed, *Utešené sklamania* (Delightful disappointments, 1977). Unlike the unsettled thematic and stylistic manner of the first book, the second concentrates on a precise set of problems and affords a clear picture of the young writer's creative *persona*. Overcoming an inclination for abstract universals, Puškáš here strives in every story to provide the action with a motivation rooted firmly in reality. At the same time he does not renounce the satirical grotesque, which assists in tearing away from within the routine veil of day-to-day life and encourages people to think about the bitter consequences that come upon us all if we lack mutual understanding or compassion for another's pain or misfortune. *Utešené sklamania* has running through it a thread of concern for the spiritual health of modern communal existence. 'When all's said and done, we are all bound to another', is the phrase in one of the stories; this principle of interrelatedness constitutes the very foundation of society. Reality lies in the perfection of the quality of relations and in the individual non-stereotyped approaches of one's fellow human beings.

Puškáš is a long way from simply dividing his heroes into positive and negative; man is complex and more often than 'good' and 'evil' what is in conflict is the 'fortunate' and the 'unfortunate' ('Stopa neúspechu' – A trail of failure), spiritual deafness and responsiveness ('Bezbolestnosť črepín' – The painlessness of fragments), unacknowledged egoism and dying love ('Interpretácia nevery' – An interpretation of infidelity) and so forth. Each time it is as if the writer were personifying the regular opposition of ideas, but the paradoxical quality of the dénouement is tailored to activate the reader's thought processes and to highlight the link between a given episode and an actual social problem. These stories are often constructed as extended metaphors; they come close to allegory; Puškáš does not, however, indulge in any didacticism or moralising. On the contrary, the author offers as a rule only the most general pointers by which the reader can, by his own endeavour, think through to the second, deeper layer of the work. Puškáš eschews spelling everything out in direct, unambiguous terms and consciously leaves room for the independent interpretation of his often mysterious stories.

The narrative of Rudolf H., for example, may be taken as an amusing joke. But the kind of bitter aftertaste left in one after reading it signals the presence in the story of a sub-text which amounts to more than just a jolly parody of the attributes of a tale of magic, of folk clichés. The author's irony is directed at all forms of artificial 'life on paper', in which everything is recorded down to the last detail, moving to patterns stipulated in advance and where all man has left is the dull role of an involuntary performer of acts prescribed from above.

By the very title of the volume, *Utešené sklamania*, Puškáš is holding out the key to a broad, polysemic interpretation of his stories. In almost every one we witness a character's self-exposure. Something unseemly which hitherto the hero had kept from himself, taking consolation in a sense of his superiority over others, suddenly, as a result of an unexpected turn of events, becomes obvious to him and to those about him. This moment of realisation is simultaneously the moment of the hero's disillusion with himself. In the author's mind it may become the first jolt towards inner self-improvement, which is what also enables the disillusion or disappointment consequently to become 'delightful'.

The crisis of an ethical lynching constitutes the main plot of *Priznanie* (The confession, 1979). As if dissatisfied by a merely partial probing of the problem, Puškáš attempts to investigate it in full psychological depth. The story analyses the very routine process of man's submersion in a slough of ethical micro-concessions, micro-retreats from the everyday demands he puts upon himself. It is typical of Puškáš that the story should be written in the *Ich-Form*. In fact, it is a long monologue by Lukáš Gregor, his epistolary confession to his father. The artificiality of the method is balanced by the scope it offers to the hero for frank and ever more ruthless self-analysis. He had not expected to turn up in a hospital bed, thereby dropping out of the chain of everyday routine, and so now he is trying to make sense of his feeling with those about him. Suddenly he has revealed to him the undercurrent beneath many of his own actions – unconscious egocentricity, the inertia of indifference and an instinctive sense of personal advantage, which had long before spawned the habit of taking more than he gave.

In this story Puškáš is testing not some sort of exclusive personality for its real humanity, but one which is ordinary, in some respects even very ordinary. It would be wrong to see in the journalist Gregor either an idler, or one who fritters his life away in the pursuit of pleasure. On the contrary, he has the solid reputation of a conscientious worker who, while unlikely ever to set the Danube on fire, would also never descend to open sloppiness. Nor could we include him in the category of the acquisitive; he has the bachelor's limited demands on life. Yet it is by this example of averagely happy human 'material' that Puškáš seeks to demonstrate the most widespread form of petty-bourgeois consumer psychology. Like the natural scientist, he subjects to meticulous inspection the germ of philistinism, which is strikingly adaptable to the defensive vaccines invented by society. There is no absolute immunity to the corrosion of philistinism in so far as it is, as Puškáš suggested in an interview with the weekly *Nové slovo*:

> sometimes even cultured, not to say appealing, and in this attractive guise it is, I daresay, familiar of any of us . . . How then is it to be recognised; how can we be sure of making the proper diagnosis? I do not think it is always easy; one needs a certain measure of ruthlessness – we all have to try to destroy the bourgeois in ourselves; in our own lives it is easier to determine how much is our essential, original self and what has the value of just tawdry imitation assumed for utilitarian, practical purposes to present man from his flawed side, for the sake of momentary success and appearances. Philistinism is not to my liking.[3]

The meticulous socio-ethical analysis undertaken by Puskáš in *Priznanie* prepared the ground in many respects for his brief novel, *Štvrtý rozmer*. This work brings together the two dominant features which have hitherto figured alternatively on the surface of his writings: the unforgiving severity of moral judgements, and a suppressed dream of ideal, harmonious relationships between people. The living embodiment of this synthesis is the work's hero, a young man with the fairly uncommon surname, Rotarides. In Slovakia, however, the hero has a famous namesake in Ján Rotarides (1822–1910), who also happened to be a schoolmaster. In March 1848, along with the poet-revolutionary, Janko Kráľ, he stirred the peasants in the villages of southern Slovakia to revolt against the landowners under the by then traditional slogan, Liberty, Equality, Fraternity. This historical fact is familiar to every Slovak schoolchild and it goes without saying that

Puškáš use of the name is more than coincidence; his hero, by education a physicist and mathematician, and in one sense a romantic, tries to inspire his pupils to aspire to 'other worlds' which have more dimensions than the world to which 'we have grown accustomed'. Once they have overcome the inertia of the stereotype, once they have whipped up their imagination, people will receive the key to such mysteries as cannot be solved by remaining confined by the usual three dimensions.

In *Štvrtý rozmer* the theoretical problems of the general theory of relativity are tied up with the everyday problems of modern man. What is understood here by the 'fourth dimension' is the general cultivation of the human spirit, humanist values of peaceful civilisation and, last but not least, the continuity of high moral ideals passed on from one generation to the next. Organic adhesion to these, creative evolution in new conditions, alone can furnish genuine guarantees that the contemporary existence of man will be fully imbued with meaning.

When we speak here of the most general sense of this novel, we are interpreting the sub-text, the deeper intention of the work, as much as the text itself. On the surface it concerns the typical vicissitudes which beset a pleasant young family, living cramped in a bed-sit on the eastern outskirts of Bratislava. It concerns the countless little pains and pleasures which Vilo, the smallest member of the family, brings his parents, the hopes and disappointments that accompany their frequent attempts at exchanging their flat; in short, it is about that aspect of life which we usually call private, intimate – or simply living *tout court*.

The central characters are far from demonstrating any kind of lofty disdain for their lack of material comforts; at particularly bad moments something amounting almost to class hatred rises in the heart of the delicate, long-suffering Tonka, a hatred directed at the owners of the grand houses and flats that can be seen from their windows. And here is the heart of the matter: no matter how urgent these problems, which continually complicate life for Rotarides and his wife and bring a note of dissonance into their personal relations, they cannot expel the most important thing from their lives, namely the spirit of inner mutual understanding, of responsiveness to another's suffering, of sensitivity to the inclinations and interests of others. The private lives of this family are imbued with a current of high humanitarian culture which seems to contribute directly to the formation of moral evaluations of even the most trifling and transitory events. Not for nothing do both Rotarides and his wife resort, in their interior monologues, to literary associations. Puškáš literally tries for size on his hero, now the smock of Rodion Raskolnikov, now the armour of the noble knight of La Mancha. Even shades of Thomas Mann, or Anatole France, surface in an entirely natural way on the pages of Puškáš's work.

Puškáš's last work *Záhrada* (*v piatom období roka*), has been appraised in detail and, which is the main thing, very recently by both Slovak (Ján Sulík and Viliam Marčok) and Czech (Josef Hrabák and M. Mikulášek) critics as a typical Puškášian tale with a thoughtful young hero at its centre, who, for a time, swims with the tide, until, after awakening from a spiritual sleep, he begins consciously to rebuild himself. It is one of the innumerable variations of the *Bildungsroman*, with such constant features of that sub-genre as the stream of self-critical consciousness, 'the dialectics of the soul', and so forth, bearing in this instance the clear hallmark of Puškáš's own poetics – a tendency towards irony, humour, paradox and the grotesque.

At the same time the book signals a new quality in the writer. Not only does he place before us, with considerably greater accuracy, and in greater breadth and more roundedly, a picture of contemporary reality (Bratislava and the provincial fringes, various social strata and groups), but he also attempts to switch from a general diagnosis of the state of social consciousness to a cure for it. It may be only partial, relative, but for all that it is no less concrete.

The tangible embodiment of the 'fourth', spiritual, dimension in this book is the orchard, planted out on the edge of a small provincial town half a century previously and attached to a minor agricultural college. With time the town has grown, and its inhabitants, now living in material security, dream of having houses of their own; they begin to insist that the orchard be cut down and the land released as building plots. Somewhere 'high up' a decision has already been taken which accommodates the legitimate interests of the inhabitants who are seeking merely to satisfy their growing expectations. Only one person, the old horticulturalist father of the novel's hero, carries on a desperate struggle to protect the orchard. To the very end, until his fatal heart attack, this insane, or as others see him, eccentric, old man stubbornly goes against the tide, yielding to neither written persuasion nor threats.

Initially, in Bratislava, young Burius hears only faint echoes of this struggle, but gradually he begins to think more deeply about it, tries to comprehend the inner logic of his rather taciturn father. Burius himself had to mature inwardly before he could understand the simple truth: his father loved his work and saw it as his main purpose in life. He had an instinct for the bond between the living and life. In addition to the straightforward benefit extracted by man from the substance of Nature, Nature herself had always existed for him as the main, even the only, source of life, not replaceable by any of the surrogates offered by civilisation. 'We have to strive for the situation', he wrote in a letter to the press, 'where every man can look at nature through the eyes of an artist and rejoice at all that is beautiful. Why do we reject – so often and so casually – everything that can protect us, make us into better people and inspire us?'

Záhrada (*v piatom období roka*) is a somewhat unorthodox title, yet one which is entirely in the Puškáš spirit. The 'fifth season' may be interpreted as meaning the time that is approaching us from the future, the time which is still allowed to man, society, civilisation. It would, however, be slightly inaccurate to view the work solely in the context of the current fashion for 'ecological prose' or even of the ecology movement itself. Problems of ecology in Puškáš are just a part of the universal problem of man's moral being, the moral responsibility of the individual to his own conscience, to the past and to the future. Thus in this novel the line taken by Puškáš intersects with another, also widely represented by Slovak literature, namely the prose of national historical self-cognition, and *eo ipso* it confirms the axiom concerning a simple, higher Nature common to all 'humanist' literature. To use Števček's definition, 'national identification' is inseparable, at the present stage of the evolution of society and literature, from the [self] identification of the individual.'[4]

This chapter is not the place to go in detail into the work of those Slovak writers who, in their individual ways, are today leading the search, in the same direction as Puškáš. They include Rudolf Sloboda, Dušan Mitana, Andrej Ferko and Ivan Hudec. However many the differences between them, they are united by a general concern for the present state of the moral foundations of everyday life.

The attention literature pays to the simple norms of human morality is undoubtedly a part of a tradition going back to Rousseau and Goethe, Dostoyevsky and Tolstoy. It also owes to that tradition the basic form in which modern writers clothe their ideas on the unprecedented scope of man's historic responsibility in the face of the ambivalent image of the liberated jinn constituted by the scientific and technological revolution, and in the face of the technocratic mentality that is so dangerously gathering force. This takes the form of the personal confession, the frank address to one's contemporaries, unencumbered by any details of theme. This appeal to common sense is often dictated, it is true, by intolerable moral pain, and by the same *cri de coeur* which has been given us such optimistically angry works in Soviet literature as Rasputin's *Fire*, Aitmatov's *The Block* or Astafiev's *The Doleful Detective*. The anguish and firm faith in man's being predestined for higher things that we find in Jozef Puškáš are drawn from the same pure spring of new 'humanist' thought.

NOTES

1. Stanislav Šmaták: 'Marginálie k mladej próze', *Tvorba* (1972), 31, p. 6.
2. Dušan Slobodník: 'Hľadanie mladej slovenskej prózy', *Pravda*, 25 August 1972.
3. *Nové slovo*, 1 May 1981.
4. Ján Števček: 'Románové koncepcie a duch súčasnosti', *Pravda*, 9 September 1987.

Translated from the Russian by David Short.

16 Magic Realism in the Prose of Jozef Puškáš

James D. Naughton

A characteristic combination of quasi-documentary realism with elements of strange fictional expressivity is apparent in Puškáš's novels and short stories. In the novel *Štvrtý rozmer* the 'fourth dimension' of the title already indicates the presence of 'something else'. The term has many layers of significance: it is the time-space theme of the physics lectures given by the central character Rotarides; it is the extra space the family desires, the extra something life requires over and above the satisfaction of material needs; it is the author standing outside his own book, the dimension of the author-creator (or indeed the reader-decoder), and the novel ends with the latter aspect in the foreground. The narrative displays odd symmetries, unlikely chances, and superimpositions of different themes offering various levels of interpretation. For example, the wife states (in a text written by herself) that she once received the same bank-note twice:

> In payment I received a marked hundred-crown note, someone had drawn a tiny little heart on it with a ballpoint pen, I almost thought it was the accounts clerk Vereš declaring his love for me in this way. . . . I paid with the note for something in a shop, but shortly afterwards the same marked banknote came back to me, when a certain man paid me my fee for copy-typing! It's true I didn't jot down the number of the bank-note, but I don't believe anyone would amuse himself by drawing hearts on every hundred-crown note that came his way. I decided that money was always the same, however hard you try, each time you find only what you just threw out. You throw away someting in front of you and immediately you pick it up, throw it away again and pick it up – like in a madhouse. Things have no meaning in themselves, until you perceive them for something else. . . . (p. 164).

The passage is open to a number of interpretations. One may take it as a literal document of an actual experience, or it may be treated as an allegory, about human reciprocity and interdependence, or the

181

need to give the world about us a human meaning, without which we are caught up in a pointless, absurd circularity. A similar anecdote is told in the short story 'Čas noci, priestor dňa' (Time of night, space of day) in Puškáš's more recent collection, *Sny, deti, milenky*: a character alleges he has thrown away a stone once and picked up the same one on the Adriatic: 'Everywhere is one place [. . .] Once I was kicking a pebble in front of me, then I lost it. I found it on an island in the Adriatic. At least, I think it was the same one . . .' (p. 13). In the novel the anecdote is part of a text within the text; in the short story it turns out to be a part of a dream.

On a broader narrative scale the superimposition of quasi-fact and fiction is exhibited by a nodal point in the plot where the husband, Rotarides, bites the bare shoulder of the sexy mother of one of his son's little friends in a supermarket where she has just picked up the last bag of oranges. It is as though he bites her smooth round golden-downy shoulder instead of a fruit, and the juice gushes out in vividly blood-red droplets:

> Nagajová turned over the pack; these last oranges were a bit small and past their best; she was just about to put them back, but then she tossed them into her basket after all. At that moment Rotarides, driven by an impulse stronger than any dampening inhibition, still bending forward, now ridiculous, over the spot where only a couple of crumbs were left, with angry, passionate force, gnawed into the shoulder, which flashed before him smooth and round, covered with golden hairs.
>
> Along with the exclamation of surprise and pain there poured over his teeth a pleasing warmth; the salty burning stream trickled down his lower lip onto his chin, and thence onto the ground, and before he looked up, he saw on the dirty marble tiles the spattered drops of blood gleaming with the beauty of real precious stones (p. 144).

The woman's daughter has been biting Rotarides's son persistently at nursery school. It subsequently transpires that she lives opposite their flat, in one of the luxury villas that block their view of the forest. He visits her to apologise and is almost seduced by her, but a newspaper report of the finding of a meteorite distracts his attention and he is saved from this surrender to his sex drive by passionate intellectual excitement. Sexual and anti-social or irrational urges meet consumerism (or consumer shortages), the housing problem, alienation from the natural environment, the dimensions of space and time, and the contrived dimensions of fictional structure, in an hallucinatory 'magic realism'.[1] Narrative credibility is maintained (the act of biting is adequately motivated), but the effect is ultimately odd and undocumentary. This results in part from the patent contrivedness of the episode within the overall narrative structure, in part from the lyrical mode of its description.

A lyrically expressive passage of the description may have simultaneous documentary validity. Puškáš may explicitly highlight this ambiguity, as in the description of the removal of a dead body from the block of flats where Rotarides lives, surrounded by uprooted old people:

> When he returned with Vilo babbling in his arms, a black car from the undertakers' was standing by the pavement. Two men in blue coats were just carrying out of the house a body rolled in a multicoloured blanket and laid out in an open coffin. They shifted their load so carelessly into the back of the vehicle that the coffin nearly overturned. He pressed Vilo more closely in his embrace [. . .] and then an unpleasant rotting smell wafted over him. In the peaceful summer afternoon, full of the jabber of children dispersing from nearby kindergartens and nursery schools, the whole event had an unreal and horrifying effect. [. . .] He called Tonka from the bathroom, but when they looked out of the window, it was as if nothing had happened outside. Along the pavement came hurrying a young woman with a string bag full of fresh vegetables. Everything is in close proximity, thought Rotarides then. The most opposed of realities. Birth and death. But it's not a poem or a metaphor. It's a housing estate . . . (pp. 25–6).

For the reader it is the other way around: it is not a housing estate; it is a fiction. Even for Rotarides the event lacks solidarity, it is ephemeral, evanescent: it is as though it had never been. The rotting smell of the corpse is swiftly gone, replaced by the woman with fresh vegetables. The odd vividness is created by contrast, small sensory touches and the ambiguity between lyrical quasi-cinematic contrivance (where scenes are made to vanish) and the quasi-documentary credibility of urban impersonality (where people are disposed of like rubbish).

Another magic element is in the introduction of an exotic object, which may be a plant or an animal, with a weird, outlandish appearance. The object is focused on and made to radiate its oddness, its otherness, and to act as a source of enigmatic mystery. A clear example in *Štvrtý rozmer* comes in an encounter with a cassowary in Bratislava Zoo:

> Behind the wire fence stood a cassowary gazing at them fixedly with its iridescent eyes. The wind ruffled its black plumage and emphasised its metallic gleam. The red excrescence on its neck hung down and shone like flame. The massive horny crest over his brow gave him the look of a creature from another planet. Rotarides froze before this exceptional beast, which was not destined perhaps for a long sojourn on this earth; it appeared stealthily and reticently, as if merely seeking its own corner in which to end its days. And yet the astonishment in the opalescent eyes seemed greater than its exceptionality; the cassowary stared without a single blink of its waxen lid at this offspring of the human race, motionlessly waiting to see if a gust of wind or some other mysterious bolt from the blue might pluck the figures from the spot, plunge them into darkness [. . .] – Kikili, – said Vilo. And at once, as though it were a magic word, the sun peeped out from behind the clouds and all the tension evaporated (p. 36).

The cassowary not only is made to represent the fragility of the threatened natural world, but also acquires a fantasy status where it anticipates figuratively the prospect of human annihilation. Fictional magic again comes into play when the boy addresses the cassowary with the children's quasi-magic spellbreaking word 'Kikili'.

The short stories in Puškáš's collection *Utešené sklamania* show a good deal of self-conscious and playful manipulation of devices to achieve strange effects. In the short story 'Neskorá tužba' ('Late desire') a scriptwriter has been drinking and gives a lift in his car to a man carrying a lamb or kid on his shoulders (the driver cannot decide which). The lamb, as it apparently is, with all its traditional literary, liturgical and other associations, becomes the object of his desire. He offers to buy it from the man, but the man will not sell and gets out of the car, at which point the story ends. The description of the animal's gaze after getting into the car demonstrates its functional kinship with the cassowary. The vivid smell of the animal may be related to the smell of the rotting corpse of the novel in its expressive and highlighting role:

> There blew, there wafted a warm, bitterish animal smell, and out of the driver's mirror there gazed a round changeable eye, with glimpsed reflections of the countryside hurtling by, but its expres-

sion remained firm and motionless; it was full of peace, inattention
and sadness. The eye had once seen what it had seen, and still saw
it now, and no one could learn what it had seen hitherto, nor what
this moment meant for it, this encounter with a human gaze . . .
Like every impenetrable phenomenon, this, too, was a source of
disturbance and attraction (pp. 12–13).

This lamb symbolises an inner peace, reconciliation or restitution,
however inchoate or illusory. It is a projection of the driver's
emotional needs, an object of obscure fixation and deranged desire:
'And yet something was lacking. A memory, a relationship, a secret?'
(p. 13) 'He wants [. . .] to convince himself constantly over and again
of the inexplicable peace and sadness of those eyes' (p. 15).

Another story from this collection 'Iba sny' (Only dreams) describes
six travellers in a train compartment, five of whom relate various
dreams they have had. The sixth, an elderly, grey-haired man, is
depicted sound asleep by the window. The man sitting opposite
claims that this man is dreaming of the other five, who would not
exist if it were not for his dream. The passengers leave except for
the two by the window. The apparently sound-asleep elderly man
has been declared dead by one of the women. When the guard arrives
he finds the compartment empty and undisturbed. The last words of
the man sitting opposite the allegedly dead person are: 'They have
evaporated and gone. Did I not say they were only dreamed? [. . .]
Everything has cracks. Both dream and reality [. . .]' (p. 56). The
reader is left to decide whether he wishes to devise a consistent
interpretation of 'what is really going on' or content himself by
decoding the story as a lyrical portrayal of evanescent dream-like
encounters on long train journeys, where one is unsure at what point
one is awake and at what point one is asleep. Fictional fantasy
and subversion of the reader's conventional willingness to suspend
disbelief are held in an ambiguous balance with pervasive elements
of psychological plausibility.

Another story from the collection involving narrative ambiguity, a
vividness of credible events combined with far-reaching uncertainty,
is *'Bezbolestnosť črepín'*. The bogus death of an ex-student turns out
to be possibly real, he may have died attempting while drunk to
repeat his trick of lying on a bed of sharp fragments of broken glass,
or perhaps one of his girlfriends had invented this story to trump the
original fraud. The first-person narrator is left struggling to find his
way in a labyrinth of fraudulent, mutually deceptive or enigmatic

relationships, in a reality of ambiguity and uncertainty, instability and lack of trust.

> Kamila took a nervous sip and kept her eyes fixed on me. I looked at her, I distended the muscles around my mouth into a smile. No, no one in the world is going to fool me! Besides, is it so important how things really are? Even if she didn't think it all up – does it actually matter? Everything is shattered anyway. Smashed.
>
> To this day I'm still not clear in my mind. And every day I'm less and less interested. But occasionally something makes me pinch my cheek or hand. I'm afraid that one day I won't feel anything at all, and everything will turn into a dream (p. 96).

The fragments of shattered glass are like a reality shattered into illusions, to which one may become so inured that one ceases to notice or care. This story fuses elements of the psychological, the epistemological and the arbitrarily fictional, but the documentary level is somewhat more firmly seated than in the preceding stories I have discussed.

In the later collection *Sny, deti, milenky* the documentary or quasi-documentary aspect seems in general to be gaining ground. The fictional structure largely relaxes into the less mystificatory role of providing a neat and often humourous plot line with little surprises and ironies rather than unsettling enigmas.

Puškáš's most recent novel is *Záhrada* (*v piatom období roka*). Its subtitle carries similar connotations to the 'fourth dimension' of the earlier novel, and may be taken in part as a playful reference to this.[2] It is a semi-autobiographical ecological *Bildungsroman* dealing with birth, marriage and death, family relations (especially father and son), work and personal fulfilment, the disorientating encroachment of the urban environment upon the traditional rural patterns of life and settlement. The son, Peter Burius, is the narrator throughout, with only a few texts of letters intruding upon his single point of view. The whole book is very much a blending of his quasi-reminiscences with a discursive tour of his inner self, the sensory and emotional texture of his recreating memory, his feelings of moral and social responsibility, his personal and social anxieties, and so on. The garden of the title is the garden of the horticultural school and family home, of childhood, of stability, of the settled rural past, of pastoral and lyric beauty, and its expressive and symbolic qualities are inseparably merged with its documentary ones. The documentary, at times message-laden, aspect of the book is transmitted through an expressive fictional evocation of a self-analysing, meditative mind. The past time of the novel is treated as a body of memory able to re-engender itself in present subjective experience, and assessed by a mind capable of critical distance. This conception of fictional recreation is made explicit, as well as being part and parcel of the whole structure of the book:

> Now I know that time which has passed through us is not lost; it sinks into the thick waters of the memory like a scroll of papyrus into the sand of the dunes and patiently waits for a favourable wind to uncover it, for an expert initiate to attempt its unwinding. At moments like this the whole surmised scroll straightens out and the events recorded on its surface shine with a fresh light, as if someone had run a miraculous life-restoring brush over their contours. Look, what relapses are these: that which gave no pain, hurts again, that which gave no pleasure, again begins to delight! (pp. 16–17)

There is a small irony here: the memory and past time are fictional, or at least fictionally transformed. The magic brush is that of the author; or perhaps one should say it is the text itself as it acts on the reader. In this sense fictional realism is always magic realism.

One notes the interpenetration of figurative landscape and discursive thought. Emotional and intellectual elements may be given sensory shape, and *vice versa*. No clear segregation is necessary. The description of a flood is a reminiscence, a vividly created event, an hallucinatory embodiment of Peter Burius's hospital delirium, a manifestation of enigmatic elemental forces, with the opposed responses of father and son, the father black and resistant, willing the restoration of stability, the son swept along in spiritual empathy:

> Turning on the hospital bed in great concentric circles [. . .] before my eyes the muddy water of the Laborec River again became an embodied force, wreaths of ropes, cables and foaming chains intertwined and tore in it, heaps of clay and sand rolled over, stones rose up with the lightness of birds' feathers; like the blackened fingers of drowned men, dry branches protruded, snagged on the pillars of the bridge or submerged willows [. . .] aspens, willows, poplars in majestic and submissive sadness relinquished their posts, descended into slumber in the splashing of the waves and floated off towards unknown distance and future time, meeting it silent, white and sinless. [. . .] Underground roamed

strange fish, getting even into the wells, whence they were fished up smoky white, blinded and almost stifled with terror, from the mysterious entrails of the earth. [. . .] And there were only two perceptions of this drama with its fatal protagonist [. . .]: the worried, gloomy, immaculately obstinate view of my father, and my perception, enraptured by its elemental beauty. [. . .] The world was flat once more, and bland as a pancake. The stagnancy, peace and tedium reigned, out of which only the worst was ever born (pp. 114–6).

Magic coincidences and enigmatic words appear again. The narrator's wife, Denisa, begins to fear the dark (her tiny premature baby is in intensive care); she declares that sight is the most vital of the senses, and the narrator reads a book beside her to help her fall asleep. The book tells him of a sixteenth-century scholar who would rather lose his sight than his hearing or his powers of speech (p. 250). In the first part of the novel a gipsy woman makes an enigmatic utterance in Romany: ' – Narodzinla pes tuke! Čavoro tuke . . . sar dubos!' (p. 89). Is it an ill prophecy? We find out only at the end of the book. Peter's sister predicts shortly after this encounter with the gipsy that she and her brother will soon be seeing each other again, quite contrary to Peter's own expectations. They do, when Peter suddenly falls ill and is sent to hospital (p. 103). Another enigmatic utterance is the cry ' – Aťa! Aťááá!' of the sick little girl who shares Peter's hospital ward (p. 126). She is from the remote village of Tarkov, where the sister works as a school teacher. In the final pages of the novel Peter visits Tarkov and discovers the meaning behind this *cri de coeur*.

There are also several exotic or magic objects in this novel. The most obvious is the ginkgo tree, which appears three times as an enigmatic landmark in Peter's passage through life. The first occasion is on a childhood visit to a large garden with exotic plants:

another journey of discovery, a visit to the former Count's garden in Kertéš, with its abundant unfamiliar flowers, bushes and one marvellous tree, which later so to speak accompanied me on my life; I saw it again at two important points; and the third tree was enormously far away from the first two, it was alone, and maybe by this mutual distancing they signalled something . . . The tree was called the ginkgo, but what all those flowers were called, I really don't know [. . .] In the middle of the garden there was a small lake with lilies and a pair of mud turtles; in a little pool, out

of which the day before they had drained the stagnant water, a
hedgehog was stuck, but the highpoint of the whole visit was a
greenhouse, full of a delicate chocolate scent and motionless
geysers of glorious orchids sticking out their glowing forked tongues
at the visitors. And the ex-gardener with the practised smile of a
seducer reached for one of the flowery geysers, plucked it like a
bud on some village meadow and gave it to mother, who flushed
to the roots of her hair, more horrified than flattered (p. 15).

The sacred tree's sexual connotations are underlined by the ensuing
erotic description of orchids and the presentation of one of these to
Peter's mother.[3] At its second appearance the ginkgo presides over
an adolescent erotic encounter and we learn of its botanic classification
from a school teacher. 'Ginkgo biloba! The rarest tree in our park, a
relic of the Tertiary, when all its related species died out. The
ginkgo, gentlemen, is one of the gymnosperms . . .' (p. 138). A
gymnospermous tree is one whose naked seeds are not enclosed in
an ovary; the Slovak adjective is 'nahosemenný' literally 'naked-
seeded'. Its third appearance marks the key point of the narrator's
acquaintance with his future wife (p. 171), who later, we remember,
gives birth to a premature baby. She has a talisman, from Bombay,
a little red sphere containing forty tiny ivory elephants, said to lose
its charm if ever opened (p. 172). They open it. One remembers that
the word 'talisman' was also used of the lamb in the short story 'Late
Desire': the lamb had been a football team's mascot.

A curious parallel occurs in *Záhrada* between the pair of turtles
(*korytnačky*) mentioned at the time of the ginkgo's first appearance
and the flat turtle-like features of the nurse who looks after Burius
in hospital: 'Her chin, nose and forehead are flat, turtle-like'
(*korytnačie*) (p. 113). And one wonders whether it is too far-fetched
to make a further association with the *korytar* or trough-maker who
puts in a later appearance (p. 264) at Bratislava market.

Closely related to the ginkgo is the fig-tree planted by the father
which grows in the school garden: '. . . like an echo of distant longing
there also appeared in the school garden, beside the cages of the
hotbeds, a makeshift glasshouse – without orchids – and scarcely 10
to 15 metres from the window on the other side of which I am presently
sleeping, a heat-loving fig-tree is to this day still struggling with the
inclemency of Nature . . .' (p. 16). It appears as a symbol of obstinate
indestructibility, fighting against all odds. Its setting and description
are graphically concrete and figuratively expressive:

Beyond the road, whose gravelly surface had more than once grazed my knees, the garden began, from the window you could see the whole of its southern part; it began with a little fence of crossed laths and a small hummock of compressed humus covering the stump of the fig-tree, which, amazingly, every spring without fail, even after the harshest frosts, again turned green; it was enough for me to see this hummock to know that it was there, that one could count on its revival (pp. 23–4).

It reappears at the time of the father's funeral, struggling up from its tumulus, a faithful eternal hydra: the word used here, 'nezmar', in Slovak signifies indestructibility. Though the garden has partly been destroyed it still looks better than on Peter's last visit in winter: 'My eyes unconsciously slid to the freshly painted lath fence, which stood unbendingly in its place: from the small hummock of humus, from the grave delineated beyond it, with promising thickness and bushiness our faithful hydra – the fig-tree – struggled up' (p. 308).

The word or concept 'magic' is used with some frequency in the novel: it describes an encounter with a girl on a train (compare the journey in the short story 'Only Dreams'): 'one whole night I spent deliriously kissing some girl . . . I paid no attention to stations, the dark, lights, distances – nothing but waves of excitation and a magic tremor without beginning or end' (p. 125). The city's alien time mode draws one with a magic force to its echoes of the remembered floods, where truck drivers become quasi-transcendent beings:

Yes – another time, that was the magic thing that drew me and that I looked for, this longing accompanied me to the banks of the Danube, where I discovered in the foamy current the echo of the old floods. Across the bridge thundering trucks hurtled, and the men behind the wheel, enthroned high above the earth, had the proud and inaccessible gazes of Ahasueruses, wanderers transversing the miserable times of ordinary mortals . . . (p. 148).

The father is seen drawing a valedictory and summatory magic circle in his imagined death scene: 'I see him standing up, describing a magic circle and sitting down again beneath the pear-tree, settled and calm, for now he has taken leave of everything' (p. 307). The treatment of Peter's wife to ward off premature delivery of her child is described as an effort to thwart the magic force of an indifferent and amoral natural order:

Five long days, again and again they pumped Denisa's benumbed body with syringes full of plegomazin; obstinately they erected an artificial barrier against the force of attraction, that magic force which was plucking at the feeble tendrils of the fruit of the mother's womb and driving it with the quiet current of the moon's tide into the light of day, just as the force of the moon's attraction drives the sea against the shore and calm havens (p. 188).

Gravity is associated with gravidity, another semi-exotic kind of wordplay: 'Gravity – that sounds almost like gravidity, I thought to myself' (p. 187).

My final example is the description of the wife extracting milk from her breasts to take to the hospital. Optically it presents a more than double image (an oscillating magic reality). The narrator finds angles from which he can imagine she is feeding an actual baby, then superimposes images of home, of painting and traditional iconography. An ironic tension develops between these and the actual situation. The illusions become more real (more vividly present) than the reality:

I imagined all the angles of view from which it might seem that Denisa was breast-feeding: it could seem so far from the back, from the side, but even the front, if an obstacle were placed in the way of the eyes to cover her lap and breasts. [. . .] Again and again I imagined that we did not live on the twelfth floor, but in the old school flat as we used to – on the ground floor –, that someone was walking along the path outside and saw over the window ledge as in a picture frame the painterly stillness of the woman's silhouette expressing the maternal bond, as it has been expressed down the ages by eyes lowered slanting to the body, head bending to one bare shoulder and elongated curve of the neck, full of humility and devotion. He would see the descending line of the arch of the shoulder, the swelling upper slopes of the breasts, and this segment of the scene, this delineated detail, as though drawn by an Old Master, would be enough for him to believe in the utter concentration of the woman on her child, so that not even in a dream would he conceive of an empty embrace and a swollen breast squeezed at the pink nipple only by fingers and the funnel of the breast-pump . . . (pp. 251–2).

It is not the explicit mentions of the word 'magic', nor the contrived coincidences and fictional symmetries, nor the enigmatic objects of fixation, nor the other overtly 'strange-making' thematic elements which constitute by themselves the essence of 'magic realism' I am trying to define here. Nor am I attempting to associate Puškáš's methods in any very direct way with the specific deadpan mystification blends of the fantastic, absurd and quasi-documentary associated with Latin American 'magic realism'. Certainly it is not impossible that this literature may have exerted a detectable influence, but that is not something which the present chapter has attempted to analyse. The quality which pervades Puškáš's writing typically manifests itself in strongly optical, often quasi-cinematographic scenes which carry oscillating superimposed layers of significance, and which are both strikingly vivid (hence quasi-real) and patently illusory or contrived (unreal, fictional, magical). They depend for their legitimacy and effect on an overall pattern in which the quasi or semi-documentary and the expressively contrived cohabit, and where elements of the exotic, enigmatic or paranormal occupy a halfway-house between 'reality' and 'fantasy'. This is a *modus operandi* which I take to be a justifiable basis for the labelling of Puškáš's style as 'magic realism'.

NOTES

1. Cf. Ivan Sulík's application of the term in Milan Pisút et al., *Dejiny slovenskej literatúry* (Bratislava: 1984), p. 811: 'young writers who do not hesitate to introduce into their prose the methods of magic (fantastic) and grotesque realism with a distinctive analytic scrutiny of reality'.
2. Alexander Halvoník and Vincent Šabík give contrasting interpretations of the subtitle in a discussion on Puškáš in *Romboid*, xxi (1986), pp. 17 and 23. They see it either as signifying another spring symbolising an approaching rebirth (Halvoník), or the new dimension of mental processing embodied in the form of the novel itself (Šabík).
3. Ivan Sulík's interpretation in an article on Puškáš in *Romboid*, xx (1985), pp. 14–17, is for me somewhat off-centre and unconvincing: 'the ginkgo tree as an intermittently recurring symbol of life, home and nature, which are at one in the final context of the ideas of the novel.'

17 The Vision of Reality in Habaj's *Kolonisti*

Karel Brušák

Ivan Habaj's *Kolonisti*[1] deals with the experience of several Slovak families who came to farm in the plain known as the Rye Island, south-east of Bratislava between the Little Danube and the Danube, when this region was ceded to the newly established Czechoslovakia from Hungary after World War I. After the dismemberment of Czechoslovakia by the Munich Agreement in 1938, the Rye Island was restored to Hungary and the 'colonists' had to move to the new Slovak Republic. In 1945, when the region was restored to Czechoslovakia, they were able to come back, but only some of them did so.

The novel is in three parts. The first book covers most of the year 1938, whilst the previous history of the colony and some of its inhabitants is sketched out in retrospect, partly by the narrator but mainly in the reminiscing of individual characters. The second and third books are devoted to the period after World War II, from the return of the 'colonists' to the Rye Island in 1945, through the collectivisation of agriculture in the 1950s, up to 1965. There is a time gap of some seven years between the first and second volume and very little is revealed about the life of the characters and almost nothing about events during these years.

In the view of Slovak critics, the novel is a socio-historical prose work,[2] belonging to the large corpus of Slovak novels with 'historical tendencies', published since the 1970s.[3] After a close look at the subject matter and its technical treatment, however, one finds that the novel cannot be classified as a specific type. The historical setting is not sufficiently emphasised to give the idea of the force of destiny, and the interpretation that the main theme of the work is the conflict between the course of history and the 'ordinary man' who becomes its manipulated object[4] would seem somewhat far-fetched. Predominantly, the work is a rural chronicle in which the historical setting forms no more than an occasional backdrop, of the type which readily absorbs elements from various types of prose. Thus, on one, perhaps the supreme level, it is a regional novel, paying much attention to the forces that determine the region's identity, by making it isolated economically and culturally. As the novel develops, the regional setting becomes metaphorical and expresses more about the *personae* whose characters have been changed by the new environment. On a closely related level, it approaches a 'novel of the soil', preoccupied with the struggle against Nature and commending the farmer's way of life. These elements connected with the soil in fact constitute the mythological side of the work and evoke the first and fundamental vision, that of Time, and the permanency of Nature versus the transience of human fate. But the work also contains elements usually associated with other types of prose. With the introduction of the Hungarian minority and the gipsies living in the region, it comes close to being an ethnical novel, and as both the *milieu* and the situation of the people are the result of political changes, it has many features of a political novel.

The thematic complexity and indeterminacy have necessarily affected the mode of narration. Unlike in most works of the rural chronicle type in both Slovak and Czech literature the narrator's discourse is restricted in favour of that of the *personae* who assume his role, or, rather, to whom he lends his voice. The involvement of the *personae* is considerable. They not only report their reminiscences, feelings, reactions, attitudes to and assessment of others, but also reproduce their dialoguising with themselves, and they talk to or argue with each other in their minds. Moreover, they take over much of the narrative function which one would expect to belong to the narrator's discourse. It has been defined as internal monologue,[5] even though this term can be properly applied only to those segments in which the *persona* uses the *Ich-Form*. As is usual in this type of discourse, the first-person voice of the *persona* alternates with represented speech, which appears either as the free indirect speech or as the marked indirect speech. In the case of the free indirect speech the reproduction of a character's thoughts and feelings by the third-person narrator preserves on the whole the register of the narrator:

> Yes, he knew the reasons why he was thinking and what he was thinking. Pal'o will remain at home on his parents' farm, he will bring his wife here; he will beget children; gradually he will take over the care of the farm; he will replace him, Peter Jakubec, when he stops working and finally depart for there above the moors, to the cemetery, next to his brother Cyril (I, p. 50).

As to the marked indirect speech, the only difference is that the third-person speech is interspersed with markers, such as 'he/she thought', 'he/she imagined', and so forth:

Now we are where we did not want to be, thought Jakubec, when the gardener went away (I, p. 153).

They will not last long, he thought, looking at the does, and where did they come from? (Lájoš, III, p. 237).[6]

In neither of these types is the character given full freedom of expression and in the view of some critics the marked indirect speech is more ambiguous than the free form because the absence of markers in the free form makes it sound more like the character speaking or thinking than a narrator's report.[7] Internal monologue in the proper sense of the term is confined to the first-person form discourse of the *personae*, and in *Kolonisti* this is the most widely used device. There is a closer interrelation between language and psychology; the syntax and register cease to be entirely those of the narrator. This happens particularly in the case of two of the most important characters, Peter Jakubec and Maruša, when the internal monologue comes close to a stream of consciousness: 'here I am next to you, in this thin shift lifted up high on my hips, don't you see it, don't you feel it, I am like freshly churned butter, just ready to be taken and spread on the bread' (Maruša, I, p. 159). Apart from the two representations of the *persona*'s thoughts and feelings, there is also what Dorrit Cohn calls psycho-narration.[8] The *persona*'s thoughts are reported by the third-person narrator after they have been processed through his mind: 'Hitler's entry into Austria opened his eyes even more; he felt the disturbances in the frontier regions between Czechoslovakia and Germany as painfully as if he were their victim, so much did the terrorist actions of the Fascists exasperate him' (Kovalík, I, p. 109). The spatial and temporal perspectives of the character are preserved but the report is too impersonal to be acceptable as the character's represented discourse.

Internal monologue has been praised by some critics,[9] and has been widely used by both Czech and Slovak novelists since the 1920s. But, as stated by Butor,[10] the autonomy of the character's discourse is rather doubtful. This is acknowledged in *Kolonisti*: 'had he to express these thoughts aloud, or to put them on paper, he would hardly know how to do it' (Štefan, III, p. 15).

It has to be recognised that even those segments of the *persona*'s discourse which are expressed directly in dialogue or soliloquy, are in fact the narrator's own and ultimately the author's constructions. Nevertheless, the *persona*'s discourse and the narrator's discourse are two separate components. Their interrelation within the structure of the text is indicative of what is loosely called the point of view, ideology, or vision, encoded in the text, or, in other words, the relationship between reality and its construction in the work.

The first impression of the narrative technique in *Kolonisti* is that of a high proportion of *persona*'s discourse (both direct and reported) together with dialogue. This seems to grow from one volume to the next until it culminates in the third. This impression is confirmed statistically. Character discourse together with the dialogue account for 35 per cent of the total text in the first, 39 per cent in the second, and 45 per cent in the third volume.[11]

On examination of the character discourse we find that apart from carrying information concerning the characters, that discourse also has an important ontological function. It incorporates historical facts into the structure. Most of these are conveyed either in the *personae*'s discourses or in their dialogues, and historical facts communicated by the narrator's discourse are in the minority. When mentioning events which could lead to controversial interpretation, he becomes impersonal: '*people* do not suspect that the Jews will go to the gas chambers' (II, p. 47) [my italics]. Occasionally he distances himself from public opinion: 'people were adding [. . .] their own biased comments' (I, p. 209). Very seldom does he allow any judgement to break into his information on history: 'The *glorious* battle for Stalingrad ended' (II, p. 48) [my italics]. All his information concerning history, either general or that of the village, is sober and expressed impartially. What he says about the Czechoslovak Legion which fought alongside the Russians during World War I differs sharply from the official Communist version in which its members are condemned as counter-revolutionaries and tools of Western intervention. In contrast with traditional Slovak antipathy towards the Czech officials and educators who worked in Slovakia when it became part of the new state, he has a high regard for the first woman teacher in the village, who came there from Northern Bohemia:

At home she must have been living like a princess, because her parents were wealthy. Certainly she did not have to depend on a miserable teacher's salary. Nevertheless, she came here, where she was most needed, and during the two years she lived here, she built for herself, not only in the hearts of the children but also in those of their parents, a lasting little memorial which many a bigwig cast in bronze might envy (I, p. 66).

On the other hand, the information provided by the characters is often dubious and at times even false:

> That's a lie, a filthy lie! We have not been left alone, even you know that [. . .] There are the Russians, Stalin has promised to come to help Czechoslovakia even without the French; it's only necessary to ask him! [. . .] Yes, the Russians will come, it's only necessary to ask them. Why don't we do it? (Jonáš, I, p. 183).

> together with women and children [. . .] I was out in the potato fields collecting colorado beetles, those greedy, voracious monsters which the American bastards were dropping on our fields from balloons (Franto, III, p. 124).

Because, with some exceptions, such as the upright and kind old Peter Jakubec with whom the narrator shows much affinity psychologically, the sensuous and greedy Maruša and the long-suffering Communist stereotype Jonáš, the characters are not clearly defined, there remains an ambiguity between subjective and objective information.[12]

Whilst, when relating historical facts, the narrator maintains a purely extra-fictional voice and keeps his distance from the characters, he openly reveals his participation in the peasant's love of the soil. In his discourse this mentality is reflected in detailed affectionate descriptions of work in the fields and of the harvest or in nostalgic pictures of village life:

> the glorious moment when the farmer's wife, blushing slightly, would cut the first slice from the newly baked bread from this year's harvest (I, p. 138).

> the young people [. . .] would remember such sleigh rides for many years, perhaps until the day they died. An endless white plain flooded with moonlight, steam under the horses' heads, the crystal-clear jingle of the bells, the crackle of the freezing snow under the sleighs, the flickering flames of lamps lost amid the plain (I, p. 37).

This attitude to the soil is expressed again and again by most of the characters:

> we live from the results of our work, not from hatred of this world or of this region which is my only home (Lájoš, II, p. 125).

who would give up land—the farmer's soul craves for it (Kamil, II, p. 29).

he was breathing in the warm fragrance of the soil, unable to have enough of it (Kovalík, I, p. 200).

This expresses the same philosophy as the works of both Slovak and Czech authors of the rural chronicles from the end of the last century and, later, by the Slovak and Czech Ruralists.[13] Július Noge has written that *Kolonisti* is a novel about the search for a new home, found, temporarily lost, and finally found again for ever.[14] In *Kolonisti* one of the women confesses to herself:

I shall again leave this region. But even as I go away, a desire which cannot be fulfilled will live within me, oppress my heart, reopen old wounds. I shall remain an Islander for ever! Like those before me and those after me, who also went away and afterwards had to fight their hidden desire to return, the desire which only the grave will stifle! (Zina, III, p. 116).

This discourse can be compared to that of the hero of V. Prokůpek's novel *Ztracená země* (Lost land, 1938): 'accept me, unknown country, because I must rest somewhere, because I must start up again somewhere, oh yes, country still foreign to me, it is the way of the world that after one's end a beginning must come, a birth after one's departure. It has to be so, if God's order is to prevail in the world'.[15] What strikes the reader in these utterances is their exalted, almost incantatory tone, reminiscent of a prayer. In the case of the hero of Prokůpek's novel, a peasant with a passionate love for the land and strong religious leanings, it is just possible to accept the connection between the character and the reported discourse. But the discrepancy between the upstart, materialist Zina who left the Rye Island to prosper in West Germany and her pronouncements is too great to be overlooked. Her voice is unmistakably that of the narrator.

In the character's discourse, both direct and reported, the reader is aware of a vision of life and death and of the passing of time. This, as might be expected in this type of prose, becomes the intrinsic theme of the novel. The narration begins with Peter Jakubec buying his brother; its turning point is the funeral of his wife, and its conclusion his meditation about his own death. Death, as the giver of peace, is ever present in the mind of the narrator and through him in the minds of the *personae*:

a small plot will suffice everyone equally, modest and greedy, scoundrel and good man, Slovak, Magyar, Roman Catholic, Lutheran and even Jew (Narrator, I, p. 9).

during a sleepless night people go out [. . .] under the stars, nearer to the eternity of the universe, up to the very threshold of the mysterious thirteenth chamber in which the future of Man is hidden (Narrator, I, p. 131).

Through the open gate he entered the territory of those whose hearts are no longer tormented by injustice, nor shaken by wrong or hopeless visions (Narrator, III, p. 300).

Those under the earth have already found the truth which the living refuse to see, and have found the way to each other (Štefan, III, p. 217).

and whenever death knocked on a neighbour's door, he was paralysed by a mute wonderment at its [literally *her*; death is feminine in Slovak] absolute power and uncompromising, unambiguous decision, which nobody can ever influence (Peter Jakubec, I, p. 10).

infinite territory, the space where he will meet again his lost dear ones [. . .] He has a feeling of enormous curiosity, whether everything will be disclosed in that coming moment, and whether he will find the answer to the question which more and more often had been whirling around in his head as his days were on the wane [. . .] (Peter Jakubec, II, p. 300).

No, not yet! Very soon I shall go to meet Katarína, he says to himself. Some days still remain for me, I still belong here; I am still a little part of the world in which *the wind* blows! Of the world where one can see the sun, the moon, the stars, a white mist over *the river* and the glistening dew on the grass! Of the world where the grove will blossom again and the vine by the house grow green, where, when summer comes, the ears of wheat will grow and mature in their ancient miraculous way (Peter Jakubec, II, p. 301) [my italics].

The wind, which never ceases to blow, is an undying witness to passing generations, the symbol of life and life itself:

you will be far away and perhaps you will not know that the wind blows over the landscape the efforts of a generation which never

> feared obstacles and drudgery [. . .] (Peter Jakubec, III, p. 180).

> the breeze which brings *the river's* fragrance and with it the echo of boys' laughter (Narrator, II, p. 252). [my italics].

The wind is personified, sharing with the people their troubles: 'Even the wind grew silent, waiting for the moment till people meet eye to eye'. (Narrator, I, p. 288). But also, in the same way as in the Slovak Symbolist, Krasko's, poems, it changes into a messenger of gloom: '*the wind* icily whispers in the dry grass among the graves and sways the branches of *bare poplars*, those faithful, silent guardians of the cemetery'. (Narrator, III, p. 300.) [my italics]. Very often, the wind is coupled with the river; like the wind, the Danube is accorded a symbolic function.[16] It moves in one direction like a clock, measuring time and, like the wind, it is personified:

> the wind which during the day had been slumbering somewhere in the river hollows, now wakes up and wafts across the fragrance of the running water (Narrator, III, p. 15).

> in the breeze, blowing from the plains, he felt the hardly perceptible yet ever present breath of the mighty river (Narrator, I, p. 189).

> and past the cottages of the new settlements the same river which flowed here centuries ago will quietly flow to the sea. The Danube continues to murmur its melancholy song. As in past ages, it looks at the new generation which swarms on its banks, which confronts indifferent fate with human patience (Narrator, I, p. 13–14).

> what if the river will not allow him enough time, what if it should surprise him and today or tomorrow bare its wolfish fangs at him?! (Mikuš, III, p. 204).

The technique chosen for the construction of a new reality necessitated the introduction of other symbols. An avenue of false acacias, planted by the 'colonists', is destroyed by the Magyars after the expulsion of the Slovak farmers, and then replanted after their return; wells are similarly vandalised. (The Magyars also destroy a symbolically Slavonic avenue of linden trees.) On the more personal level, there is the wall dividing the house of the two estranged brothers which is pulled down after their reconciliation. And, finally, there are Western cars owned by the upstarts who have betrayed the simple, hard ways of Lipová Osada by going away, and for whom the car implies compensation for the emptiness of their lives.

The views of the narrator and *personae*, which are identical within
the larger context of the basic theme of the novel, also coalesce in a
specific sphere of the lives of the villagers, eroticism or, rather,
sexuality. The attention paid to sexuality in *Kolonisti* is somewhat
reminiscent of Zola, even if the treatment is more restrained.

the gipsy women [. . .] gathered their coloured skirts up high above
their thighs; they held them under their chins with one hand whilst
with the other they were sending secret signals to the inquisitive
men from the village hidden behind the willows, who devoured
them with hungry, leering stares (Narrator, III, p. 278).

his burning breath, made hot by the impatience of the coming
moments burns her with the power of fire worthy of the moment
of the conception of a new human being (Narrator, II, p. 170).

she bends back, half-closes her eyes, with her nipples propped
against the man's chest like lightning conductors (Narrator, I,
p. 118).

God moulded woman from malleable material; when a tough man
breathes on her, she softens; before you know where you are she
loses her sight and hearing; she is deprived of her good sense; all
inhibitions fall away from her, and when she beings to enjoy
herself, Amen, darkness! (Peter Jakubec, I, p. 153).

he imagined her in her half-empty bed, scanning the darkness with
her big eyes and sighing, tormented by desire for that to which she
was accustomed, and which she had missed for a long time (Vinco,
I, p. 115).

Vinco does not want it much even when she shows herself to him
in her transparent shift; in vain she warms the featherbed for him
with her body, as if May Day of '38, when she had been with him
for the first time, had never happened, as if those wonderful
moments were only a dream, because, when she compares them
with nights as they are now, it makes her angry. How very different
they are. But for her everything is just as it used to be; she warms
very quickly but Vinco is no longer the old Vinco; he doesn't get
excited looking at her curves; he doesn't rush to bed first, he is
not inflamed by the old fire, and when it happens at last, it is more
like a marital duty which the husband wants to get through as
quickly as possible. (Maruša, II, p. 167).

in vain men pretend to be indifferent to her womanhood; in vain some frown when they meet this pretty widow as if she were infected; he knows what is going on within each of them; he knows the forces and desires battling inside their bodies! He is convinced that if they could, these hypocrites would not hesitate, oh yes, any of them, would jump on her (Vinco, I, p. 114).

From this brief investigation of the relationship between the narrator and *personae* in *Kolonisti* it may be deduced that the narrator assumes a double role. He acts as both a narrative voice proper and simultaneously as the instigator and controller of the characters' discourse. But not even in his first role does he remain a purely extra-fictional narrator. At the beginning he states:

> The river also borders and observes that part of the left bank which is before our eyes. It is only a small section, something like a sample, but it contains the most important features of the whole. Perhaps it will be adequate for our intention [. . .] Let us approach; we shall begin with a description (I, p. 14).

That beginning of the narration suggests that the narrator is not merely an extra-fictional voice; gradually the reader realises more and more that he is not an omniscient narrator telling a story and recording the discourse of the characters:

> from time to time there would arrive in Lipová Osada one of these [. . .] fellows [. . .] who were despised *by us* [našinec] from the bottom of our hearts (I, p. 153) [my italics].

> During his fifty years many things have befallen Peter Jakubec, and, *I would guess*, all the things which can befall a man (I, p. 9) [my italics].

There is an even closer indication of how the narrator ranges himself with the *personae* who, although participants, possess only incomplete information: 'Galambová Jolanka, how was it with you really? With whom did you conceive the baby due to be born in only a few weeks' time when you decided to drink the bleach from that bottle?' (I, p. 9).

A narrator of this type who identifies himself with the characters and, at the same time, induces them to share with him an integral worldview, must necessarily be proximate to the author, not implied but historical. This affinity was pointed out in connection with Habaj's short stories: 'It seems that he does not even narrate his story – we feel him rather as a narrator within the story itself, as he moves in the world of his protagonists in humble kinship.'[17]

To fictionalise his world view, the author uses a mode of narration which has been criticised as monotonous, insufficiently dynamic, and difficult to follow:

> The style in the third part of the trilogy moves along in a monotonous, sleep-inducing flow, just like the whispering of the leaves on p. 75.
>
> The alternation of monologues, first-person and third-person narration (the author's discourse) has no precise legitimacy, at least not one to be traced on first or second reading. To be frank, it makes the reader's orientation in the text quite difficult; it is difficult to follow who is being spoken about, and to whom the internal monologues belong.[18]

But this criticism is based on a misunderstanding. The mode of narration in *Kolonisti* could hardly be otherwise. It is dictated less by the choice of the author than by the imposition exercised by his worldview – the belief in eternal values, a cosmic order, peace and reconciliation, almost a religion in which the name of God is not mentioned.

This philosophy was not entirely in tune with the ethos of the *milieu* in which the work was produced. No author can be entirely independent of a *milieu*'s influence and its traces in *Kolonisti* are clearly discernible. In the contention between the two mutually disparaging ideologies the immanent ideology prevailed. Its impact caused the rejection of the modes prevailing in much of contemporary fiction, a return to more traditional components and their combination in a new structure. It is in this respect that *Kolonisti* is an important and, as far as it is possible to speak about the 'originality' of a work, an orginal novel.

NOTES

1. Ivan Habaj, *Kolonisti*, I (Bratislava: 1980), 288pp.; 30 chapters; average number of pages a chapter 9.6; print-run of 10 000.
   II (Bratislava: 1981), 315pp.; 20 chapters; 5.7 pages a chapter; print-run of 10 000.
   III (Bratislava: 1986), 301pp.; 20 chapters; 15 pages a chapter; print-run of 5000.

2. I. Sulík, 'O Habajově trilogii široce i úže', *Literární měsíčník*, XVI (1987), p. 103.
3. V. Petrík, 'Historizujúce tendencie v slovenskom románe sedemdesiatych rokov', *Slovenská literatúra* (1985), pp. 482–500.
4. Ibid. p. 499.
5. Július Noge, 'Na ťažkej trati bez rekordu', *Romboid*, 6 (1987), p. 78.
6. The name of the character concerned is given whenever necessary.
7. Seymour Chatman, *Story and Discourse: Narrative Structure in Fiction and Film* (Ithaca: 1978), pp. 201–2.
8. Dorrit Cohn, *Transparent Minds. Narrative Modes for Presenting Consciousness in Fiction* (Princeton: 1978), p. 11.
9. 'Un procédé excellent (surtout si on juxtapose les monologues intérieurs de plusiers personnages) pour montrer combien chacun est enfermé dans son point de vue et se fait des événements et des êtres une idée singulière.' M. Raimond, *Le Roman depuis la Révolution* (Paris: 1968), p. 274.
10. 'Le monologue intérieur prétend restituer la réalité du vécu, mais comment se fait-il que ce language ait pu arriver jusqu'à l'écriture? A quel moment l'écriture a-t-elle pu le récupérer?' M. Butor, *Repertoire II* (Paris: 1954), p. 66.
11. Proportion of characters' discourse (C), dialogue (D), and narrator's discourse (N) in percentages:

	C	D	N
Volume I	15	20	65
Volume II	13	26	61
Volume III	30	15	55

12. The most important historical facts mentioned (a) by the characters: Czechoslovak mobilisation in 1938, I, p. 109; the Communist Party meeting in Košice the same year, I, p. 149; the question of Soviet help after the Munich Agreement, I, p. 183; the progress of the war in summer 1945, II, p. 8; the Trianon Agreement, II, p. 136; the agreement on the transfer of population in 1946, II, p. 230; the elections in 1946, II, p. 244, (b) by the narrator: the Land Reform in 1919, I, p. 13; negotiations of Tiso with the Hungarian Government in 1938, I, p. 209; mobilisation in 1944, II, p. 53; the formation of the Czechoslovak People's Democracy in 1948 and the collectivisation of agriculture, III, p. 47.
13. One of the examples of Ruralism in Slovak literature can be found in Kvetoslav F. Urbanovič, *Oráčina* (Bratislava; 1933).
14. Noge, 'Na ťažkej trati bez rekordu', p. 77.
15. V. Prokůpek, *Ztracená země* (Prague: 1938), p. 11.
16. The river topos is as common in the Czech and Slovak literature as in Western literature, for example, J. Morávek, *Zpáteční voda* (Prague: 1977) (new edn); M. Urban, *Živý bič* (Prague: 1929); cf. Virginia Woolf, *The Captain's Death Bed* (New York: 1950), p. 27: 'It is we who change and perish. But the river Wensun still flows.'
17. J. Tužinský, 'Ivan Habaj, 7 poviedok', *Slovenské pohľady* (1984), 10, p. 134.
18. Noge, 'Na ťažkej trati bez rekordu', p. 78.

18 National Antiheroes: Symbolism and Narrative Voice as Coded National Identity in Oľga Feldeková's *Veverica*

Norma L. Rudinsky

One of the distinctive elements of Slovak literature is its coded exploration of national identity and national history. Perhaps paradoxically, this characteristic appeared only after the formation of Czechoslovakia in 1918. In the nineteenth century, Realist novelists did not question who they were since Slovaks were quite aware that they were the Upper Hungarian Slavs. Later, however, when they were together with the Czech nation the question of Slovak identity became important – and not only because, for a time, the Czechs insisted that the Czechs and Slovaks were one nation; that was the battle over 'Czechoslovakism'. Perhaps the Slovaks themselves became fascinated with the question of how they had 'survived' for a thousand years 'under the Magyars' without the support-systems most other nations had: without their own political infrastructure, without a distinct cultural centre or even a geographical area which was purely their own, and especially without any separate codified literary language until the 1840s. Beside the question of *how*, there arose the question of *what* had survived.[1]

The lack of great historical events to write about forced certain characteristic technical features upon the literary treatment of Slovak national identity and history. In the absence of kings and kingdoms as head and home for the nation, Slovaks had to enhance the common people and, in a few cases, the gentry, by mythic symbols. Instead of having heroes doing great deeds, they had antiheroes, raised to great enough heights to become heroic. National symbolism alone became simplistic and even reductive, so the best writers began to

205

refine their metaphorical content by variations in narrative technique. This change fostered complex and intellectually interesting treatments of otherwise somewhat over-simple and uninteresting characters. Of the many examples of such development, I shall briefly consider four major novels on account of their probable stimulation of these changes as well as their later influence on Slovak prose and, I assume, on the brief novel, *Veverica* (nickname, otherwise 'Red squirrel') by Oľga Feldeková.[2] I do not intend to prove specific influences, but one can at least make fruitful analogies apparent.

Milo Urban's *Živý bič* (The living scourge, 1927) is constructed on the symbol of the scourge as an instrument of justice, and it shows the villagers becoming the living scourge to punish their oppressors after finding their self-respect in recovering their 'lost hands' and, as the novel's last line says, finding 'liberty'.[3] Urban's Orava village symbolises the Slovak nation in the standard historicist view of the Slovaks as the downtrodden victims of foreign usurpers in the Slovak homeland. In addition to its ideological verisimilitude, however, Urban uses the symbol Expressionistically to reveal the inner force of the village rebellion, its instinctive, unconscious, impulsive nature.

Mythic symbols for Slovak identity are basic to all the work of Cíger Hronský. In *Jozef Mak* (1933), the eponymous hero is the Slovak Everyman, 'natural man', stronger than steel and harder than stone. The two women he loves are also mythic – the dark, passionate Maruša and the fair, sacrificial Jula.[4] Hronský's use of the mythic symbol, however, is more complex and ambivalent than Urban's: his characters are not victims of outside oppressors but of their own natures. This complexity of characterisation is far stronger in Hronský's *Písár Gráč* (Gráč, the clerk, 1940), where Hronský's ambivalence approaches *Angst*.[5] Significantly, here Hronský is dealing with the present, or at least the later interwar period, and it is a measure of his artistic skill that this mythic symbol for the Slovak present is a sort of descent into Hell through Gráč's conversations with the dead Alojz Greškovič and a purification, as Gráč throws off the dead weight of his World War I experience and prepares for a new life of love with Jana.

The mythic symbolism of modern novels by Vincent Šikula and Peter Jaroš reflects what Slovak Marxist historians emphasise as the Slovak share in central European history: survival and rebuilding.[6] To represent this Slovak past, both Šikula and Jaroš use artisan families of builders: carpenters and bricklayers. Jaroš's *Tisícročná včela* provides a compelling image of Slovak history taking place in a millennial beehive through love and work, sex and toil, exemplified in the Pichanda family of bricklayers.[7] The male Pichandas are mythic working men like Adam Hlavaj (Urban's novel) and Jozef Mak (Hronský's novel): more or less an archetype.

This archetype receives more complex treatment in Šikula's 'Majstri' trilogy.[8] Besides the master carpenter Guldan, who embodies the pride-in-work ethic, and his youngest son Imro (the mentally sick ex-partisan whose happiness and that of his wife Vilma are destroyed in the Uprising and the subsequent partisan war), Šikula describes the village boy, Rudko, who appears also as a young adult. Šikula achieves an original view of the Uprising by showing it from the oblique perspective of a family living in western Slovakia, where in historical fact almost no action occurred, instead of central Slovakia the actual location of the historical Uprising, where, naturally enough, most Uprising fiction is also set. His oblique view of the Uprising is analogous in a sense to the peripheral place of the child Rudko in the novels, and while I may be guilty of overstatement if I say that Šikula evokes the symbolic child who is the only one to say the King has no clothes, the trilogy is clearly permeated with the belief that the perspective of childhood carries an innocent truthfulness that must not be ignored. When Šikula first began writing from his oblique perspective on the Uprising, he was accused of disrespect and trivialisation, but most critics now acknowledge that he was using Imro and Rudko in much the same way as earlier writers had used such antiheroes as Jozef Mak.[9]

So far I have referred to the controlling symbols in these novels as they functioned alone, but in fact they are given their connotations by technical innovation, the second characteristic way in which Slovak national identity is coded into literature. This innovation varies the author's point of view or narrative voice.[10]

Urban's privileged, reliable, omniscient author-narrator in *Živý bič* comments on the events described, and, more important, judges these events, showing outrage, disgust, pity, admiration and, finally, joy. These narratorial emotions, which provide the tone of the novel, fully support its symbolic effects and ensure its unity. With Hronský's *Jozef Mak*, however, the narrator's voice is manipulated. The omniscient narrator supplies the characters' thoughts and their subconscious, unrecognised desires and fears (as does Urban's narrator), but Hronský's narrator also talks directly to his characters and thus assumes a role in the novel where his emotions and judgements contrast and refine those of his chief characters. The voice of Urban's narrator is only stylistically different from the voice of the chief character Adam Hlavaj – their ethical content is the same. Hronsky's narrative voice is intellectually different from Mak's voice. In the terminology of Dorrit Cohn, Urban has a 'consonant' and Hronský a 'dissonant' narration.[11] By setting the novel in the last third of the nineteenth century, Hronksý could show two Slovak consciousnesses: the old passive, inarticulate mentality of the peasant Mak and the appreciative but radically more subtle and intellectualised mentality of the narrator. This duality allows Hronský to claim Mak as a Slovak Everyman, but simultaneously to distance himself from Mak and to disclaim him as not the whole of the Slovak reality, since the intellectual commentator is also part of Slovak identity. The novel's tone, and the emotions of pity and respect the reader feels for Mak's speechless dignity and the women's helpless suffering are modulated by the historical focus and moral definition supplied to us by the sensitive commentator.

Hronský's *Pisár Gráč* seems to have the opposite point of view from that displayed in *Jozef Mak*: the first-person narrator is Gráč himself. Yet this unified point of view is only apparent: Hronský plays with the reader, for example hiding from the reader facts about Jana which Gráč already knows, and not letting us see at once whether an incident is real, remembered or imagined. So again we are distanced from the myth, and Hronský can both claim the symbol as legitimate for the Slovak experience and disclaim its single meaning, by indicating to us that the ostensible narrator Gráč is unreliable. Our interpretation is forced onto us by authorial silence rather than authorial comment. Then, however, the last fifth of the novel (with the cutting of the willow tree and the death and funeral of the boy) shows a more usual 'consonant' narration until the final conversation with the dead, which clearly ends in Greškovič's silence. Thus, Gráč's spiritual turmoil and eventual wholeness become apparent through the novel's symbolic action combined with the various changes in its narrative voice.

Jaroš's *Tisícročná včela* employs one straightforward narrator who provides the Slovaks' place in the larger historic picture by means of what I am tempted to call a documentary or newspaper narrative, in which news dispatches on war and revolution draw parallels and analogies between history and the actions of the Pichanda family. With Šikula's 'Majstri', we come to a complex narrative technique where the author identifies the narrator with an individual character in one part and with a child's point of view in another. This might be a common literary technique, but it had previously been only rarely exploited in Slovak literature. Child narrators are peculiarly rich in their paradoxical invocation of both the triviality of a 'mere child' and the child's spiritual freedom from onerous, hypocritical adult rules, *à la* Huck Finn. The child's voice also supplies dramatic irony whereby the reader understands what the child sees or reveals but cannot yet comprehend. The adult narrator of the first novel of the trilogy is partially identified in the two later novels with a certain Rudko, who is sometimes still a child, but often also an adult remembering and commenting on his own childhood. This narrator adds a complex, subtle personality to a cast of characters otherwise fairly simple. Though Šikula does not address his characters like Hronský, he constantly speaks directly to the reader and carries on long 'discussions' with 'himself'. The narrators of most of the earlier novels I have referred to explicitly control and explain the action and characters, but Šikula's ostensible narrator is deliberately made to appear out of control and unable to catch the whole truth of his subject. For example, he assumes various roles outside his narrative function, claiming to be a conscientious historian striving for the detailed truth of his epoch, or a moral philosopher carefully expounding absolute goodness. Then he again returns to his literary function and elucidates the conventions of fiction – forcing the reader into a sort of Brechtian alienation from the same verisimilitude that the fictional conventions are meant to establish. Like Hronský in *Gráč*, but to a far greater degree, Šikula makes the reader resolve all this deliberate mystification and establish a secret communion with the actual author by bypassing the ostensible narrator.

Throughout this seemingly chaotic narrative with an otherwise simple plot, Šikula maintains a surface lightness, folksiness, and deliberate trivialisation of everything he says, even while insisting on his seriousness. He deliberately plays the fool, and thus invokes the holy fool, the underdog against tradition, the seeker after a new truth. More than in the other works I have mentioned, Šikula's symbols merge with his narrative voices to disclaim a simplistic picture of Slovakdom. The breadth of his reference to various literary conventions, disciplines, events, and alternative evaluations of those events, gives his work a stylistic (though not necessarily a philosophical) complexity that Urban and Hronský's (but also Jaroš's) novels lack.

It may seem pointless to compare a slight novel of under 100 pages to fully-fledged novels, but the differences in length, like the similarities of symbol and narrative technique, are telling. Oľga Feldeková's *Veverica* is set in an Orava village during the critical period of collectivisation in the late 1940s and early 1950s. The work constitutes a mixture of allegory, parable, realistic fiction, and history, but we are led to understand its mythic symbolism of Slovakdom by the author's dedication to the Finnish poet who had told her that the Finnish word *orava* means 'red squirrel', which is also the nickname of the chief female character, the young village girl Žofia whose hair turns a beautiful red after the death of her father.

In *Veverica*, Feldeková has been inspired by Slovak Surrealism and the 'magic realism' of Latin American writers with their grotesque, violent, disconnected, fantastic events dressed in realistic detail and held together more by the reader's questions than by narratorial answers.[12] Magic realism as a literary form is said to appear where an old peasant society clashes with a new industrial society, because the established, accepted social forms are challenged by new norms which disrupt old symbolisms and create new signs.[13] Feldeková shows the peasant society of the Orava region, and by extension of Slovakia, as it is being replaced by the collective farm, and, indeed, by factories as they are built in the countryside. Through a number of Christian symbols, she also shows the changed position of the Church; however, here her symbols are multivocal, and sometimes her point lies not in the symbol but in its trivialisation, as in the episode with the herbalist or folk healer. On one level Christianity is reduced to a superstituion and we seem to enter a post-Christian world where the old institutions are outdated like the old farming methods. For example, the student priest leaves the seminary and becomes a surveyor, and the female narrator's family runs the gamut of beliefs: her grandparents are still filled with village superstitions and sectarian prejudices, while her mother has a more reasonable, commonsense faith and her father is an atheist. On another level, Feldeková seems to condemn only the corruption of Christianity, not its essence, and only the church members who do not practise true Christianity like, for example, those who in the child's dream fight over the food distributed.

Despite its Latin exoticism, Feldeková's use of magic realism fits naturally into the fantastic tradition of the Slovak Lyrical Prose school of the 1940s and thus appears almost domesticated. The work's employment of varying points of view manifests the influence of Šikula's narrative technique. Feldeková's first-person adult narrator tells us she observed the first of the events described in the novel at the age of three, but she explicitly doubts her accuracy at that early age and has puzzled over their meaning since toddlerhood. Thus, immediately on the first page, the reader is presented with an unanswerable question about the comprehensibility of events that have to be taken on the bases of only faith and logic. This intellectually limited child's knowledge is relieved by comments from the now grown-up narrator, and her frequent sardonic humour undercuts the innocuous pretence that a child had observed the action – the sardonic quality is closer to Hronský's tone in *Písar Gráč* than to that of Šikula's cheerful, ostensibly garrulous narrator. Less important, the reader also senses an autobiographical basis to the novel: the reader suspects that the adult narrator is the author who was born in 1943 and had grown up in Orava, and so the reader feels a reassurance of a sort (cf. Hronský's silent presence in *Gráč*) in that the meaning must lie within the apparent mystery.

The mystification is indeed extensive. Žofia, the young girl nick-named (Red) Squirrel, is a victim figure who becomes pregnant but will not reveal the name of the father, apparently her young neighbour Jožko, who has just entered a seminary. There are numerous fantastic incidents involving Slovak folklore: Žofia's baby turns into a bird; a Pole from Cracow marries Žofia because he loves this baby and later he kidnaps the child and disappears; the future priest's mother becomes mute and her eyeballs turn inwards when she is laid into by a woman whose son is accused of the baby's paternity; in the child's grotesque dream the young seminary student distributes morsels of meat to swimmers who fight each other for the meat but drown anyone who succeeds in grabbing a morsel; some time after Jožko leaves the seminary, he is killed in a mysterious accident with a threshing machine drawn by a beautiful black horse, all of which appears to signify corruptible nature and death as well as Jožko's priestly vocation. If Žofia represents Slovakia, or Slovakdom, one wonders whether Jožko represents the Church, and his hypocrisy the failure of Christianity. Jožko's death could be construed as deserved punishment for his previous moral fault; it is also made mysterious by the atheist father's premonition and the 'miraculous' signs following that premonition. Yet the fantasy is not sustained; for example, Žofia moves to Budapest, marries a concert violinist and forgets Slovak. One wonders whether this is some political allegory. That is conceivable though not likely. Nevertheless political satire certainly occurs when a silver aeroplane drops thousands of leaflets with the single word 'Happiness' printed on them during collectivisation.

Disparate, discontinuous violent symbols are linked with the faithful realism, terse intellectuality, and precisely cadenced dialogue which characterised Feldeková's earlier stories. Unfortunately, she has an occasional clever-cleverness of style, especially with the strange sounds overheard by the child – a female erotic sound (Žužiju) and a male erotic sound (Chlch, chlch) which echo the poem 'Už a este' (Now and still) by her husband Ľubomír Feldek, but which lack the more abstract, philosophical connotations inspired by the poem.[14]

In the final paragraph (which changes from retrospection to 'nowness') the narrator assures us that the meaning of the events finally becomes clear to her as she opens the door to a beautiful red squirrel and a new dawn. Only here do we possibly awaken the mythic symbol of Slovakia as Nature. Here the squirrel, which means both Orava (and by extension, Slovakia) and the girl/mother, acquires an abstract significance which colours and offers an interpretation to all the disparate mysterious details of the novel's plot. This world is perhaps post-Christian, or perhaps just unChristian, but it at last becomes a natural and hopeful world. We are reminded that Nature herself is mysterious and unknowable, yet fecund and optimistic: after the Slovak girl has disappeared to Budapest, a beautiful new squirrel appears with the new dawn. As an image for Slovakia, the tiny, cosy, provident, but untamed, squirrel is a strikingly original heroic antihero.

Veverica has been neglected by Slovak critics. The only serious review I am aware of condemns its self-destructive 'playing' with the plot and the 'onslaught of poetic fantasy' to which the plot falls victim.[15] Alexander Halvoník's basic criticism is that 'a more demanding aesthetic principle requires more explicit social content and more serious meaning' than he sees in *Veverica*. Yet one can scarcely ask for a more serious meaning than the one I have sketched in this chapter. The reviewer also fails to see the dual point of view. The contention that the adult narrator brings to the subject only doubts about its literal meaning and gives 'no new qualitative knowledge' could only be written by a reviewer who has forgotten such works as *Pisár Gráč* and *Majstri*.

Feldeková's *Veverica* accomplishes the same double function of depicting and alienating a simplistic historical view that we saw in the longer major Slovak novels I discussed at the beginning of this chapter. One might argue that, to a great extent, such a double function is possible in a brief work only because it echoes the symbols and narrative voices we already know from its predecessors. The similarity of location and theme in Urban's *Živý bič* is evident but the analogies to Hronský's symbols and Šikula's complex narrative technique are, perhaps, less obvious.

Any 'national literature' carries codes identifying it as 'national', but the extent to which Slovak prose fiction is coded to explicate national identity and history seems to be exceptionally great.[16]

NOTES

1. I have discussed the historical factors affecting Slovak identity in 'The Context of the Marxist-Leninist View of Slovak Literature, 1945–69', *Carl Beck Papers in Russian and East European Studies*, no. 505 (1986), pp. 1–34.
2. Oľga Feldeková, *Veverica* (Bratislava: 1985). It has been translated into Hungarian by Ferenc Ardamica, *Mokus* (Bratislava: 1987).
3. Milo Urban, *Živý bič* (Prague: 1927).
4. J. C. Hronský, *Jozef Mak* (Martin: 1933). *Jozef Mak* is one of the few Slovak novels translated into English (Columbus, 1985).
5. J. C. Hronský, *Pisár Gráč* (Martin: 1940).
6. As summarised in Vladimir Mináč's 1969 essay *Dúchanie do pahrieb*, 'From blood and sweat, from pain and work, was born the civilisation of this piece of the Earth . . . Others could build cathedrals and castles: we had to rebuild our hovels over and over again . . . We stopped the Mongols, Turks, and other Asiatics, not by our swords and heroic deeds but by outlasting them.' I quote from *Súvislosti* (Bratislava: 1981), p. 96.
7. Peter Jaroš, *Tisícročná včela* (Bratislava: 1979).
8. Vincent Šikula, *Majstri*, *Muškát* and *Vilma*.
9. This continuing controversy over Šikula's view of the Uprising appeared in the periodical, *Slovenské pohľady*, nos. 3, 10–12 (1977) and 1 (1978). The later consensus is summarised by Vincent Šabík, 'Staré a nové čriepky do portrétu Vincenta Šikulu', *Romboid*, xxi, 10 (1986), pp. 19–29.
10. I have more or less used the categories suggested by Wayne C. Booth in *The Rhetoric of Fiction* (Chicago, 1961), especially Chapter 6, 'Types of Narration', and Chapter 8, 'Telling as Showing: Dramatized Narrators, Reliable and Unreliable'.
11. Dorrit Cohn, *Transparent Minds: Narrative Modes for Presenting Consciousness in Fiction* (Princeton: 1978), pp. 26–33 and note 10, p. 275.
12. This inspiration is mentioned by Slovak critics in conversation but does not appear in the only three brief and basically unfavourable newspaper reviews of this book that I have found. When asked whether she was comfortable with the description of 'magic realism' for her *Veverica*, Feldeková replied that she had indeed been influenced by Gabriel García Márquez, but also felt annoyed at critics who treated her stories as mere descriptions of observed events; she had wanted to show she too could write fantasy (conversation, 16 December 1986, Bratislava).

214   *National Antiheroes*

13. This is Frederic Jameson's definition in 'On Magic Realism in Film', *Critical Inquiry*, 12 (Winter 1986), pp. 301–25.
14. Ľubomír Feldek, *Poznámky na epos* (Bratislava: 1980), pp. 51–2.
15. Alexander Halvoník, 'Hra s príbehom (osudná)', *Pravda* (Bratislava), 1 August 1986.
16. I am extremely grateful to the International Research and Exchange Board (IREX) for making it possible for me to carry out my research into modern Slovak fiction in Bratislava (1986–7).

19 In and Out of Reality: Dušan Dušek

Sonia I. Kanikova

In 'Death and the Compass' Borges tells of a detective who rejects the single hypothesis about the motive for the murder of a certain Talmud scholar. He rejects it on the one hand because the chance factor is too great and on the other because he considers that reality does not have to be interesting, but hypotheses have to be. The detective declares, 'Before us we have a dead rabbi and I would favour an entirely rabbinical explanation'.[1] He takes a highly complex path to the murderer and his motive; this path leads him into a trap which the murderer had by pure chance set for him.

On my first reading of Dušan Dušek's short stories,[2] I ascertained that reality was not interesting; unfortunately, I did not even find a dead rabbi. As a result I found myself having to take a complex path to track down an absent absolute motivation.[3] I was faced with a series of uniform incidents: the *dramatis personae* are situated somewhere between their desires and life. There are variants, characters at various stages of frustration, but the reasons for their problems remain initially unclear. The action of the stories seemed to hang in a psychological vacuum, to be connected with the characters only externally.

The problem of unrealisable desires is a frequent subject of literature as a whole. The apparent absence of an internal relationship between the action and the characters in Dušek's texts led me to consider the relationship between action and characters' desires in literature. My examples of this are random, since I have chosen to take such a complex path. In the *Iliad* Paris is dissatisfied with his life as it has been; he feels the need to add something to that life, and so he adds Helen. That turns out to be a temporary satisfaction of his desires, since on top of Helen he also adds a war to his life; the fulfilment of his desires motivates the narrative. *La Tentation de Saint Antoine* represents an instance of dissatisfaction with existing (that is, realised) doctrines; those doctrines appear to St Anthony insufficient for his personal faith, and the motivation for the whole narrative is his desire for faith. Faust's desire for knowledge provides

215

Goethe's narrative space. Indeed longing or desire or quest is the most general motivation for literary narration.

One might go as far as to say that every text is the visible representation of insufficiency or lack. The text fills in what was insufficient or lacking. If I may take the individual's life as a circle, I take for granted that the circumference of that circle is broken or contains gaps in every human being. The insufficiency or lack may not be visible in the central characters of the text, but it will always be evident in the author or narrator. Insufficiency will in some form or other always constitute the impulse for narration. A character may appear not to suffer from any insufficiency or lack and to desire simply to move from point A to point B. In this case that desire becomes the reason for the narrative. That constitutes an example of insufficiency's being expressed by the text itself, not by the inhabitant(s) of the text. The desire to travel does not need psychological motivation in the case where the character's travelling simply instigates a different narrative. K. in *Der Prozess* desires nothing. He is, however, alive and that fact at least signifies his desire to be alive. (K. has not made use of the essential human freedom, the freedom to kill oneself.) The eponymous hero of Hašek's *Švejk* appears not to desire anything; nevertheless all his adventures might be said to express the will to say alive; the narrative gains its motion as a result of that will. The motion of the narrative in *Der Prozess* is entirely different; Josef K. does not even desire to be alive. He does not, however, have any negative desire either; he does not want not to die. He understands he is there, alive. He is uneasy at being alive. Thus there exists the possibility of his having some desire, and thus of some culpable desire. That awareness provides the narrative motion. In *Švejk* the insufficiency lies in the text, in the lack of death. In *Der Prozess* the insufficiency consists primarily in the anxiety of living, the necessarily broken circle. Secondarily, however, the text imposes insufficiency on the reader; the reader is made to see death as the only answer to anxiety, death as the only completion of the circle. Insufficiency makes for motion; sufficiency or non-lack makes for stasis. Where the circumference of the life circle is unbroken, where there are no desires, there is only an end to life and to narration.

The text fills the gap in the broken circle. That filling represents an organisation of reality. Thus the text, while it signifies insufficiency, also represents the urge to replace that insufficiency with an organis- ation of the world which does not correspond to the author's or the reader's immediate perception of the world. The text constitutes, then, the opposite of insufficiency; it removes the author's insufficiency. The text is the desired addition, that part of life which is lacking. It contains the organisedness life does not possess. The insecurity engendered by insufficiency disappears. It is replaced by the palliative security of the posited organisedness. We may, however, have a text which merely describes the state of insufficiency. It is not that it fails to offer a solution (which the reader hardly demands of a text), but that it fails to register the dynamism of living itself, life as the motion inspired by insufficiency. Such a text does not, in fact, contain a narrative, but an explication. In such a text one finds only a fake narration. The text may still fill the gap in the broken circle, but the text is not organised. The text itself consists in non-organisation, chaos, something which cannot fulfil the circumference. The chaos naturally produced by insufficiency is supplemented by additional chaos rather than by organisedness. This textual state may be exemplified in Dušek's works. In Shklovsky's words, 'Narration demands not only action, but also anti-action; it demands non-correspondence'.[4] If a text contains no non-correspondence, but only correspondence, the text lacks motion and therefore does not constitute a narrative. There is no tension between individual characters or between characters and action. If A loves B and B loves A, there is no story; there must be a third element, a non-correspondence, to give motion to an action. An action can be entirely formal. A loves B and B loves A, but A has to go away or B turns up late at a rendezvous. The result of that is the potential for action. It is, however, only a potential and that potential can itself become part of something entirely formulaic. Something must prevent narratives falling into mere formulae. Defining that something is not easy.

In some texts there is action and dénouement and apparently the law of non-correspondence is fulfilled, but still the narrative remains fake. To try to explain what I mean by fake narration, I take the perhaps unconsciously Freudian Dušek's 'Svetlonoš' (light-bearer or Lucifer or Venus; *Poloha pri srdci*), where the characters are passive, even if they appear to do something; that is the norm in Dušek. In this tale a boy has come into conflict with his mother and has run away from home. His mother waits for him in their flat and suffers pangs of conscience; then she leaves the flat to look for him. The boy returns together with a neighbour whom he has just become acquainted with. The boy's mother returns and finds them at the flat door. The story ends with the following:

> The boy was standing by the door of the flat talking with their
> neighbour from some storey higher in the building, a thin fellow
> wearing only boxer-shorts and a sweat-shirt, holding a ping-pong
> bat and wiping the sweat from his forehead with his sleeve. He
> said 'Hello' to her. And when she was saying 'Hello' back, she
> could not keep her eyes off him; finally she had to smile at him.
> When she started to look for her hand with her keys, she found it
> resting on the fellow's shoulder.[5]

This ending resolves the tension between all the actors in the tale.
The reason for the mother and boy's coming into conflict lies in the
fact that he wets his bed almost every night – something which goes
very much against the grain with his mother. The boy loathes wetting
his bed but is incapable of doing anything about it. The tale's
beginning actually concerns the cause of this bed-wetting – from the
boy's point of view. That cause is, on the one hand, Venus, on the
other, a certain fear. Venus 'will not let him go to sleep'. In his
insomnia he hears soft footsteps from the next room, as well as 'the
sounds and fragments of words [. . .], sighs and [. . .] kisses.'[6] Venus
comes to the boy's room and:

> listens at and whispers into the keyhole of his bedroom door, calls
> him, haunts him; the path was always open, since his mother never
> shut the door onto the balcony, although they lived on the ground
> floor; she airs the flat all night, but that is a lie; she actually leaves
> the door open only so that the torch-bearer, the morning star,
> Lucifer, would have easier access to his room and so be able to
> torment him.[7]

The boy provides a further explanation for his bed-wetting: 'It takes
him ages and ages to go to sleep and, once he is asleep, he sleeps
much more soundly than other people; he is not aware that he needs
a pee and so, once more, he wets his bed'.[8]

In the course of the day the boy runs away from home because he
has two arguments with his mother. The first takes place in the
morning, when his mother looks at the school record he has to carry
with him and finds there a remark that he had received a black mark
for behaviour at school. After a long row, the boy admits he had
been key-hole peeping into the girls' lavatories. That admission elicits
a smile from his mother. The second argument takes place in the late
afternoon when his mother discovers his wet bed. He answers his

mother's shouting by stating 'that is was not his fault and that she ought to shut the window leading to the balcony, if she wanted him to on living'.[9] From this the reader understands there is some motive unknown to him for the mother's leaving the door to the balcony open. Her primary excuse is that she could not bear remaining in an unaired flat for eight hours. Then she is afraid that her son is reading her thoughts, that he knows she is hoping that some man will come through that window. The reader does not know whether some man actually uses the window or whether its openness really only results from the woman's desire. Whatever the case, the woman's thoughts contain a sensation of guilt towards her son. (She also feels she cannot actually stand up to her boy, and that she ought to try to be friends with him.) By this time it is clear that the text concerns a certain insufficiency, that is a lacking husband/father. That insufficiency makes the woman and her son unhappy. When that insufficiency appears likely to be removed, the tale ends. The scene at the flat-door seems to indicate the narrative's goal: a man has been found. His presence immediately reconciles mother and child.

This reconciliation would lack verisimilitude if the reader were not earlier in the story given some information about the mother and child's sense of insufficiency. That insufficiency might have a psychological or some other derivation. Perhaps the psyches of the mother and child have been traumatised by the absence of a man/father in the house. The mother's behaviour towards her child is hysterical. The child has hysterical somatic reactions – his incontinence – with which he punishes his mother.

The boy's words that his mother, by keeping the balcony window open, does not want him to go on living, are parallel to his fear of Venus's entering through that window. When the boy is running away from home, his first thoughts concern Venus, but Venus not in connection with bed-wetting, but with the fact that Venus was the same thing as the torch-bearer, Lucifer.

On that same day the boy had been reading a book of horoscopes which he had taken from his mother's room. In that book he had read the traditional astrologists' tale concerning the origin of Venus. From other thoughts of his we learn that Venus, the morning-star, disturbs him more than might be usual in his nocturnal anxiety. The text does not provide any immediate meaning to torch-bear (Lucifer), but puts Lucifer into an astrological context and so the reader may derive a meaning which changes the significance of the boy's nocturnal anxiety. Generally, Venus symbolises love and sensual pleasure. In the horoscope Venus is femaleness and motherhood. According to the astrologists' tale Venus (Lucifer) may also symbolise male sexual potency or activity. The transformation of female into male, Venus into Lucifer, may suggest the mother's willing introduction of Lucifer into the boy's room, but it may suggest the hermaphrodity of the mother for a boy whose father is absent. Furthermore that transformation may have a basic Freudian meaning for Dušek; it may represent the boy's jealousy; thus the interpretation of the boy's bed-wetting as a punishment of his mother is further supported. The boy also suffers some vague sexual anxiety as a result of Venus's existence as the morning-star, as the boy's female opposite number. That parallels the sexual awakening represented by his peeping-tom activities in the girls' lavatories at school. The narrator/author tells us that Lucifer 'received a place in the heavens, because he was a lamp which also shone in the day-time, the bright planet which always hurries after the sun into the wet sea so that in the early hours he could reveal himself as the [female] morning star, showing mankind the way'.[10] The 'wet sea' is connected with the wetted sheets in the text, the oral-tradition and Freudian identification of water (sea) with women, as well as with the neighbour's drenched sweat-shirt at the end of the text.

The boy's wetted sheets themselves represent sexual dissatisfaction or restlessness. Wetness has three meanings: literal wetness (the sheets), woman (genital secretion), and male wetness (the solution). Previous to the final scene the boy had watched the neighbour playing ping-pong and the sweat dropping off him. Male wetness represents male strength for the child, as later, for the mother; for her it also represents the male capacity to solve. What first appeared to be a situational psychological problem of manlessness for mother and child turns out to be, far more than anything else, a sexual problem.

In this story Dušek declares sexuality the fundamental problem of life. Sexuality is the force which influences all mental and physical activity. Sexuality is the motivation for Dušek's narrative. At the same time sexuality constitutes the meaning of the narrative. If the motivation and the meaning of the text are one and the same, the text is a fake narrative. Not only is the fake narrative typical of Dušek, but also sexuality tends to be those fake narratives' central concern. The action, the chain of events I have isolated in 'Svetlonoš', has no meaning of its own. This action is a fake story. We learn what the text actually intends to say only from the metastory.

In 'Svetlonoš' the metastory is what provides us with meaning. The action contains only the results of the premised meaning and has no life beyond the premise. We may compare the fakeness of the narrative with ritual acts, which manifest only the visible part of a given myth. If the acts are isolated from the myth, they lose their essential meaning. They become an empty form into which anyone may place his own meaning, but such a meaning is merely an interpretation. This interpretation cannot reconstruct the myth which had given birth to the form. The key to ritual is outside the ritual. The key to the fake narrative is also not contained in the fake narrative itself.

The story, the fake narrative, of 'Svetlonoš' is one of the possible stories which life proffers. The story is the *sujet* in the broadest sense of the term, and for the author it plays the role of an empty form. The author is free to attribute to the story any meaning he chooses. By attributing a definite meaning the author expresses a definite view on life. The more believable the story is, the more believable is the view (meaning) which claims to be its explanation. The attempt to make that view the only possible explanation of the story renders the author's view not only the story's explanation, but also its motivation.

In other words, the view is what made the story take place. Thus the apparently real becomes unreal because its only life lies in the author's view. The unreality of the story and its complete fakeness result from the reduction of the meaning of life to one view. A particular view has imprisoned life. The actors in such a narrative are as unreal as the story itself. The actors are also merely the product of the author's view. They cannot have any other psychology than that which the author's view can give them. The action of the story is not a product of the actors' characters, but of the author's view. The action is created to express a view and the actors are a product of the action. The construction of the narrative does not lead by its action; the view has turned into the narration and illustrates itself. The view has taken over the functions of narration and thus no narration actually exists. The view is not subjected to verification, as would be the case if the narration were fulfilling its proper function. The view does not explore reality. It considers itself to be reality. It has been narrating itself as the only possible reality.

Here we see the vicious circle inherent in Dušek's works. It constitutes the source of his imagery, of the specific functions of his language and of his themes. The viciousness of this circle lies in the fact that the author's view is not verified. Productive insufficiency is lacking in Dušek's works.

In contrast, in real life the insufficiency concomitant with living forms the basis for productivity. Insufficiency produces both the banal events of life and the world of ideas. Views or opinions are produced by the insufficiency of explanations for existence. Views on reality seek to constitute the missing part of the circumference of the broken circle, which expresses insufficiency. Views, however, necessarily return to reality to verify themselves. Only reality is the criterion for the acceptability of a view. Even the most improbable-sounding view can be accepted by reality as a genuine component of reality, since such a view is capable of expressing the whole beauty of endless insufficiency, the endless quest which has no goal. The truth of the matter is that life does not actually seek explanation; life is realised in the beauty of seeking.

That slightly alters the conception of insufficiency as I initially employed the term, when I was speaking about Paris's dissatisfaction. In fact what is lacking is not actually important. What is important are the possibilities insufficiency engenders: eternal seeking and narration. Narration is nothing but a part of the seeking. Narration is the faithful depiction of seeking and also its travelling companion. Insufficiency is the condition for there being no end to seeking, to narrating. The meanings of what is found will always be put in doubt by further findings. The meanings cannot constitute the goal. The goal cannot be the meaning either. Therein lies the problem of the vicious circle of Dušan Dušek's works. Dušek lacks insufficiency.

He lacks insufficiency not only because one assumed view, the pansexuality of existence, has become the organising principle of his fictional world, but also because this fictional world has no other contents except the contents of the author's view. There is no room in his texts for productive insufficiency. Dušek's fictional world is a world regulated by one all-explaining view. The only thing which can be lacking in that world is what the view dictates people are lacking. The narration and the actors form a construct of the author's view and what can be lacking has to be a part of that construct. The delivery of what is lacking is the only dynamism in the text which excludes the possibility of non-correspondence. It is like the delivery of the final word to a sentence, when the sentence is so clear that we already know what that final word must be.

For example, the only dynamism in the tale, 'Slamienka' (Straw basket, *Poloha pri srdci*), is between the point of a woman's sexual frustration (she is, naturally, an old maid) and the point of the realising of the sublimation. The tale actually concerns the path leading to a subliminal picture.

The tale, 'Dvere' (Door, *Náprstok*), is a typical manifestation of the autorealisation of the meaning. In this tale we are presented with a woman who has an inexplicable passion for funerals. Equally inexplicable are the passages in the story which are meant to describe the flow of her thoughts, where the reader hears about a longing for grief, about tears, her and other people's tears, a longing for the locking of windows and doors, for locking altogether, a longing for old age and for the experience of death (in others and herself). It appears that no explanation is offered for this unusual behaviour. The story could theoretically consist in only the description of such desires, but the text provides an explanation in the form of a Freudian slip. The concentration on the fact that the central character had forgotten to put her knickers on, her Freudian slip, has the sole aim of emphasising her frustration. Various allusions to that frustration are scattered about the text. If we put all these allusions together, we discover that she is frigid and that her funeral mania constitutes a sublimation of her unsatisfied sexual energy. This is a typical Freudian conception of behaviour. The tale, 'Závoj' (The veil, *Náprostok*), also concerns sexual frustration, the frustration of a woman who cannot find a husband and who has a strong yearning for marriage. Her life is composed of making drawings of wedding anniversaries in accordance with the metal or gem conventionally linked with those anniversaries; at the same time she invents appropriate dress and banquet menus for the celebation of the anniversaries.

The long title-story of *Náprstok* comprises several cases of sexual frustration. It offers rich material for an analysis of the constructing of the vicious circle. The text is composed of 27 episodes linked by a common main character, Adam, and other figures who appear in several tales in the book. The stories of *Náprstok* are put together as a collection of glimpses of a small town and its inhabitants. The book has the subtitle, 'A few idyllic photographs taken by the postmaster, Emanuel, borrowed from an old album and published privately as postcards'. The stories are set in the early years of the Czechoslovak First Republic. Concerning the title-story, Dušek himself writes on the blurb that it is a detail: 'At the beginning [of the book] there is a general overview, then a few partial views and at the end [the title-story] a detail'. In the story we find, apart from Adam, his friends Dominik, the old man Podoba, Adam's wife Katarína, and so forth. 'Náprstok' contains episodes from the Great War, pub anecdotes and biographical sketches. The omniscient narrator relates events from within and from without.

If observed superficially, the text appears not to conceal any deeper meaning and does not constitute an apt depiction of the period setting. The incidents in the text could happen at any time in history. The characters do not clearly belong to a concrete period. Except for the fact that we hear of individual characters who had spent time in the trenches, everything that happens could be placed in some other period. The linking principle of the episodes is associatively constructed, but the reader sees no guiding rule in the associations. Furthermore, the associative principle is not consistent. Usually a *motif* or individual word from the last sentence of one episode is linked with the first sentence of the succeeding episode. In one case the striking of a clock at the end of one episode prefigures an episode concerning Dominik's alarm clock. The mention at the end of another episode that Adam and Katarína had got married constitutes the reason for the next episode concerning the fact that Dominik had not been at their wedding. This episode, however, actually concerns Dominik's war experiences. Another episode ends with the words, 'bolo, bolo, všetko bolo – a všeličo inač ako malo byť, bolo, bolo, ale čo . . .' (it happened, happened, everything happened – and all sorts of things happened quite differently from the way they should have; it happened, happened, but so what . . .' and the next episode begins with the word, 'Nebolo . . .' (It didn't happen . . .).[11] The episodes are not in chronological order. Most of them could be put somewhere else in the cycle without impairing the text. The only line of development which evolves consistently is the gradual revelation of Adam's problem, his unsatisfied sexual desires, which, at the beginning, are only hinted at. Soon these desires are manifested more directly in something like interior monologues. Only at the end of the cycle do the hints and Adam's thoughts fuse into the larger problem of sexual frustration. Only then does the fact emerge that this problem actually forms the foundation of the whole long short story. The hints really do not begin until the ninth episode: 'In the night he would change into a dog and run out of the house, driven and summoned by the scent of a bitch, by saliva and a message from other dogs . . . He could not sleep. Whole bouquets and wreaths of stimulant odours breathed on him from out of the darkness . . . The lixivial smell of genitals intoxicated him . . .'.[12]

This allusion to Adam's state is overwhelmed by the context so that the reader still remains lost as to where the main theme of the cycle lies. A little later matters become clearer. Adam thinks about a past mistress and about his wedding night, when Katarína had not submitted to sexual intercourse. Adam is jealous of his sons because, when Katarína hugs them, their heads rest on her bosom. He wants to drive them away, unbutton her blouse and press his head between her breasts. When he borrows his wife's bicycle and jumps on it to ride himself to work (this is, incidentally, the only mention of some life in Adam other than the life of sexual frustration), the saddle, on which Katarína had been sitting a short while before, excites his sexuality: 'What he would have most liked to do was to sniff the saddle and, perhaps, even kiss it'.[13] The fact that his sexual desires as regards Katarína had never been completely fulfilled is related to the reader in an episode in which Adam reels off all the things which had not come to pass. In fact, all those things amount to one thing, sexual desire from his wife. That is immediately followed by a description of the sublimation of Adam's desire: 'Adam worked out his revenge: escapes and maps'.[14] In his imagination he travels about the world and everywhere he has beautiful mistresses. Here we come across his favourite Red Indian, Enide, with her naked, glistening, full breasts.

At one point Adam is arrested for stealing the bicycle and is kept in police custody for several hours; the reader never knows whether or not this event had actually taken place. His interrogation had absurd elements, since he goes to the police to complain that his bicycle had been stolen and finds himself accused of stealing it. The explanation of the whole episode, his experience of the sense of guilt and his fear of punishment, comes in a sentence, about which Adam is uncertain whether it had ever been uttered: 'From now on there'll be no more travelling to jungles, no more Red Indian girls, no more Africa!'[15] Immediately after his spell in custody the problem of his frustration is completely revealed. The images which form in his mind are linked with earlier images, and his whole behaviour acquires a new meaning for the reader. His previous desire to turn into a dog becomes even more pronounced and is now connected with a desire to become a railway engine. The locomotive is given a direct correspondence with sexual intercourse. 'It was not enough to change into a dog . . . He ought to change into a locomotive. To whistle or blast a horn . . . To release steam into pistons – and to let some steam out as well . . . To move his wheels and then his knees, too . . .'[16] The meaning of the whole cycle is expressed in Adam's last vision, in which sexual images placed in an immediate context of desire unveil the hidden significance.

My interpretation is incomplete, since it describes only the experience of Adam, and that only fragmentarily. In fact, all the elements of 'Náprstok' are suffused with erotic meaning. The old man, Podoba, is frustrated by his old-manly impotence. Podoba appears in the collection's first story, 'Piesok' (Sand), where he is introduced only with the following words: 'I cry out to Heaven and no one hears me! These sparrows! They have it off on chimneys, on roads, on fences! Flipping hell, I'm the only one who has nothing! And then they say it's May'.[17] In 'Náprstok' Podoba shows Adam a furry black rabbit skin which he always carries about with him. He tells Adam he always has it with him because he had once had a woman like it. Podoba goes on to tell Adam, 'As long as your drake raises its head, everything's all right. Don't forget that'.[18] Birds as penes are omnipresent in Dušek. Penis-birds constitute his most frequent image, an image which serves as a key to unlock his not very secret sexual chambers.

The author exploits the Freudian polysemy of lexical items. The primary meanings of words tend to be replaced by their figurative meanings. These figurative meanings are erotic. In Slovak the word *vták* means bird but has the vulgar erotic meaning penis (cf. English cock). Dušek's exploitation of secondary meanings does not, however, end here. He replaces the word *vták* by all manner of specific bird-names; *kačer* (drake), *kohút* (cockerel), *vrabec* (sparrow), *holub* (pigeon) and so forth. In this connection the verb 'to fly' assumes erotic meaning in Dušek. Bird's feathers become an emblem of sexual potence. Feathers, however, are compared with human body hair, which, when dense, likewise signifies sexual potence. The hair on one's head also has erotic meaning for our author. Elderly impotent men or sexually inactive women are always described as having one or two strands of hair on their heads. The erotic significance of head hair is the same in all his texts, but this significance is actually revealed only in openly erotic scenes. It is unnecessary for me to quote further instances to indicate the auxiliary function of language in relation to hidden meanings. The linguistic identification of all manner of objects with sexuality creates chains of significance which are directed towards erotic meanings. The transition from one meaning to another becomes possible thanks to the existence of a rule-system, a code which is given by the premised significance.

The rule-system is far from complex and the reader will quickly become familiar with it. Dušek depicts his frustrated figures in their fixation with their own bodies and bodily secretions. Sweat, saliva, tears, sperm, love-juice, urine and faeces appear in Dušek's texts as frequently as birds. In fact, birds and secretions are concomitant. Old Podoba, for example, constantly speaks about his stool and observes his urine with great intensity. Adam and he compete in trying to urinate over the grass on the other side of a fence.

Dušek is less vulgar, perhaps, when he depicts women's erotic imagination. Katarína associates erect penes with flowers which have a mauvish colour and conical blossoms. Female odours are also more delicate than male. Katarína makes scents out of these phallic flowers which she applies to her body. With these scents Katarína experiences her body as an object of desire. The author, however, describes that as a sublimation. Her physicality is linked with her children.

In 'Náprstok' wetness and fire are directly connected with erotic activity. Here we find images which appear inexplicable in other texts. For example, *zápalky* (matches – also: 'inflamers'), 'little heads with fire' are identified with penes. A great deal is written about hens and cockerels. The function of these images is revealed in the subliminal actions of old Podoba. His cockerels are introduced thus: 'First the hen was mounted by a cockerel who was normal, but before he could get going, another cockerel came running up, a cockerel who had been crazy from birth; he knocked off the normal cockerel and leapt up onto his place so that he could show everyone who was boss. Podoba helps another of his cockerels to remain in place during copulation, 'he held him on with trembling hands – and that gave him his greatest pleasure'.[19] We may consider this an entirely subliminal act, because in his attacks of senile forgetfulness, when he does not remember his name and certainly not his age, the old fellow imagines he has cockerel blood in his veins. In 'Náprstok' no space is not filled with erotic meaning. The non-existence of anything beyond that meaning is so evident that, if something extraneous to that meaning appears, it is either a vulgar joke or a facetious comment like 'Men and women are the worst people in the world'.[20] No human communication is possible beyond erotic meaning. When Adam is at the front and intends writing a postcard to his wife, he is incapable of thinking of anything to say except the Slovak cliché, 'As a souvenir of my life as a soldier, Adam'.[21]

The very title of the collection, *Náprstok*, as it is explained by the author on the blurb, symbolises sexuality, *na*; *prs*; *tok* (for/onto; breast; flow/secretion). In the story itself he plainly links the thimble with Gyges's ring. Further on in the blurb the author says the book is 'a game with three sevens'. It is not clear what he means; he could be referring to the seven main orifices of the body or the Protestant seventh Commandment ('Thou shalt not commit adultery' – or in Slovak, 'you shall not fornicate'.) Seven is also the climacteric number. In occult literature seven is the number for hidden water and for arcane knowledge (perhaps, then, for Dušek, the Freudian perception of self-knowledge).

Noting the insertion of erotic meanings into words makes it easier for us to define the term 'fake narration'. When we read Dušek we actually read two texts because of his manipulation of language, the fake text and the essential text. The individual word only denotes its connotation, its hidden meaning. In this Dušek repeats his vicious circle on the linguistic level. This vicious circle lies in over-denotation. Over-denotation manifests a tendency to obliterate insufficiency. Insufficiency of language is defined by the fact that the semantic possibilities of a word are unlimited. A word is understood as a form into which meanings can be continuously inserted. Dušek takes a word's primary meaning to be an empty form which is filled by a figurative meaning. In Dušek that figurative meaning is always erotic. That constitutes the assassination of insufficiency. In this reduction of plurality to singularity one may see the fundamental flaw of Dušek's works. All possible stories in the world are reduced to one story. All words are reduced to monothematicness.

Critics in the discussion review of *Náprstok* (*Romboid*, 1986) maintain that Dušek's works contain themes like the return to childhood (history), the native town/village and so forth. We find the same thing in what critics say in the blurbs to Dušek's works. Such a determination of themes is itself empty. Dušek's themes have nothing to do with 'home', history and so forth. In fact none of the great themes of literature is to be found in Dušek: guilt, love and death. These themes cannot be there because Dušek's sexuality theme cannot contain them in any significant form.

In the story 'Potok pod potokom' (The stream under the stream, *Kalendár*) erotic meaning invades ever more territories of life. In this tale all manner of natural objects acquire meanings from the landscape of the body. It is a ritualist's celebration of the identification of everything with Eros. Trees are phalluses. Leaves are body hair. All vegetation, terrestrial and aquine, represent body-hair or hair on one's head. Insects symbolise pubic hair. The sea–shore represents the contours of the vulva. Sea-urchins, oysters and mussels represent female genitalia. Shoals of fish are streams of spermatozoa. And so it goes on. What we have is total copulation of all natural phenomena.

This is all written in earnest by Dušek; he manifests no humour in erotic matters. The narrator hero of 'Potok pod potokom' shows the reader this conception of the world as a model for the overcoming of sexual frustration. We may also consider this story as a laying bare of the author's method.

Dušek's wild passion for reducing everything is directed towards a definitive ending of erotic insufficiency, even to the extent of fusing the male and female in hermaphrodity. Hermaphrodity in the broadest sense was contained in the very structure of the fake narration, in linguistic identification leading to monothematicness, perhaps in the very mechanism of the fitting of a single meaning into the empty form of individual words. Hermaphrodity as a solution to sexual insufficiency is presented to us directly in the story 'Holokrk' (The bare-necked hen, *Poloha pri srdci*). This 'holokrk' is a bisexual hen which becomes a hermaphrodite. In this tale hens and cockerels are subliminal images of an elderly couple. The woman has only three hairs on her head and the man has lost his 'cockerel's hooves', but sometimes he hears them clinking in the distance. Before they lose their hair and 'hooves' the man has a favourite hen and the woman a favourite cockerel. When each slaughters the other's favourite bird and make soup out of them, they lose their hair and 'hooves'. When all other possibilities of sexual activity have gone, hermaphrodity remains as the only solution – in the form of the 'holokrk'. This is the extreme form of self-sufficiency. The reader sees in that a certain narcissism which goes beyond the sexual. Insufficiency has fulfilled itself.[22]

My chapter presents only one possible interpretation of Dušek's works. I have concentrated on the main part of the author's texts. The oppressive, monotonous presence of the human body, and the exclusion of all life outside the physical, the disintegration of time, and the suggestion in these texts that everything had always been the way Dušek presents it; all this is flabbergasting. I found a strange connection between the behaviour of his figures and the possible cause of that behaviour. The only key which offered an explanation of that connection was the doctrines of Freud.

No text, however, can be a definitive utterance on any matter.

NOTES

1. I quote from the Russian selection of Borges stories: Jorge Luis Borges, *Proza raznykh let* (Moscow: 1984), p. 105.
2. Dušan Dušek has published the following books for adult readers: *Strecha domu* (The roof of the house) (Bratislava: 1972); *Oči a zrak* (Eyes and sight) (Bratislava: 1975); *Poloha pri srdci*; *Kalendár* and *Náprstok*.
3. Cf. Tsvetan Todorov, *Poetika na prozata* (Sofia: 1985), p. 98.
4. Viktor Šklovskij, *Theorie der Prosa*, trans. Gisela Drohla (Frankfurt/Main: 1966), p. 63.
5. Dušek, *Poloha pri srdci* (Bratislava: 1982), p. 62.
6. Ibid., p. 56.
7. Ibid., pp. 56–7.
8. Ibid., p. 57.
9. Ibid., p. 58.
10. Ibid., p. 56.
11. Dušek, *Náprstok* (Bratislava: 1985), p. 142.
12. Ibid., p. 121.
13. Ibid., p. 156.
14. Ibid., p. 143.
15. Ibid., p. 173.
16. Ibid., p. 174.
17. Ibid., p. 28.
18. Ibid., p. 148.
19. Ibid., p. 129.
20. Ibid., p. 130.
21. Ibid., p. 132.
22. The concept 'insufficiency' is used by Angel Angelov and Dimităr Dochev in their so far unpublished lecture, 'Razmyshlenia za individualnostta na texta, predizvikani ot analizite na Leo Spitzer, za koyito toi i vsichky ostanali spomenati v doklada imena nosiat iztsyalo otgovornost' (Thoughts on the individuality of the text suggested by the analyses of Leo Spitzer and for which thoughts Spitzer, like all other persons mentioned in the paper, has full responsibility.) The authors employ the term 'insufficiency' in connection with the question of the possibility of genuine communication. They state that 'signs conceal not simply a given reality, but also real insufficiency. We might add that they conceal unconscious real insufficiency' (TS, p. 10). The term 'unconscious' is used in its psychoanalytical sense. The authors' idea is that we cannot overcome our own selves and that the body is the main obstruction to our taking part in a dialogue – with a text as with individual human beings. Angelov and Dochev conclude that an ideal cannot be general; an ideal is always somatically individual.

20 Language, Paralanguage and Metalanguage in Karol Horák's *Súpis dravcov*

David Short

> Comic dialect is humor plus anthropology.   *Leo Rosten*

Karol Horák was born in 1943 in Katarínska Huta, in the Lučenec district of south central Slovakia. He went to university at Prešov and now lectures on Slovak literature at the Arts Faculty there. At the same time he is active in both the professional and amateur theatre in Prešov and has written or produced a number of plays. Some of his work has been performed on the wireless.

His prose output has been more slender, but no less successful. His first prose work was *Cukor*, a novel which won the publishers' annual prize. It is the story of a mother who undertakes something like a pilgrimage, northwards from where she lives, to barter tobacco for sugar. There is no sugar in the house in the period immediately after the end of World War II when the supply system has yet to return to normal. For similar reasons, this ageing, almost saintly woman, is reduced to hauling her sack of tobacco across the country on foot. The immediate motivation for the trip is the perhaps imagined sugar-craving of her pregnant daughter and any possible danger lack of sugar may present to the unborn child of the woman's daughter. On her journey she has to contend with the hostile conditions of the mountains in winter and encounters a mixture of kindness and hospitality, greed, hostility and bleak indifference among the many people she meets on the way.

Since *Cukor* is not the topic of this chapter, I shall say nothing of its lyricality, its interpolated stories, its graphic portrayal of some of the characteristics and consequences of the war and the Uprising for 'independent' Slovakia, or of the contrast presented between utter selfless good and 'bourgeois materialist' baseness. Suffice it to say that *Cukor* is an emotionally appealing story, economically told, which avoids the sentimentalisation into which its subject might all too easily have led the narrator.[1]

Many critics have referred to experimental aspects of *Cukor*, but it is not surprising that even more is made of the experimental nature of *Súpis dravcov*.[2] *Súpis dravcov*, for which the literal translation of the title is totally inadequate, is a short work consisting of two *novelle*, each with a title of its own, 'Zánik dialektu' (The demise of a dialect) and 'Kurz jazyka' (The language course).

'Zánik dialektu' is the beguiling story of the efforts of an ageing philologist to capture the last remnants of a particular, hitherto undescribed, local dialect in the mountains of Slovakia as evidence for the history of proto-Slovak migration. It is an acutely felt personal mission to collect and collate material on the language, at all costs, before either he dies or the dialect is wiped out through interference from incomers once the network of main roads reaches the area. (There is an element of realism within the general theme in that the book appeared at a period when work was proceeding apace on the Slovak national dialect atlas, though this background barely encroaches on the text beyond one passing reference to the needs of the Academy of Sciences [p. 11] and a couple of references to the atlas as such, for example, p. 44.) The old dialectologist is accompanied on his wanderings by a local sixth former who, by his age and background, finds the whole enterprise rather ludicrous. Nevertheless he does accompany him to the various poor cottages where speaker-informants thought to be good examples of the dialect live, though he declines to be fully involved in the interviews. He remains an observer not only of the linguist's 'follies', but also of the environment, which is so backward that he, unlike the scholar, cannot wait for modernity to reach the area. The scholar eventually dies, abruptly, in the middle of a wake, which was almost an ideal setting for making notes on the dialect in which he is interested. He leaves behind him his tapes containing what the reader has seen as interpolated tales told by the informants. Their subsequent fate is left entirely open, though the reader is probably correct in surmising that all the work, and the tramping over the hills to do it, had been in vain. Dialect and dialectologist die together, and the wake is as much for the dialect as for the deceased.

The second story, 'Kurz jazyka', describes a week spent by the central character at an intensive language course organised at his place of work – the kind of thing that does occasionally happen. In other words, there is once more a background realism, but as with

'Zánik dialektu' it has no direct bearing on the story. The action, such as it is, for it is even more underplayed than in the first piece, is in the narrator's bewildered piecing together of what had happened after he had been on a pub-crawl with his friend. They had fought over a woman; he had bashed his friend's head against a wall; he remembers the friend's falling and banging his head again on a railway line: he recalls dragging him off to the school equipment room to recover, and finding him dead the next morning. He simply does not know whether he had killed him, or whether his friend had fatally injured himself. All this takes place against the background of, indeed merges with, the language course, which is conducted by a direct method, involving shutting out one's native tongue and beginning the foreign language from the position of a languageless child who has to learn *ab initio* how to name things, form simple utterances and so on. As the main character's mind is blanketed by post-alcohol amnesia, so the classroom is often blacked out, for the projection of slides and films. The story concerns not only language, but also conscience and consciousness, reality and illusion, cause and effect, and also it attempts, to adapt Halvoník, a striking juxtaposition of the ontological situation and a situational model.[3]

One theme of both pieces in *Súpis dravcov* is, then, language in various manifestations.[4] 'Zánik dialektu' concerns the conservation of a language, a dialect, on the brink of 'death', while 'Kurz jazyka', superficially at least, concerns the 'birth' of a user's second language. What is at first sight remarkable is that there is more than a hint that both activities are of questionable long-term value, indeed are ends in themselves,[5] at least as far as the main characters are concerned. What makes it so remarkable is the sheer breadth and depth of language-consciousness, found in Slovak writers in general, but in Karol Horák in particular.[6] The perceived demise of the dialect with the scholar's own death,[7] in other words, its (ultimate, probable) disappearance but for the artificial form of his notes and tapes, together with the failure of the language course, which had little chance of success from the outset, indicates perhaps that language, real living language as speech, is what is paramount. In the surviving dialect-speakers the dialect is not dead, inconsequential to them though it be, and, for the students of the language course, their *own* language and the ability to express their needs and fears in it is the supreme – and an inevitable – necessity. All this underlines the truisms that speech has priority over writing and that we use our language faculties far more in oral communication than in other manners. These underlying facts are quite proper to the domain of a writer otherwise associated with drama. Formally 'Kurz jazyka' owes a great deal to the dramatic text,[8] and in 'Zánik dialektu' it is far more important to have the philologist's informants talk to us direct, in the interpolated stories, than to be given any details of the kind of notes he makes or of how he intends to process his taped material. In short, Horák, while using a language researcher and a foreign-language student (and perforce a teacher) as his main props, characters from the realm of both pure, descriptive linguistics (dialectology) and applied linguistics, is not actually interested in linguistics as such. The uses of language here become a literary study, *par excellence*, far removed from the dryness of which Horák would, presumably, accuse contemporary linguistics.

It is perhaps interesting to note that in 1984–85, five years after the appearance of *Súpis dravcov*, an open polemic was pursued between writers and linguists. It began when B. Kapolka complained that the Slovak literary language was a burden and mere status symbol. For the linguists F. Kočiš (*Kultúra slova*, [1984], 18: pp. 289–92) took up the cudgels against this view, arguing for a more imaginative use of language, particularly on the wireless, and encouraging professional language-users to invite the cooperation of linguists more regularly. Most of the issue number 4 of *Kultúra slova*, 19 (1985), was then self-defensively devoted to challenging the charges of the anti-linguistics brigade and seeking to demonstrate that Slovakia's linguists had always sought to tread carefully between warranted standardisation and the excesses of purism. This particular skirmish is one reflection of the constant disquiet over the language prescription and standardisation that is so notorious in societies (Slovak, Bulgarian, Czech, French, Russian, Spanish and so forth) which have official bodies to keep tabs on the state of the language.[9] I have found little direct reference to the function of the title *Súpis dravcov*,[10] but it is tempting, among all the predators which one might discern in the work, to see the linguists or philologists, scavenging[11] among the output of the literati, as fairly high on the list of possible interpretations.

The two stories are not closely linked in plot or content, though Halvoník argues persuasively that the second offers a key to the first. They both, however, encompass a wealth of ideas on language, some more, some less explicit. Most of them can be distilled down into the overall idea that language, at all levels and viewed from whatever angle, is fraught with paradox.

The first paradox is that between the total freedom of spoken language, speech, and the constraining effect of written language. This is not an original ideal by any means. However, the evidence for the paradox is here presented with unusual subtlety. The difficulty for the writer is in getting it across using the only permanent method available to him, namely the written text, which involves a degree of unavoidable, rather than deliberate, self-irony of which he is doubtless aware. In 'Zánik dialektu' the freedom of the spoken form can be seen in several ways, in the main one of which is the very elusiveness of the dialect which the scholar is seeking to capture. Not for nothing is he described by the *Ich* as a *lovec motyľov* (butterfly hunter) or *naháňač motyľov* (beater, as in the hunt, of butterflies). The butterfly is not easy to catch; it flits from place to place, as do the scholar and his lethargic guide in their search for the dialect.[12] Moreover, butterflies have only an ephemeral existence, as does any one, synchronically viewed, stage in a language. With the primacy of spoken language comes man's freedom to name things, imitatively, or however he likes. In 'Zánik dialektu' this freedom is used to the fullest. Throughout, whether in the *Ich*'s narration, or in the interpolated tales spoken by Palenícka and Ján Poljovka, there is copious paralinguistic invention in the shape of phonetic (rather than onomatopoeic) representation of sound. Some is conventional, such as *bum, bum* (p. 10) for knocking on a door, but open to development for a more determined, agitated hammering – *bam-bum-bam-bum-bumdy-bum* (p. 11); others we have in an already developed form, such as *drindidrin* (p. 23) and *drandadran* (p. 23–4) for the sound of a mandoline, *pamparárampampam* (p. 71) for a funeral brass band, *blingcingilililingicingiling* (p. 40) for a shop bell, *ech, ech, ech – prt, prt, prt* (p. 35) for an old van staggering uphill, *hŕch, hŕch* (p. 54) for a dog growling, *hau-haf-auvuvií* for a hesitant and *auveuveuúú* (p. 64) for a determined, desperate howl of another dog lamenting his master's death, *fufufu, dududu, žíít, cveng-beng* and *rach-rach-rach* (p. 33) for a motorbike proceeding up-hill and down dale on a dirt road, and then the human sounds, from *achichuchichíí* (p. 20) for girls giggling in church to *achrap* (p. 11) for a businesslike spit, *trúút* (p. 11) for nose-blowing, *cvak-cvak-cvanky* and *cingi-cangi* or *cungi-cangi-cung* (p. 25) for the clatter of teeth and jaws during an epileptic fit – with the nasal consonant for one gold tooth, or *acheichú* (p. 16) for a cough. An extension of the same principles expresses various actions which may or may not be connected with sound, such as *cupi-lupi* (p. 10) for a brisk walk, *štipi-lipi* (p. 10) for a goose pecking at the scholar's trousers, *žmur-žmur-žmúri* (p. 11) for a cat blinking in the sunlight, *klap-klip-klap* (p. 12) for footsteps on (presumably) a wooden floor and *mľadzgi-mľadzgi* (p. 16) for fallen apples crunching underfoot. A significant feature of all of these is that they function freely in syntax as verbs, adverbs, nouns or interjections; all that is possible in Slovak with onomatopoeia, but usually it is far more limited. Little attention is paid to the device in grammer and relatively few instances are recorded (recordable) in dictionaries;[13] such works are by nature constraining and at variance with the freedom I am concerned with.

Some of the items in this class are developed morphologically to become 'true' verbs, as in *brumbrumká* (p. 42) for a mumbled *aa* with the lips closed, or *guliguligúľala* (p. 23) for a metaphorical star rolling across the sky (actually the movement of a gold tooth during a song).

This freedom of noises and the linguistic freedom to (re-)create them as primary meaningful speech sounds is complemented by a folksy tendency to create ricochet expressions, such as the standard *láry-fáry* (here: 'casually', p. 30), the Slovak-Hungarian rhyming synonym compound *fúz-bajúz* (whiskers, p. 33) and *kocúrik-košťúrik* (tom-cat, p. 24).

Another area of free linguistic creativity is punning. The effectiveness of the puns varies. Among the effective are *Šakový mal figy, teraz má figu, figy mám ja* (p. 37), based on 'figs' and a sense of 'fig' akin to the English 'not care a fig', and the double characterisation of the teacher as *ľavý bečok* (left back, dimin.) and *ľavoboček* (bastard) (p. 53).

Just as sounds and actions need to be named, so too do unique entities, in other words places and persons. In 'Zánik dialektu' there is ample evidence of the 'natural', or obsolescent, patterns of giving personal names, the various devices for distinguishing among male members of the same family – 'senior' versus 'junior' versus 'middle' *Ivanič Ján*; *Ivanič Jozef* the I, II and III; the nicknames based on alternative reduplicated consonants: *Ivanič Nanaj*, *I. Papaj* and the scatological *I. Kakaj* (pp. 9–10);[14] and the 'free' variation between nominative singular and genitive plural for adjectival surnames in the case of *Poudruhý, -ých*, the teacher. On top of that we have folksy surnames themselves, such as *Čušpajsík* or *Poljovka*, which originate in nicknames. Toponyms are equally clearly folk-descriptive, but the only linguistic fun involving them is the name of the main village, *Vyslanka*, whose original, also scatological, name *Vysranka* would once not have mattered, but has been switched as sensitivities developed. At the same time this is a side-swipe at the politically motivated habit of changing place-names that has been perhaps more widespread in Slovakia than any other territory given to such games.

In 'Kurz jazyka' the 'freedom of the spoken language' is manifested only marginally. The only elements of paralanguage are the quasi-verbal *gagaga* and *kvakvakva* (p. 111) of empty, meaningless talk at the farewell party after the course (symbolic of the total lack of real communication throughout the enterprise), the graphemically inventive *PḰKK* (p. 103) for the sound of a projector, and the pseudo-Magyar counting-out rhyme used by a child playing with a dog – *án, tán, tabo kán, ertek, bertek, baran, bokoš, cirik – pes* (p. 99). 'Kurz jazyka' also contains puns, including quite an involved pun involving *hrbolec* (heap, lump), *hrob* (grave), *hrb* (hump), *chrbat* (back) (p. 90), which serves to concentrate attention on the importance of the *hrbolec* of soil stolen from a grave and its being the only bit of usable (real, natural) soil for potting houseplants in the unnatural urban gravel, concrete and steel environment of the city. In the domain of names, the character who may or may not have been killed is called Číž (siskin), and some of the linguistic invention, including one cliché that is perhaps a pun, centres on the bird-world. *Číž* itself is onomatopoeic, which is appropriate in a work of this nature, and, like other names, it can be played with: by diminutive-formation to *čížik*[15] and by nick-name transfer to *Čimčarára* (a normal Slovak representation of twittering). This is used in answer to a subsidiary question under Question 13 in an oral exercise based on 'an outdated textbook' which looks increasingly like a police interrogation. When the *Ich* is presumably affected by his conscience, his clock *čipčali* (went cheep-cheep), and a quasi-witness's quasi-statement about the night Číž died refers punningly to *dvaja nočni vtáci* (two night-owls, literally 'birds of the night', p. 100), that is Číž and the narrator, whose name we do not know, but for whom Číž is not unlike an *alter ego*. The other name which is played with in 'Kurz jazyka' is *Ildika*, the (living) girl over whom Číž and the narrator had quarrelled, and the name on the grave where the soil was purloined. It is tempting, in the light of what we know of the narrator's attitude to nature, the countryside, 'real' soil and so forth, as opposed to the town, to see in Ildika also a near-anagram of *idylka* (cosy idyll); the cemetery with its rank grass and flowers is a cosy idyll in contrast to the brutality of life beyond its walls.

The opposite side of the freedom and primacy of spoken language is the constraining effect of the written, which is invariably portrayed as ludicrous. The narrator of 'Zánik dialektu' makes the scholar's vocal renderings and annotations of stress, rhythm and intonation totally ridiculous – in his rendition of *čo vám včely ušli* as *tatátatátatáá*, written down as *čo vám – čiara* (dash), *čely – oblúk* (arc) *usli – tátararáá*: *vlnovka* (wavy line); the irony is that the utterance he is recording was in any case *čo vam čely* (that is, colloquial *včely*) *uleteli* (p. 15). His *rarirará, rarúreri* and *oblúčiky – vlnovky – čiarky* and so on become satirical refrains debunking Academe. The very descriptions of the scholar as he tries to 'entrap' the dialect by his recordings and notes is also pejorative. He is a rather silly butterfly catcher (an allusion to *Lolita*?), an incompetently predatory tom-cat, the whole proceeding is conducted as a mission – not a scholarly mission, but a military campaign, for he wears ex-army boots; he attacks (*je v útoku*, p. 10) the village geese by kicking at them; he bellicosely (*bojoven*, ibid.) hurls stones at dogs; his fist is *v akcii* (in action, p. 11) on the schoolhouse door; he is *na pochode* (marching up and down, p. 12) as he explains things to the teacher; hearing that the destructive impact of the new road is closer than he feared, he packs his bag and *jedna, a dve, a tri, a štyri, a päť a šesť – cvak* (one and two and three and four and five, click – his bag shutting, or heels clicking, p. 13), before heading into the *terén* (terrain, ibid.), and he calls *popol a síru* (fire and brimstone) down upon those who would destroy the dialect he wishes to save. His militant approach to his work is not just a portrayal through the eyes of the *Ich*: for it is not by chance that his own account of the general dialect division of Slovak entails the word *nájazd* (incursion, p. 18) to explain the separation of West from East Slovak by the more distinctive Central Slovak, or that modern interference between dialects is viewed as *násilie* (violence, p. 14) perpetrated against an old language. Whether he is to be seen as a brusque, business-like soldier on a campaign or a knight in shining armour, he is still as ridiculous as a would-be language-trapper. The irony is that his death means his efforts are brought to nought, but his is not the death of a tragic hero.

In 'Kurz jazyka' there is a more open criticism of the unfreedom of written language, and other 'unnatural' registers of spoken language, chiefly the language of authority. The falseness of the textbook questions is an obvious case, and the criticism is all the more forceful because the textbook used so closely approaches a police interrogation. The text of a presumably internal circular concerning the reasons for the course's being established is an exemplar of officialese; it is couched in automatic phrases like *Pre potreby vzdelávania* (in the interest of education, p. 79). The language of literature is shown to be debased in a parody of the *Natureingang*, the setting of time and place and the introduction to the hero in a detective novel, here masquerading as a 'retelling in one's own words' of a story in the language class (p. 96). The language of widespread injunctions is also shown up as of dubious merit: waxed-paper beer beakers are inscribed *Po použití zničte* (Destroy after use, p. 111); the authoritarian teacher does just that, but by throwing one on the ground and jumping on it. It is no accident that Horák has here worked into his text a superficially innocent and perfectly proper piece of advice, but one which is expressed in the imperative, involves the semantics of destruction and is then distorted in the observance by the main representative of authority in the story.

The second paradox of language which Horák investigates is that of language as both living and dead, as an evolving organism and a fossil, as an instrument for the original writer as opposed to the laboratory specimen of the linguist, or language as the property of the individual as opposed to the collective. It is essentially an opposition of points of view, roughly collateral with the natural and the unnatural.

The linguist in 'Zánik dialektu' is overjoyed to find in the dialect of Vyslanka a relic of the state of Slovak five to seven centuries previously. It is not dead, but he is treating it at best as a living fossil, which he (foolishly) wants to petrify in his notebooks and tape-recorder. He is affected, however, by blindness to the fact that close inspection shows very little difference indeed between the language of his two main (aged) informants and that of his young guide. Furthermore he is tacitly portrayed as inhumane or anti-human, not only in his treatment of dogs and geese, but in his failure to realise that the dialect is only interesting (that is, archaic) because the village is so backward – electricity is a recent innovation, some cottages have only compacted earth floors, and people are still terrified of aeroplanes. (Using a concept close to them, one old villager inventively describes a biplane as 'flying yokes' [*jarmá*], p. 46.) The most imposing building in the village is the school-house, which is served by a teacher who never completed his training course (he had been thrown out for failing dialectology) and who is also best known for his erstwhile prowess as a footballer. Even the new road is intended to serve the commercial interests of a nearby quarry and will benefit the villagers only secondarily.

The opposite of the linguist's 'unnatural' attitude to language is the more 'natural' attitude of the writer of literature, demonstrated (actually paradoxically) by the existence of the work itself. Features mentioned earlier – the exploration of the freedom to switch word-classes, to invent words or to introduce and mingle a wide range of lexical levels – standard, poetic, dialectical, expressive and vulgar, can all be described as 'natural'. Part of the paradox is that this is literary artifice and experiment with form, taking the language registers to places they have not been before.

The victory of the 'natural' attitude is achieved in two ways. One is in the human approach to the character called (tellingly) Šakový (almost 'Everyman'), bearer of not only what the scholar could describe as a *hnusný* (disgusting) interdialect, but actually of the most amazing idiolect. There are far more linguistically fascinating elements in his speech than in that of any other character; that exemplifies the view that the individual is more important than the group; and it is the writer, through his narrator, who has given us this closely observed picture without learned commentary, not the scholar.[16] The second way by which the victory of the 'natural' is achieved lies in the very fact that the scholar collapses and dies. The drunken local vet does try to revive him, but the chief irony is that he might have been saved, had the road which he had so damned been built. While the road might well 'destroy' the purity of the dialect, it will serve the people. It will also probably create linguistically and otherwise more individual characters through the greater mobility it will facilitate, and so might become the salvation of even such dry-as-dust undesirables as dialectologists. Note also that the place from which the new road is to be built is called *Žiaľ* (sorrow, grief, or 'what a pity!').

The 'natural' versus 'unnatural' theme in 'Kurz jazyka' is connected largely with the foreign-language learning process which is inherently an unnatural process. In the extreme method selected the learners are required to put their mother-tongue out of their minds, which demands an enormous, perhaps superhuman effort at pretence. For with it they are expected to blank out minds and memories, which survive by nature in mother-tongue preconditioning. That this is a well-nigh impossible psychological exercise is underlined from the outset by the fact that the teacher, called a *komentátor*, and having about him much of the policeman or 'Big Brother', is portrayed as a man in a white coat. This suggests that his charges are mentally deficient (which they would be if the method of tuition had a sound basic premise) and alienated. The idea of alienation becomes dehumanisation where the students become variously *predmety* (objects; in 'Zánik dialektu' the scholar's informants are also occasionally so labelled) or just ciphers (numbered 1, 2, 3 as questions go round the classroom), and people in a picture become 'animate nouns'.

Moreover much of the teaching is conducted in the dark; thus the only perceptible things in the environment are sounds and smells. It is not surprising that the unnamed central character is desperate to find himself, be himself, by dashing off to the natural world of the woods – *vrútiť sa do lesa: čistinka – lysina – lúka*,[17] which becomes a refrain. A comparable list: *strom – kameň – dážď – slnko* (tree – stone – rain – sun) also becomes a refrain, re-humanising the girl-student, 'No. 3', to whom the self-searching narrator attaches the Hungarian name Ildika.

A possible third paradox in this work lies in the conceptions of language as a prison and language as a free agent. It is perhaps better seen as part of the opposition of the first paradox (freedom of spoken language *versus* constraints of written language), but it has overtones which put it on an altogether different plane. More is made of it in 'Kurz jazyka' than in 'Zánik dialektu'. A connection also with the second paradox is that prison is an unnatural state, and the course is conducted in a prison-like atmosphere. It is compulsory; the *komentátor* may be seen as much as a warder as any other kind of authority; the building where the course is held is in the country, but it represents not the freedom associated with the country as in 'Zánik dialektu', but a miniature of the city as prison, an unnatural closed environment; through the teaching method employed, people become metaphorically locked in things and things in people, until there is no fundamental difference between them. The pupils become locked in the (unnatural, constrained) fairy-tale world of the picture they are supposed to describe. In the dungeon-like classroom words lose, rather than gain, meaning: all that registers with the narrator at one point is the *nežné trenie jazyka o pery* (the gentle friction of tongue on lips [p. 86]; the nearest we get to the illusion that language is being dispensed with as required, the organs of speech working on in their pre-linguistic way). The main image of words as a prison comes at the opening of chapter 5. Here words enter the mind subliminally, surreptitiously, now lulling the receiver to sleep, now jerking him awake, but they *udržujú stále v zajatí* (keep one constantly captive, p. 102). The old words (ideas, memories) have had to be put away, but the new words offer no security. They are so overwhelming you cannot hear yourself breathe; they deaden the senses and it is a struggle to crack their shell and enter their world. Liberation appears to come at the end, with the party held to mark the completion of the course, and for a moment the text reads almost like something out of 'Zánik dialektu', with more paralanguage, more puns, more playing with names. Outside the classroom the *Ich* almost becomes himself again. The complication is that he is tied to the city, the elusive chimera Ildika likewise, and the new language which he has not adopted has somehow deprived him of meaningful speech. His mouth has grown over leaving nothing but a hyphen. And it was in the hostile city that Číž's still unresolved death took place, on which his memory remains blank, and neither language can help him. The irony of the situation is the belief of some students that possession of a foreign language *eo ipso* offers another form of liberation. For the teacher, probably thanks to his linguistic know-ledge, is being posted to Mexico as a diplomat and the students suspect that they too may now have better chances of travelling *von* (out, p. 111). This is the source of a triple pun, which ironises the situation even further, given that puns have previously been used in a purely playful non-destructive way. The semantics of *von* cover: a) 'getting out of prison', here present only tacitly, b) 'going abroad', which is how it is first used by the students in reference to their own chances of matching the teacher-diplomat's future, and c) 'leaving the classroom to go to the lavatory', which is how the teacher-as-teacher interprets it in replying to the student's question.[18] All three meanings emphasise the position of authority and privilege of the 'teacher' as ruler of the microcosm and thus of rulers generally. The whole leaves us with the sense that there is no third paradox, that plainly and simply language is imprisoning; but the other side lies essentially in the freedom of the natural (first two paradoxes) and in the fact that it is language itself that has enabled the author to see a situation, make the point and, like the psychiatrist's patient made to talk out his problem, be liberated. In this sense 'Kurz jazyka' ought to be optimistic, but it is only optimism tempered by the parallel, non-linguistic plot of post-alcohol amnesia and the outstanding problem of Číž's death.

Language as a prison barely comes into 'Zánik dialektu', but there are shades of it when, during World War II, Šakový had been labelled a Czech because of the quaint language patterns in which he is trapped, and the authorities try to expel him to the German

Protectorate of Bohemia and Moravia. His linguistic anarchy is mirrored by his refusal to be tied to any place of origin at all, or his insistence on being from where he happens to be at any given time. A man for all seasons and places.

Horák is an outstanding observer of language in use. This is evident both in characterisation and in the reproduction of individual speech. In 'Zánik dialektu' the *Ich* is a schoolboy, and his language has not only the general richness of rural speech, but is also rich in the expression of irreverent schoolboy attitudes to teachers (the teacher is *bývalý nepriateľ* [my former enemy, p. 12] and the school door is *pekelná brána* [the Gate to Hell, p. 10]) and authority generally, including the Church. We see this in his use of metaphors from sport, mostly athletics and football (the dialect hunting trip itself is *puť, klus, atletika s prekážkami* [a hike, a trot, an obstacle race, p. 10]) and in the language of the textbooks from a variety of lessons, entirely appropriate to his mock indulgence for learning in the presence of the scholar, the teacher and the schoolhouse itself. His description of the village houses in un-Slovak Slovak as *drevenokamennohlinasté* (wooden-stone-mud, p. 9) is redolent of the geography textbook; the village's being deserted at harvest time reminds him that it would be a good opportunity for the Turks to attack and pillage (the Turkish period, obviously important in local history has also given rise to the nickname 'Bajazid' for the teacher and once-renowned left-back, after Bayezid I, the sultan who defeated the Hungarians); the high style of literature, in fact a parody of lines 3 and 4 of the opening stanza of Andrej Sládkovič's (1820–72) *Detvan*, a classic with strong patriotic associations, surfaces in his introduction to the village itself: *dedinka Vyslanka zvaná, mať stará chýrnych ožranov* (a village, Vyslanka by name, mother old of fabled drunks, p. 9); and of course language lessons have left their mark: the *Ich*'s attitude to language is neatly conveyed by a simple parsing exercise: *pedagog sa s nami lúči podstatným menom plus slovesom: na nárečie – srať* (the teacher bade us farewell with a noun plus a verb: sod the dialect! p. 14). (At this point we do not yet know why the teacher should have such strong feelings on the subject.) Although the language of the *Ich* is fundamentally the same as that of the older informants, some of his metaphors show him to be of the twentieth century, despite the backwardness of his village. Thus the sight of the cane reminds him of *mapy detského zadku, podliate klobásy poludníkov a rovnobežiek* (maps of a child's bottom, swollen weals of longitudes and latitudes, p. 13), and the description of the priest (a character otherwise associated with sporting metaphors) becomes (*ako*) *pásák, vlastne teda pásáčik do kopca ťahá* (like a [caterpillar] tractor, actually more a mini-tractor grinding up the hill, p. 19). The switch to the diminutive here is typical of the language of the *Ich*, whose indulgent attitude to the strange ways of adults is largely conveyed through diminutive forms, a pattern set in the arresting opening paragraph, with its *pinklík* (duffle bag), *ruksaštek* (rucksack), *hatižáčik* (back-pack), *bagančičky* (boots), and the later *ceruztička* (pencil), *papierik* (paper), *obalček* (folder), *magneťáčik* (tape-recorder) and countless others. It is also a manifestation of the liberation of language in that it is a resort, beyond the normal measure, to a device that is already present in it. Similarly liberating is, for example, the *Ich*'s destruction of clichés in, for example, his *sedemmílové tenisky* (seven-league trainers, p. 19).

For his part the scholar is characterised by his one-track-mindful dialectological researches. Most of the metalanguage, the language about language, appears in his speech, but unlike the *Ich*, who is aware of actual verbs and actual nouns, the scholar is concerned with what come to appear as unreal irrelevances: his *zvyšky cirkumflexu* (remnants of the long falling tone) or his imperfect transcriptions of the *rarirara* type. This pompous scholarly discourse and the urgency of his getting back to process his material contribute to his portrayal as a quixotic figure.

The teacher in 'Kurz jazyka' is also very simply characterised by the language he uses, from his formulaic opening *Vážení priatelia* (respected friends, p. 80), to his long-winded sentences and individual lexical items such as *kádry* (personal files, ibid.), *evidovať* (register [misused], p. 109) and *najefektívnejšie* (to greatest effect, p. 80), and high incidence of imperatives. His discourse is hardly individual, but it is at least as well observed as a type of some of the genuine individual speech patterns in 'Zánik dialektu', whether they are those of the informants specifically being studied by the scholar, or of the other characters whose speech is simply reproduced by the *Ich*. The variety of styles or registers in *Súpis dravcov* is not just in the different longer discourses or consistent speech patterns that characterise, but also in the register-changes brought about by individual incidents. Thus the dry-as-dust scholar becomes a normal, linguistically inventive Slovak when he is made angry by attacking geese, and he produces the expletive *gunárisko gunáriskové gunáriskovité* (approximately: ganderish gandery gander, p. 10); at the party towards the end of 'Kurz jazyka' we have the well observed soppy emotionality of the tongue-tied drunken bureaucrat-teacher, including the possibly telling stutter *sing-sing-signnálnych sústav* (sing-sing-signalling systems, p. 111): how well Sing-Sing prison is known to the Slovaks I have no idea, but the stutter which matches its name stands adjacent and in apposition to *reči* (speech), which could underline further the language-prison theme. If deliberate, this is the most sophisticated pun in the book.

Horák's skill with language is not just in the observation and reproduction of patterns of speech, not just 'linguistically literary'. He has his own purely literary skill as well. Suffice it to recall the description of, for example, Čušpajsík's epileptic fit (pp. 25–8), the scene at the funeral as everyone tries to pile into the hired bus-trailer (p. 65), or any passage involving action, such as Šakový's motorbike or van proceeding across the country, the corpse bouncing in the coffin on the back of the lorry (p. 67; corpses generally have a rough time in *Súpis dravcov*), Poljovka's expropriation of Šakový's groceries (a lesson in how things fall off the back of lorries; pp. 36–7), or the turning over of Poljovka and many others.

The two stories, while containing elements of both the natural and unnatural poles, are nevertheless fundamentally each representative of one. 'Zánik dialektu' is rich and creative on a purely linguistic and stylistic level; language here explores its own nature by the hand of the writer, who endows it with a wealth of alliteration and assonance, rhyme and rhythm and enlivens it by inventive diminutive formation and the incorporation in the text of the 'given', the linguistic heritage, not just of dialect, but also of proverbs, sayings, nursery rhymes and folk songs. It is dynamic and made more so by frequent use of asyndeton, by lists of especially graphic, often onomatopoeic verbs and verbal nouns and countless other devices. 'Kurz jazyka', in its 'freer' moments, also has all of these elements, but the free play is generally absent. What is left is an adventurous attempt to smash the rigidity of linguistic formality (officialese and highly artificial and regulated foreign-language learning). The variation of form: dialogue as in a play, or film, static film clips, 'normal' narrative, gives us just short jagged splinters of the larger picture. 'Zánik dialektu' contains a warning, given that a dialect is a language too, that nothing should interfere with the freedom to create what an unfettered language offers; 'Kurz jazyka', is a depressing picture of the other extreme, a warning against regimentation, against setting a 'course' (*kurz*) for man or his language, against giving language a fixed (that is, limited) value (*kurz*).

The work's critical reception has largely been positive, most writers appreciating that Horák is using language to talk about language. I would agree with Sulík that in Horák we have a rare and bold experimenter in a literature and at a time when few avail themselves of the spontaneously generative capacity of language.[19] On the other hand I cannot agree with Truhlář that underlying the scholar's dialect and folklore researches is the less symbolic, 'more solid' search for the meaning of life and its mosaic quality.[20] Truhlář also believes that 'Kurz jazyka' is too fragmentary, complicated, sophisticated and recherché. Čúzy considers the fragmentation an asset, though he confines his assessment to method and content, saying nothing about language, either as vehicle or subject. Oddly, Čúzy also consistently misquotes it as 'Kurz jazykov' (languages course). Ján Jurčo also gives the work a positive reception,[21] concluding that the reader will gain a 'powerful, ethical, cognitive and an aesthetic experience from it'. On 'Zánik dialektu' he refers to the style 'charged with sub-text' and on 'Kurz jazkya' to 'a number of semantic zones and associations', but refrains from spelling out what the subtext or associations are. Karol Tomiš[22] singles out 'Kurz jazyka' as the sole exception in recent Slovak prose to 'search for aspects of reality so far undiscovered by literature, for new means of expression and unconventional formal procedures'. The least positive view of the work is Peter Andruška's.[23] It denies that the subjects are new and unknown and says they are simply not normally discussed, or are discussed in other terms. Then, having characterised the particular novelty of Horák's method, he denies him any primacy, though he does not say whom Horák is following. What is worse, he criticises Horák for burying man and reality beneath a welter of words, making his demonstration of what language can do an end in itself, unworthy of an above-average writer. The only Czech reaction to the work I have found,[24] which appeared a year behind the early Slovak reviews, is unreservedly positive; it notes the formal elements of drama and originality of style and is unique in mentioning the linguist's death. Otherwise it is restricted to retelling the 'plots' while appreciating that the language and style are unequivocally paramount, but as form and material, not subject.

All the critics pick up the fact that *Súpis dravcov* was written before *Cukor*, though published after. This suggests it was perhaps a trial run for some of the modes of experimentation in which Horák indulges. Its shortness would then account for the widely perceived density, or intensity, of the role of language which becomes somewhat reduced in *Cukor*. Thematically *Cukor* is also less controversial, and its success 'eased the passage' for *Súpis dravcov*.

All the critics have agreed that *Súpis dravcov* is a work of great humour, which is undoubtedly the case, but applying more to 'Zánik dialektu' than 'Kurz jazyka'. Some writers have classed it as grotesque, which is only partly true;[25] while there are undoubtedly grotesque elements, there is far more humour of other kinds – parody, slapstick, satire, not to mention the purely linguistic humour underlying some of the points discussed earlier. Throughout the book Horák is a literary and linguistic magician, and nothing better sums the work up than Rosten's prescient observation that 'there is a magic in dialect which can liberate us from the prisons of the familiar'.[26]

NOTES

1. *Cukor* has been widely reviewed, but one of the most sensitive and thoughtful accounts of how it differs conspicuously from the mainstream of modern Slovak prose is Alexander Halvoník's 'Slávnosť pohybu', *Romboid*, 15 (1980), 7, pp. 80–2.
2. Halvoník alone plays down the experimental qualities of *Súpis dravcov*: 'It is probably pointless to emphasise the "experimental" nature since what is unconventional in it is organically tied in with its content and is unlikely to have any deliberate programmatic status'. Ibid., p. 81.
3. Ibid.
4. Indeed Horák, in an interview with *Rozhlas*, 1980, 51, p. 24, describes it as the protagonist.
5. In his review of the work, 'Vizitka prozaickej vyspelosti', *Večerník*, 17 April 1980, p. 5, Ivan Sulík accepts as an entirely positive matter that the scholar is trying selflessly to retrieve the dying linguistic and folklore heritage of the village, which is itself indifferent to its cultural heritage. By contrast, Ladislav Čúzy, 'Poetika a interpretačné možnosti (nad prózami Karola Horáka)', *Romboid*, 17 (1982), 4, pp. 22–6, notes that doubt is cast on the value of such work. He believes the intent is purely satirical of collection-mania, unsupported by any positive results, and would doubtless agree that this is a portrayal of the type of 'intellectuals [who] place too high a premium on the sheer ingestion of data' (Leo Rosten, *The Return of Hyman Kaplan*, London, 1959, p. 18). This too is not entirely fair since we do know the kind of conclusions the scholar hopes to reach.
6. Another recent example of transparent linguistic (as opposed to literary) language consciousness, but exploited to effect in literature, is Ivan Hudec's 'Saský genitiv, vokáň a ja' (The saxon genitive, circumflex and I), which is an extended play on certain orthographic devices in English and Slovak, including a sideways look at the consequences of the conceit for dialect. The story is in the collection *Záhadný úsmev štrbavého anjela*

248   *Language, Paralanguage and Metalanguage*

(Bratislava: 1987), pp. 132–9.
7. It is unfortunate that the scholar's death is not mentioned by reviewers. Clearly to do so would be to deprive the readers they hope to encourage to turn to the book of the discovery of the dénouement, but without mentioning it they deprive themselves of a whole line of reasoning which this paper will seek to follow. 'LC' in *Nové knihy*, 27 November 1980, p. 1, comes closest, but fails to see how it makes a denial of his other claims for the book.
8. A point noted by Čúzy, though in terms of the film scenario, and by the author of the entry on Horák in *Encyklopédia slovenských spisovateľov*, (Bratislava: 1984), vol I, pp. 204–5, who describes it as a *scénická montáž* (scenic montage) and a work 'more vocal than specifically literary and book-like'. This neatly encapsulates the irony of having to express in writing, which is permanent, that which is essentially transient.
9. Ivan Sulík's review contains a foretaste of the debate, attacking the anti-linguists and using Horák as an example of what can be done by the linguistically sophisticated writer. I believe his view of Horák is thus far correct, but Horák is a 'literary linguist' with no pretensions to being a 'linguist' as such. I suspect the idea might horrify him.
10. Sulík's review mentions the *dravci* in inverted commas, but it is by no means clear who or what he thinks they are. Implicit in Halvoník's review is that 'dravosť' (rapacity, impetuosity) is a ravenous, dynamic yearning for knowledge, closely associated with the 'pohyb' (motion) of the review's title (see note 1): 'a transformation of movement by means of artistic language, a testing of language's capacity to capture that which is transitory, ever-changing and never standing still alongside that which is constant and unchanging, an investigative [also 'reconnaissance'] shooting of the word at big-bellied banalities, suspected anaemias, relative voids and much-vaunted certainties' (p. 81).
11. My image of scavenging is meant entirely non-technically. There is in any case no proper word for it in Slovak paradigmatically opposed to *dravec* except the rare loan-word *saprofág*, which the common readership would not know, although there are species-specific terms suggesting in particular carrion-scavengers (cf. the Slovak translation of the first version of this paper in *Romboid*, March 1988). If my image were taken strictly, it would be an insult to literature in general and Horák in particular. For scavengers haunt the dead and putrescent while predators, *dravci*, prey on the living. If my interpretation of the title of *Súpis dravcov* has any foundation, then it would also require acceptance of the view that literature, as well as language, is a living organism.
12. The parallel with Don Quixote has not escaped reviewers, for example, Halvoník or Čúzy, in their respective reviews, see notes 1 and 4.
13. One such is *pif*, occurring here and there in 'Zánik dialektu', and *frng* (here *fŕŕng*, p. 58).
14. This type of name-giving has been another target for linguists in a variety of articles in recent issues of *Onomastický zpravodaj* and *Recueil linguistique de Bratislava*, which adds to the topicality of *Súpis dravcov*.
15. If one wished to stretch the view that Horák is 'having a go' at the linguists, even this name is worthy of note. *Číž* is a dialect word for the

siskin; *čížik*, in full *čížik obyčajný*, is the well-established name for the bird, but under recent changes in nomenclature it is now officially called *stehlík čižavý*. While the appliance of science has thus brought members of *carduelis* together terminologically (for example, siskin and goldfinch – *stehlík obyčajný*), it has also committed the double silliness of deliberately divorcing Slovak further from Czech, a 'policy' that caused raised eyebrows on both sides of the Carpathians when it was at its height, and of elevating an onomatopoeic (more or less) nonce-word, *čižavý*, which does not even figure in the dictionary, to the status of a species-specific adjective.

16. The speech of Šakový, far more than of any of the characters, has such linguistic distinctiveness that, in its creative (that is literary, not linguistic) transcription, it 'seduce[s] the eye to reach the ear and [is] orchestrated in the brain'. (L. Rosten, *The Return of Hyman Kaplan*, p. 14).

17. This is a good example of Horákian deftness with language. From *les* (forest) he switches to *čistinka* (a forest clearing, bearing the semantics of *čistý* – pure, clean), thence to the near-synonymous *lysina*, but referring to a treeless patch not necessarily in the forest, then to *lúka* (meadow), a far larger open space, joined to *lysina* by alliteration. By a switch from the genitive *lesa* to the nominative of the other three expressions he has also achieved word-final assonance, a typical piece of the sound-consciousness so much more at home in 'Zánik dialektu', but rare in the world of 'Kurz jazyka'.

18. This is just one example of the vulgarisation of language and the philosophy of language in which the teacher indulges.

19. *Kapitoly o súčasnej próze* (Bratislava: 1985), pp. 111–12.

20. Břetislav Truhlář, reviewing *Súpis dravcov* in *Slovenské pohľady* 96, (1980), 10, pp. 119–20.

21. 'Prekvapujúci prístup k životu', *Pravda*, 61, 149, 26 June 1980, p. 5.

22. 'Na ceste umeleckého dozrávania', *Slovenské pohľady*, 100 (1984), 4, pp. 10–30, especially pp. 29–30.

23. 'Próza ako experiment', *Nové slovo*, 22 (1980), no. 29, p. 20.

24. Zuzana Bělinová: 'Přínos slovenské prózy', *Literární měsíčník*, 10, (1981), 5, pp. 117–18.

25. For a detailed recent appraisal of the grotesque see R. B. Pynsent's 'Čapek-Chod and the Grotesque', in Pynsent (ed.), *Karel Matěj Čapek-Chod: Proceedings of a Symposium* (London: 1985), pp. 181–215.

26. L. Rosten, *The Return of Hyman Kaplan*, p. 15.

21 The New Composite Poem in Contemporary Slovak Verse and its Relationship to the Development of Slovak Prose

Marián Kováčik

Poetry ranges from a simple lyric poem like a nursery rhyme to extensive lyric compositions with strong narrative or dramatic tones. The uniqueness of the individual fate can be expressed by the sovereign form of the sonnet as well as by an epic in its various cultural historical versions. Though it is clear that the effectiveness of a poem does not depend upon the number of its lines, a poet who has achieved a certain degree of human and artistic maturity, usually tries to express his individual intellectual and emotional experience in a more demanding form. In the Slovak poetry of the last 30 years that form is represented by the 'composite poem', which integrates the results and methods of the classical literary genres as well as the achievements of the new poetics of the twentieth century.

The genre which has at various stages of its development been labelled epos, lyrical epopée, short epic verse, broadly-based epic poetry, verse cycle, narrative poem, poetic montage, and so forth, has a tradition stretching back to the dawn of Slovak poetry. Slovak neo-Classicists and the Romantic poets of the Štúr period, Realists and poets of the Slovak *Moderne*,[1] Proletarian Poets,[2] Slovak Surrealists, as well as poets who reached creative maturity only after World War II, all contributed to the development of the genre. In 1956, evaluating the poetry of the early 1950s, Alexander Matuška (1910–75), one of the greatest Slovak scholars and critics in this century, saw the problems of further expanding epic tendencies in Slovak lyric verse thus:

Demands for epics and for 'epicisation' are heard. But these demands do not seem to be entirely justified, for, quite apart from the fact that few poems lack a narrative element and an element, however small, of plot, they will lead to [. . .] even greater descriptiveness and poverty of ideas and to giving even less care to poetic form. Epicisation diverts poetry from one of its basic tasks, that is, to bring the actions and activities of life to a standstill and observe them by means of establishing their meaning, that is, to illuminate things and make them understandable. Epicisation, all right, to a certain degree. But these one-sided demands for the epic by no means offer salvation; they embody purely superficial advice and belong among those sorts of remedies that cure no one and nothing. At least not that imprecise, unconcise, long-winded Slovak lyric verse of ours.[3]

Matuška's scepticism sprang from the knowledge that poetry cannot overcome its own wretched condition merely through formal, in some cases only formalist, changes to its awkward appearance; poetry had to undertake a much more fundamental regeneration of its creative abilities. It is true, however, that in the 1950s works of poetry were written that belong to the basic canon of Slovak socialist literature, works expressing in an artistically fruitful manner the poet's active, committed attitude to the new movements in society. But the beginning of the 1950s was also the period when poetic mediocrity with its glorifying rhetorics, its black-and-white vision and greyness of expression was thriving. Thus this phenomenon, nowadays called 'schematism'[4], became one of the many problems that literature had to face and solve in the spirit of the social changes inspired by the XXth Congress of the Communist Party of the Soviet Union (1956). It was particularly the younger poetic generation and primarily its artistically progressive members (Milan Rúfus and Miroslav Válek) who made for the '*perestroika*' of those days. Their platform was the monthly *Mladá tvorba*, founded in 1956.

The beginning of this process of innovation is characterised by the young writers' critical attitude towards earlier literary practice and, most of all, towards the unimaginative results of that practice. Together with a definite worldview, they stress the moral importance of veracity in art. The individuality of the author and his own unique style (and at that time an author had to fight for the right to sadness) are again considered to be the *sine qua non* of creativity. There was no question of any attempt to weaken the bonds between the artist and society or to achieve ivory-tower stature for the artist, but rather

to surmount the barrier between the purely subjective and the poetic
expression of belonging to a society, while the writer still preserved
his or her autonomy. This endeavour to make interaction between
the individual and the collective more effective could be brought
about on the basis of the authentic intellectual and emotional
experience of the poet. The young writers of this period also showed
an intense interest in the Avant-Garde of the earlier twentieth century
and its predecessors. Free verse, association, rich 'modern' imagery
are used more and more. Poets start making extensive use of sub-
text, and an active attitude is demanded of the reader. A poetic trend
called Concretism emerged (nothing to do with Concrete Poetry)
which programmatically emphasised the aesthetic, sensual effect of
poetry. When these poets actually got writing they were not as one-
sided as their programme suggested. Many talented authors began
to write poetry in this period, but there is no doubt that the most
important role in this creative atmosphere was played by Miroslav
Válek, not only in his poetry itself, but also in his contribution to
defining what modern socialist poetry was. In his conception the idea
assumes that dominant position as the bearer of the poetic in the
poem; further, the realistic nature of poetry is stressed, but that does
not exclude the exploitation of 'modern' means of expression; Válek
also demands continuity with national and socialist poetic traditions.
This programme is considered valid to this day, and it still forms the
foundation for bold, wide-ranging works of verse.

The contemporary composite poem is an attempt to create a
comprehensive, but also concise, universal artistic treatment of an
open-ended series of polymorphous, often inconsistent, realities from
today's world; it is an endeavour to understand these realities'
relations with the individual and his historical perspective. This new
type of verse has its source in a broader, more intellectualised
personal, but also collective, experience than the purely subjective
lyric poem; it tries to depict life in a more complete form than had
its predecessors. It is based on the assumption that any reality can
serve as impulse and subject of a poem; at a certain stage in literary
development that could even be a reality that had previously been
considered taboo for poetry. The new composite poem consists in a
number of fragments of approaches taken from other genres and
forms of art, such as narrative fiction, film and journalism. These
components do not usually form any semantic or chronological
progression but contribute, each in its own way, to the total ideological
and aesthetic effect of the composition. In this multi-genre compo-

sition the epic (narrative) plays an important role. In contrast to traditional epic verse, however, the epic (narrative) does not serve here to create a story-line of characters, but to lend the work a profounder message than it would otherwise have. The composite poem relinquishes the monologue form of utterance of the lyrical *persona*; that *persona* is normally replaced by a more objective narrator. Its aim is not commentary but the actual re-creation of states or events within the space of the composition. In spite of the fact that the new composite poem differs in many respects from standard lyric utterances, because of its greater capacity to express subjective feelings, it demonstrates a profounder lyricality than earlier types of poetic expression, even though it does not employ the usual means of lyric verse.

It takes from narrative fiction the deliberate use of an audible narrator, the presence of various characters, dialogue, the employment of situation frameworks, and also the action itself, where the *sujet* of the action, its chronologically non-linear side, is emphasised. Film-making provides methods like sudden cuts, changes in angle of vision and montage that give the stream of memories, experiences, thoughts and events its special pace. Another principle used in the composite poem is that of polyphony, that presents, in the form of dialogue, movement or chorus, a variety of voices which may often appear to be in disharmony. The interplay of various chronological levels and variation of space are other characteristics of this new composite poem.

Substantial innovation will be found also in the language. The language of composition becomes democratic; the writer takes off his poet's buskins, leaves the hermetic world of conventional meanings, rids himself of clichés, sentimentalisations and substitutes all this with exact, natural means of expression. He may use the language of science and technology or sport or indeed the slang of various social groups. With such new language comes a new imagery, based not only on elementary poetical tropes like simile or metaphor, but also on the interaction of the larger structures (a microstory or a sequence). A composite poem is nearly always in free verse and its rhythm depends on language organised according to intonation. When rhyme is employed it occurs in unusual positions.

Typologically, the new composite poem follows on from the method used by Apollinaire in 'Zone' (*Alcools*), but it subordinates his purely associative principle to more marked ideational and compositional aims. If a unifying plot dominates the work, its other semantic planes will be decisive. This penetration of a wide range of literary means of expression into all levels of poetic utterance is characterised by Stanislav Šmatlák as poetic syncretism or genre syncretism.[5]

All these elements give the composite poem a new quality, a higher degree of 'artistic knowledge' of the basic problems of human existence and their relation to society is brought about by an optimal harmony of the discursive reflection, imaginative thought and emotional expression. This knowledge is deepened by a unique linking of the intellect and the poetic imagination.

Válek played a key role in the forming of the new programme for verse; in his own verse the new composite poem prevails. Válek constantly compares and contrasts contradictory historical and personal experiences. Šmatlák characterises Válek's poetry as 'the collusion of brain and senses', and he describes its new form thus:

> It is especially in the development of Válek's poetry that the traditional type of intimate lyrical utterance is gradually replaced by a new type of poetic syncretism. In it, the semantic elements relating to the inner situation of the lyric subject meet and cross the paths of the sort of *motifs* we know from epic and dramatic representations. This creates a relationship of objective comparability between the semantic and compositional structures of the poem and the form of the outside world in all its complex, but basically identifiable, inconsistencies.[6]

So Válek's composite poems, in their qualitatively new form, become a creative inspiration also for members of the poetic generation who made their starts in literature only in the second half of the 1950s and who created their own variations of the new sub-genre, poets like Ján Buzássy, Ľubomír Feldek, Mikuláš Kováč or Jozef Mihalkovič.

The efforts to overcome the boundaries of the traditional lyrical utterance in the new composite poem and the development of Slovak prose fiction have many common features. New Slovak fiction also feels the need to express veracity, to make its own authentic statement about the objective world and to renew its formal apparatus. It is, however, poetry that, because of the new course it takes and because it is more adaptable than prose, plays the leading, inspirational role in the beginnings of *Mladá tvorba*. Though inexperience prevented young fiction writers from presenting full verisimilitude, they succeeded in expressing their own vision in a new way that links the prose-writer Rudolf Sloboda with the Concretists, and indeed Sloboda became something like an honorary member of that group. Later on, the traditional provinces of poetry and prose were extended to the point of their mutual penetration. While the purpose of narrative tendencies in poetry was to heighten its objective validity, prose, originally inspired by the tradition of so-called Lyrical Prose (for example, Šikula), made use of poetic devices to give its message inner depth. Initially prose and poetry shared a common set of themes that is particularly linked with the world of childhood and adolescence with its social, historical and geographical determination; in prose and verse immediacy of expression is stressed, as well as lyrical sensibility and imagination. In their means of expression poetry and prose both prefer *sujet* to the carefully constructed plot; they also share their accentuation of the sub-text, their creation of streams of experience and ideas and their underlining of the personal concern of their narrators. These two apparently contradictory approaches, the objectivisation of the poetic message by the use of narrative (epic) or dramatic elements and the subjectivisation of prose by the introduction of lyrical elements, are made one by their common goal, that is greater truthfulness.

The development of literature, like any other development, has its natural laws and limits. In the 1960s exaggerated emphasis on subjectivity and, most of all, negligence of the social relations of art led to an ivory-tower mentality and thus a loss of communicativeness in some Slovak poetry and prose. The remarkable products of Slovak fiction in the 1970s and 1980s demonstrate that Slovak literature has succeeded in overcoming this 'inverted schematism'. And it was again poetry that took the initiative in highlighting the close relationship between the individual and the collective at the beginning of the 1970s.

Mature Slovak fiction writers who have used their individual experience to give their works inner depth and have established their own unmistakable hallmark, are now facing the task of undertaking a more complex treatment of reality. In their broadly conceived historical novels, the phenomenon of genre syncretism is as present as it is in the contemporary new composite poem. Typical examples of this syncretism are Peter Jaroš's *Tisícročná včela* and *Nemé ucho, hluché oko*, where we find the optimal harmony of the grotesque, the absurd, the picaresque novel, and historical document and journalism on a pronouncedly realistic background.

The development of Slovak prose over the last 30 years has led on from a search for the personal, unique expression, from an effort to express the individuality of the author, to a more objective, but still authentic, representation of humanity and its world. This development is analogous to the development of the Slovak poetry and the new sub-genre of the composite poem.

NOTES

1. The Slovak *Moderne* included the poets gathered in the anthology, *Sborník slovenskej mládeže* (Budapest and Prague: 1909) and the periodical, *Prúdy* (Budapest: 1909–14; Bratislava: 1922–38), like Janko Jesenský (1874–1945), Martin Rázus (1888–1937), and Vladimír Roy (1885–1936), the last two of whom in their early work continued and developed the innovations of the Slovak Symbolist Ivan Krasko (1876–1958) who was also part of the *Moderne*. They attempted to liberate verse from Realist and nationalist ponderousness. Rázus, however, later in his career became a fervent nationalist poet and prose-writer. Incidentally, he and Roy spent some time in the United Kingdom before World War I at the invitation of R. W. Seton Watson.

2. Slovak Proletarian Poetry came onto the scene when Czech Proletarian Poetry had already failed; the convention is to call Ján Poničan's (1902–78) first collection, *Som, myslím, cítim a vidím, milujem všetko, len temno nenávidím* (I am, I think, feel and see, I love everything, only darkness I hate, 1923), the beginning of Slovak Proletarian Poetry. In fact in 1923 there were very few Slovak proletarians anyway. Ladislav Novomeský's first collection, *Nedeľa* (Sunday, 1927) was strongly under the influence of the School. Probably the most successful writer of Proletarian Poetry in Slovak was Daniel Okáli (1903–88) whose slim collection, *Ozvena krvi a zápasov* (Echoes of blood and struggles, 1932) did not see a new edition until 1973, when other Proletarian poems of the 1920s and 1930s were included.

3. Alexander Matuška, *Od včerajška k dnešku* (Bratislava: 1978), pp. 51–2.

4. Editor's note: 'schematism' is the eastern-bloc term for Socialist Realism as 'personality cult' is the term for Stalinism or 'stagnation' for Brezhnevism and all results of the 'Brezhnev doctrine'.

5. Cf. Stanislav Smatlák, *V siločiarach básne* (Bratislava: 1983), p. 115, and 'Kritici diskutujú o Kováčikovom Medzimeste', *Romboid* (1984), 11, pp. 13–15.

6. Stanislav Šmatlák, *Dve storočia slovenskej lyriky* (Bratislava: 1979), pp. 473–4.

22 The Translation of a Literary Work into a Projective Form: Papp's *Kára plná bolesti*

Slavomír Magál

Papp's first prose work, *Kára plná bolesti*, appeared when he was already a man of 40. It was appropriately described by critics as a compromise with Lyrical Prose. The author depicts a social problem of considerable gravity using the form of a lyrical ballad with only minor elements of actualisation. This resulted in shortcomings and controversial points in Papp's work and it affected the author's approach to the reality reflected, which oscillates between a social critical attitude and a 'poetic' depiction of the depth and strength of human life.

Historically speaking, *Kára plná bolesti* represents a departure from the subject-matter and compositional methods of the time of writing. It also constitutes a return to Lyrical Prose, a stage in the history of Slovak literature which had ostensibly long completed its development. However, in spite of the difficulty in defining its form, the story of two outcasts contains some qualities of general validity illustrated by the unshakeable faith of man in the possibility of better conditions for life. This inspired attempts at reviving Papp's work in the form of a theatre production (adaptation by Jozef Mokoš, directed by Juraj Svoboda at the Nová scéna in Bratislava, 1984), or the film of the same title produced by Slovak Television in collaboration with Slovak Film in 1986.

Studying the translation of conflict between period and sub-genre into another (projective) art form allows us to analyse the vitality of the lyrical current within Slovak prose and its potential in a new historical situation. *Kára plná bolesti* is an intimate story about two friends, Jakub and Majo, both of whom often find themselves in conflict with the surrounding world. Their characterisation is simple: both excessively trust people, who invariably abuse their trust. The characters' internal conflict with the outer world results from their

inability to conform with the prevailing spirit of determinism and to
develop, grow and simply live with the totality of human relations
marked by unfavourable social circumstances and the war.

The action is considerably weakened to the benefit of a 'higher
objective' – ideology. A basic contradiction is shown to be the
contradiction between the individual experience of men and their
indifference to others in everyday encounters. The story itself emerges
as a rounded set of minor episodes which, along with the precisely
outlined axis of the main story, offers an insight into the complexity
of the characters' thinking and acting. The fact that the key characters
are revealed through both contemplation and action induces a
considerable degree of tension in the reader. This is the basic attribute
of the subsequent projective adaptation. Because of the characters'
fundamental decency and their faith in humanity, they are very much
themselves despite their social handicap as model personalities not
only in the literary but also in the projective dramatic presentation.

From the point of view of its composition Papp's work recalls a
mosaic pieced together from short dramatically charged adventures
with a strong tragic background. Contemporary criticism put Papp
somewhere behind the trio Hronský, Švantner and Šikula, apparently
more because of their affinity of type and their common use of Lyrical
Prose elements than because they considered Papp an opportunist
imitator. The definition of the basic relations between the characters
through action was of immense benefit for the 'projective' adaptation.
As a rule, the conflicts carry in themselves the germs of new
meanings and starting points for the development of the story. The
determination of characters by action simplifies the dramatic vision
without necessitating lengthy explanations of the peripeteias through
dialogue. For example, the dramatic climax in Jakub's relation
towards his sister Tereza during their fight does not constitute only
the culmination of their conflict, but also the source of one of the
key *motifs* – the feeling of guilt for the fatal lot of Tereza. Similarly,
Jakub's fight with the circus strongman represents above all his
desperate struggle to find his place in society – any society and at
any price.

In these binary meanings, the emotional and lyrical levels of the
novella do not pose problems for subsequent visual interpretation
and do not even lead to communicative short-circuits of the kind that
occurred in previous film versions of Lyrical Prose novels, for
example, Figuli's *Tri gaštanové kone*, Chrobák's *Drak sa vracia*. In
this regard it is an advantage for the film adaptation of *Kára plná*

bolesti that each conflict contains a moment of decision-making. The characters become aware of the human responsibility for their actions. Jakub and Majo's freeing the doe-hare, when they find out that she is with young, is typical of this awareness. The author does not encumber this episode with verbal ballast. He leaves room for his reader's thinking and allows for an organic association of images and the interpretation of the symbol.

Papp does not develop large monumental themes or look for world-shattering heroes. Like Šikula, he choses outcasts and eccentrics living on the margins of society. Their simple life is determined by a great ideal which finds its expression in one chapter title, 'There might be such a place somewhere'. The characters have exceptionally strong sensual perception; they live in close contact with Nature and they consider details more important than the world as a whole. They are used to free decision-making as one of the few advantages of existence at the bottom of the social hierarchy. Every intervention from the outside means a new shock for them. Their desire to affirm their own human and social values is emotionally impressive. Jakub in particular rebels directly and convincingly against senseless military drill and against the character named Mara of Husťák, who in a naive application of some kind of 'people's' capitalism attempts to deprive him of the only privilege he has ever had in his life – the right of exclusive ownership of the cart in which he carries water from the spring, an ownership which is useful to the community.

The social machinery with Mara as its extended tentacle not only invades the integrated world of the two main characters; it also becomes the symbol of a spider that prevents people from behaving according to the principles of humanity. Mara's death and the end of society as it existed before the war are organically interconnected. They represent a catharsis engendering new hope in spite of the fact that Jakub is finally left alone at the mercy of unknown forces which ruin all the values of the natural life he had been living before.

The authors of the film version had to face in the first place the principal contradiction inherent in the lyrical depiction of poverty and suffering. The efforts to overcome this contradiction were evident in the rewriting, or rather writing-up, of the original story, in the enrichment of its *motifs* and the concentration of the theme, which consists in a fair number of episodes, into four chapters representing the seasons of the year.

An emphasis on historical reality and its influence on the human mind could have added a more specific motivational basis to the original story. The film version did not, however, succeed in bridging the gap between the level of expression on the one hand and the level of meaning on the other. The lyrical style of the *novella* was replaced by a similarly kaleidoscopic film narration and an impressive, visually inventive and inspired, though less functional, imagery.

In the projective version the story particularly resisted a precise period characterisation of reality. The war scenes, constituting a new formal frame for the work, could not compensate for the reduction in the typological features of some characters (the priest, the butcher, the indifferent figures of soldiers and officers of the Slovak Army). In an effort to add dynamism to the story, 'mystical' elements, such as the character of the crippled 'village queen' are emphasised. Consistent motivation of the behaviour of all characters is lacking in the film and is replaced by a deluge of social peculiarities and eccentricities. This future limits the space for penetrating under the surface of the events.

Like the *novel* itself, the film version concentrates on the relationship between the two friends patiently carrying their load of pain, a relationship that is emotionally impressive but psychologically not entirely convincing. Neither in the book nor in the film do Jakub and Majo search for the causes of the situation in which they find themselves; they seek an escape by looking for a promised land. At first they did not consider revolt in any form. More often than in the literary original, the magic formula 'this is where you were born and this is where you've got to live; you won't find happiness elsewhere' occurs in the film; it is expressed by the exalted old woman.

From the point of view of motivation, the story acquires a flavour of an almost mysterious determinism which, in view of the time and place of the action, cannot be understood as a plausible source of the principal characters' behaviour and thinking. Reality is not the objective of artistic presentation for the film makers. What they give us is mostly a simplified background to a story about the blighted pursuit of human happiness. Moral and abstract lyrical meanings which are the main qualities of the work, appear in the film to be isolated from reality and are illustrated by clichés.

Sophisticated dramatic construction of the plot and a professionally perfect visual stylisation do not necessarily guarantee the creation of a good film even when the original literary work is both dramatically substantial and thought-inspiring. The projective adaptation of Slovak Lyrical Prose in the past had demonstrated that it was not enough to repeat and paraphrase the greatest possible number of symbols of external reality contained in the literary originals or to condense them further. Film-makers have to present a new definition of these symbols. This is a precondition of any true interpretation. As Jakub's cart, worn out by time and stony roads, gradually disintegrates under the continuous pressure of its heavy load, the idea of the film cannot cope with the superabundance of visual inventiveness and symbolism.

The fact that the composition of the image consistently draws on a number of distinct levels, and that a visual and acoustic counterpoint is used to draw together several different *motifs* constitute the most important creative contributions of the authors of the adaptation, the script-writer Zuzana Križková and the director Stanislav Párnický, to the message itself and to how it is perceived.

Unlike in his previous films, the director did not insist on an exclusively dramatic linking of episodes. His episodes often work like an emotional tornado which evokes states of awakening. Not just the awakening of Jakub from his dream, but also the awakening of the country and the nation into a new social reality. The director draws upon the same arsenal of expressive means of modern cinematography, for instance on colour coding, where he uses a red diaphragm every time blood appears in the picture. Similarly polyfunctional is the shooting of several initial sequences in black-and-white to document the actual situation, to underline its everyday character and general validity and to differentiate it from the lyrical (colourful) tones of the story.

In addition to the equality of space and the importance assigned to both principal characters, the overall effect is enhanced by an impressive visual culmination of dramatically loaded situations (that is the absurd departure of Major, the death of Tereza, Jakub joining the army). However, the *motifs* which are not firmly based in the literary and dramatic form and which function as complementary elements to the original literary structure (the boys from Hitlerjugend, the soldiers, the hypocritical priest, the prostitution of Mara) appear obscure and unconvincing in the film version. The rediscovery of the well-spring as a symbol of the life force is too sudden for its significance to be fully perceived. The final march of the living and the dead gives the impression of being a reference and a tribute to the trendy cinematographic clichés of the recent past.

The comparison of the literary and cinematographical work shows the unresolved problem of the inadequacy of a lyrical framework for stories with social content. The problem of how to present homogeneously specific historical reality within the framework of an essentially transcendent lyrical story. Originally, in Lyrical Prose there was just one time dimension: internal time determined by the scope of human life. Novels and *novelle* lacked accurate historical context and geographical location. These, however, are the principal attributes not only of the effective presentation of an important aspect of reality from a social point of view, but also of a specific form of film narration.

It seems that the problem of merging two structures (lyrical framework and social content) can be solved only by artistic compromise. Papp appears to have attempted the depiction of typical characters from a deprived milieu within a lyrical story. At the same time, he wanted to show that humanity and a desire for fulfilment in life survive even at the very bottom of the social hierarchy. On the other hand, it might be precisely at the bottom that the author finds humanity's existence in a pure form. The author abstracts the subject from the specific social context and only at the end of the story does he define the state of deprivation as a result of a definite social system. Inevitable consequences of this approach are the introduction of an historical perspective and the optimistic end of a tragic human situation.

The highly-charged metaphorical language and style of the Papp's *novella*, as well as its theme and composition, represent an uncommon combination for Slovak literature. This fact points to one of the inorganic ruptures in the development of modern Slovak prose and its premature loss of some elements which could have led to further development. The actualisation of the Lyrical Prose techniques as presented by Papp in the late 1960s and its transfer to the level of the projective arts demonstrate that the historical interruption of its evolution had prevented a spontaneous materialisation of specific new literary quality.

Kára plná bolesti is in many respects, in the literary as well as in the film version, a corrective to the schematic social chronicles of the past. In the period of its appearance it can be measured both by the past state of Slovak prose fiction and the present state of Slovak cinematography. In the literary form it appears to be semantically outdated and to have no prospect for resuscitation in the wider context of the national literature. In the projective adaptation, the very fact that the *novella*'s version of Lyrical Prose hovers around the intersection between the lyricising ballad and a story with a definite social content indicates that the door to inspiration by one of the soundest traditions in Slovak literature is by no means closed.

Index

Dates of birth and, in a few cases, death of modern Slovak prose writers are supplied. For translations of individual works' titles, readers should look first at pp. 37–9. Otherwise translations come at the first mention of a text.